Digital Photography with Adobe® Photoshop® Elements

Gavin Cromhout Josh Fallon

First published April 2002

Trademark Acknowledgments

friends of ED has endeavored to provide trademark information about all the companies and products mentioned in this book by the appropriate use of capitals. However, friends of ED cannot guarantee the accuracy of this information.

Adobe and Photoshop are registered trade marks of Adobe Systems Incorporated and are registered in certain European countries. This mark has ® appended thereto. Adobe Dimensions is a trade mark of Adobe Systems Incorporated.

Macintosh is a registered trade mark of Apple Computer, Inc.
Windows is a registered trade mark of Microsoft Corporation.

Published by friends of ED
30-32 Lincoln Road, Olton, Birmingham, B27 6PA, UK.
Printed in USA
ISBN: 1-903450-80-2

Digital Photography with Adobe® Photoshop® Elements

Credits

Authors
Gavin Cromhout
Josh Fallon

Technical Reviewers
Darlene Billmair
Nyree Costello
Vicki Loader
Rick Truhls

Proof Readers
Victoria Blackburn
Jon Bounds
Luke Harvey

Indexer
Fiona Murray

Commissioning Editor
Jim Hannah

Technical Editors
Libby Hayward
Adam Juniper

Author Agent
Mel Jehs

Project Manager
Simon Brand

Graphic Design
Deb Murray

Managing Editor
Chris Hindley

Gavin Cromhout

Gavin Cromhout lives in Cape Town, South Africa. He studied art formally at the University of Cape Town, formally sleeping through all the lectures. Gavin is currently working on a website for the Innovation in Communication award, between looking for whoever has his coffee mug (which is actually used for tea).

If you'd like to get in touch with him, you can reach him at: gavin@lodestone.co.za. Gavin would like to once again thank Alison for her help with editing, and would like to dedicate his part of the book to his grandfather Ray Ryan, the greatest landscape photographer of his time.

Josh Fallon

Studio artist turned graphic designer Josh Fallon, 24, resides in Los Angeles, providing illustration and web design services. Fallon's illustration work has been featured by Adobe.com, Computer Arts Special magazine, and in the book New Masters of Photoshop. Fallon currently works full-time as an in-house corporate designer and part-time as a freelance illustrator/web designer. Aside from keeping freelance clients happy, he stays busy working on the continual development of pet project DesignLaunchpad.com, a resource where beginning graphic designers can go to get practical advice on design. Fallon's work can be seen at FallonDesign.com.

Table of Contents

Ladies and Gentlemen: Photoshop® Elements

That sound you hear is the trashing of photographic equipment and the glug of chemicals as they flow down plugholes. Across the land, darkrooms are being lit up, and computers are being installed ready for the biggest revolution to hit photography in over a century – digital cameras!

Well OK, so maybe analog photography will stick around for a while yet, but there has never been a better time to get into the digital workshop. The digital camera market is booming, with cheaper models being given away free with new PC packages. On top of this, Adobe has issued an affordable version of the closest thing there has ever been to software white goods: Photoshop.

Adobe® Photoshop® Elements is for everyone. It's designed to carry out all those little tasks you wondered about when you got your pictures back from the local processing shop. It just makes pictures *that little bit better.* Also, as we're about to show you in the chapters that follow, it can do a whole lot more. Whether you want to be creative and off the wall, or whether you want to be practical and maintain that little bit of photographic dignity, Photoshop Elements more than meets the mark. It has strength and subtlety, and in these pages we cover it all.

This book is aimed at people interested in photography. The beauty of Photoshop Elements, we find, is that it enables anyone who doesn't necessarily have roots in professional photographic techniques to carry out really quite sophisticated tasks. Rest assured that at no point in this book do we get carried away using professional jargon. All the techniques are explained in simple and easy-to-understand sections, and by the end of it you'll wonder how you ever managed without Elements!

The CD

This book comes fully equipped with everything you need to manipulate your mini masterpieces. First off, if you don't have it already, you'll want a copy of the software! On the CD you'll find a free 30-day trial of Adobe® Photoshop® Elements.

Throughout the book, walk-through tutorials will help to reveal the power placed at your fingertips by Photoshop Elements. These tutorials are based around image files supplied by the authors, and every file can be found on the CD within individual chapter folders.

If you have any problems with the CD don't hesitate to contact us at support@friendsofed.com and we'll do our best to help you out.

Layout Conventions

We've tried to keep this book as clear and easy to understand as possible. So, we've only used a few layout styles to avoid confusion. You'll notice that all the screenshots in the book are taken using a PC rather than a Mac. This is just for consistency and to keep our book looking nice and uniform, so sorry Mac users! You can be sure that if there is any difference you should be aware of, we will point it out in enormous letters. Both PC and Mac keyboard conventions have been used, so you'll see CTRL, CMD, ALT and OPTION given throughout the text.

Practical exercises will appear under headings in this style:

DO THIS TUTORIAL NOW

...and where we think it helps the discussion, we'll break things down into numbered steps:

1. like this
2. and this
3. and this

Finally, if we think there's something particularly important you should bear in mind, we will highlight it:

> *So you'll know not to skip over it!*

Support

friends of ED is committed to offering online support for all of its titles. If you have any questions about this book, please mail support@friendsofed.com and one of our support team will get back to you. It's what we're here for, and we'd love to hear from you!

If you have any general questions about friends of ED, you might like to check out our web site at www.friendsofed.com. There you will find a message board to post any general Photoshop questions. There is also a host of other features up there – interviews with renowned designers, chapter samples from other books, and up-to-date information on forthcoming projects. So, if you're wondering where to go after you've mastered Photoshop Elements, this is the place to be!

1 Getting started in Photoshop® Elements

Like much of the current wave of new technology, digital photography breaks down barriers and opens doors. Armed with a digital camera and an image-editing program as intuitive and flexible as Photoshop Elements, home users are offered the chance to create beautiful images that outshine those of the professionals. Let's take a look at the benefits of using digital cameras over analog models – it will help us understand where we're headed, and exactly what Photoshop Elements is trying to do for us. After that we'll have a go at opening a file, having a play with it, and then saving it. You'll soon see how quickly you can get to grips with image manipulation!

A digital revolution

Digital cameras have only been around for the past seven or eight years as viable consumer products. Interestingly enough, the technologies that led to the development of today's digital cameras are rooted in the 1970s, when Kodak and other companies began working on filmless technologies in hopes of creating a rival to traditional photography. Through the 80s and early 90s several companies came out with digital cameras that captured images at **megapixel (million pixel)** resolutions, but they were not practical for consumer use. It wasn't until 1995 that the first consumer digital cameras were released, and since then they have become an increasingly attractive proposition for professionals and amateurs alike.

Comparing digital and analog

You might be surprised as to how similar the process of capturing images using a digital camera is when compared to using a traditional camera. With a traditional camera, when you click the button to snap your photo, the shutter briefly opens and closes, exposing the light-sensitive film inside to the light given off by whatever you just shot, and pretty much burns that moment on the film.

It's more or less the same process that occurs when you use a digital camera: you point and click, and the shutter opens and closes to expose the inside of the camera to the light of your subject. The difference is that with a digital camera, the light is not captured by film, but by an electronic device called a **Charge Coupled Device** (**CCD**), which records the visual data and transfers it digitally to whatever sort of storage media you use in your camera. So this is what it means when digital cameras are called **filmless** – the film of a traditional camera is replaced by the combination of a CCD and some form of digital storage.

Zooming in: how they work

So with the basic difference between the two types of camera in mind, what is the difference between the types of images they produce? With a traditional analog camera, you would most likely have your film developed into prints, and retain the negatives for safekeeping should you want to reproduce the photos or perhaps have larger prints made in the future. You get quality images, but unfortunately unless you own a photo lab, what you see is what you get. You are powerless to change your photos once they are shot, so you'd better hope you like them!

With digital, however, as long as you don't lose or erase the original shots, you'll always have fully-editable images to work with. Color correcting, framing, sizing, manipulating – you can do it all, and the only limitation is the quality of image your camera is capable of capturing. Digital images are measured in pixels – the more pixels your CCD can capture the closer your photos will come to resembling images captured using analog cameras. As you can imagine, as mainstream digital camera technology progresses it is becoming a rival to traditional photographic images – most popular digital cameras are currently capable of capturing anywhere from 1 to 4 megapixels. This might sound like a lot but when you zoom in close enough you can still see the individual pixels as opposed to the natural grain of traditional film.

So while digital cameras may not always initially capture such quality of images as analog cameras, it is the power to edit and share digital photographs *after* the shooting that is the major selling point for digital photography.

Introducing Adobe® Photoshop® Elements

So you have a digital camera and are interested in altering your photos. Maybe you want to change the contrast, adjust the color, crop the image, remove redeye, or perform any of several other adjustments. Well, there are several free image-editing programs that can do this, and there was probably one that came free with your camera's software.

Photoshop Elements, however, can do all of these tasks easily and intuitively, and that's just the beginning. With this program you can prepare your images for the web (including animated images and web galleries with customizable templates), create panoramas from multiple images, combine several images, text, and graphics on multiple layers, and create sophisticated effects with built-in filters and styles, to name only a few.

Throughout the course of this book we'll cover the features that are essential to you, the digital photographer, and ensure that you come away with the power to alter your photographs in any manner that you desire.

Layout of the program

Let's take a few minutes to get acquainted with the different aspects of the program's interface and what their functions are. These will be brief introductions – they will be covered more fully over the course of the following chapters.

Opposite is a shot of Photoshop Elements, as it looks when you first launch it.

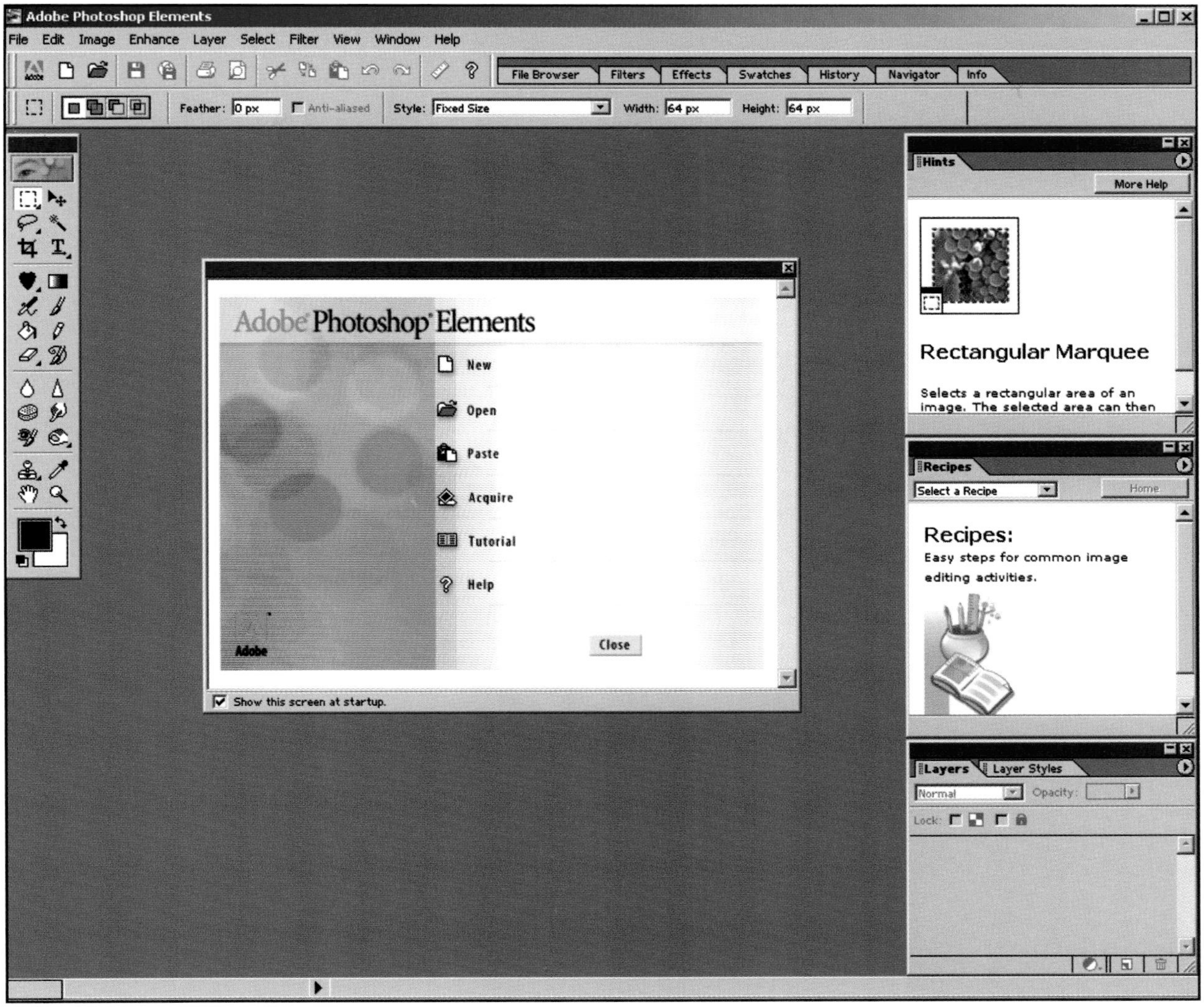

The Toolbar

The Toolbar gives you access to the main tools you'll be using while working with your images. Tools for selecting, moving, painting, drawing, blurring, sharpening, zooming – and so on – are all to be found here. This is also where you select the foreground and background color, which will come into play when we fill selections and use the gradient tool.

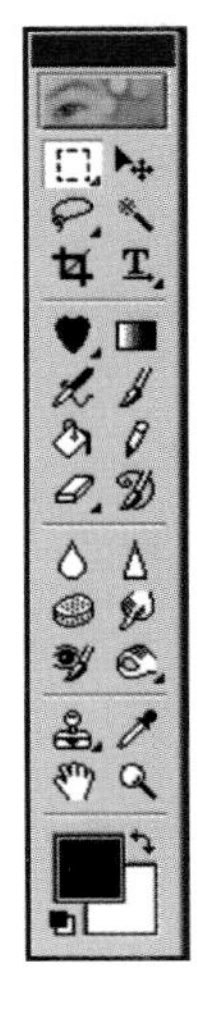

The Options bar

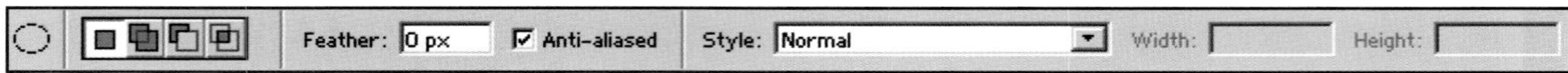

The Options bar changes according to what tool from the Toolbar is selected. The image here shows the Options bar for the Selection tool (notice how the icon for the Selection tool is shown at the far left of the bar). Be sure to take note of the Options bar whenever you select a tool from the Toolbar so you can experiment with the different settings available for each tool.

Palettes

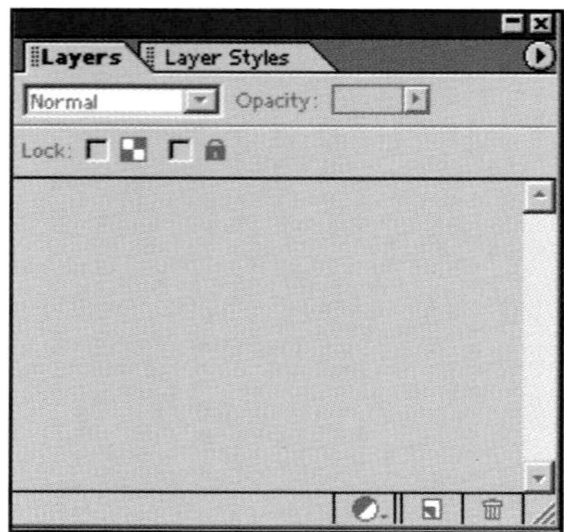

Palettes are simply a way of organizing the different features of Photoshop Elements. They are very useful for improving workflow and customizing the interface to however you desire. Palettes can be moved anywhere on screen, grouped together (you can see above how the Layers and Layer Styles palettes are grouped), and even stored in the Palettes Dock to maximize screen space. Let's face it, this is an important feature, because getting the hang of all those palettes covering your photograph is quite hard to stomach.

The Palettes Dock

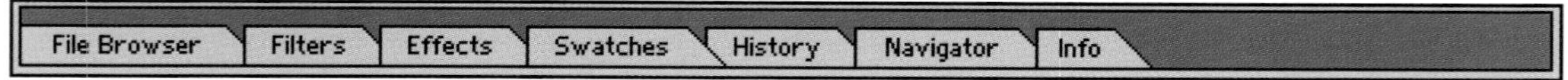

The Palettes Dock allows you to store your palettes in a centralized location, which is essential for those working on a small monitor. To use the dock, simply drag a palette by its tab and release the tab in the dock, or close the palette to automatically send it to the dock. The tab will then be available in the dock, and can be accessed by clicking the tab to reveal the palette's contents.

The Canvas

The canvas is the main working space for editing your images – any image you open is on its own canvas. You can alter the canvas by resizing or rotating it. In the top bar, the canvas displays the title of the image you are working on, the color mode you are working in (which we will cover in greater detail in later chapters), the size you are viewing the canvas at, and the dimensions of the canvas. At the bottom, the canvas also has a popup menu for displaying several other settings of the current document, as seen in the screenshot below.

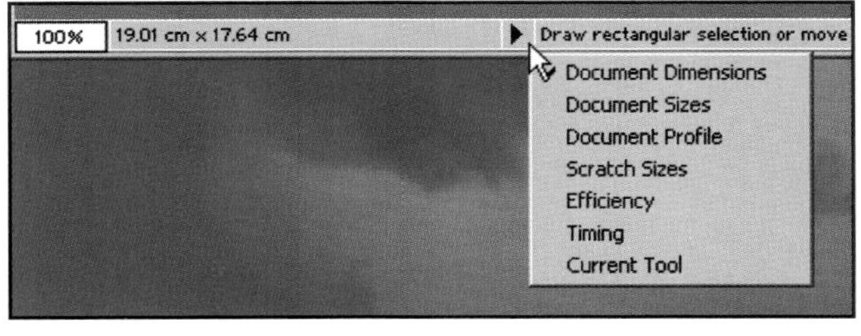

PC

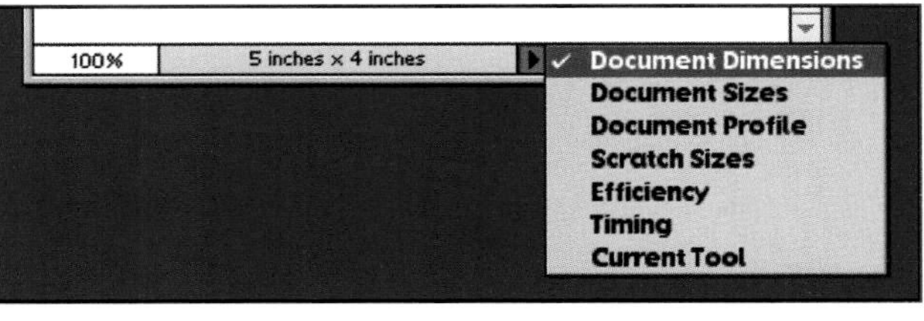

Mac

Menus and the Menu Shortcut bar

Many features of Photoshop Elements that are available through toolbars and palettes are also accessible through the main menu. There are also main menu shortcuts located below the menu bar for common tasks such as saving, opening, copying, and printing.

Okay, so we've had a wander around the Photoshop Elements interface, now let's not waste any time getting our hands dirty here. We're going to **open** up a picture in Photoshop Elements, we'll **crop** it and then we'll add a quick frame effect using a **layer style**. If some of these terms sound at all foreign, don't worry, all will become clear – for now let's jump in.

1. If this box is still open then click the Close button at the bottom to get rid of it.

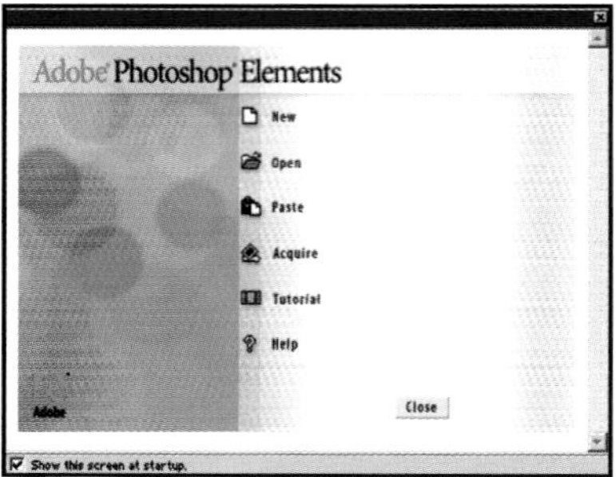

2. Locate the **File Browser** tab toward the top of the screen. Get used to using this – it provides quick access to the files of your computer without having to use any of the typical **File > Open** dialog boxes. Click the tab and notice the interface that opens up.

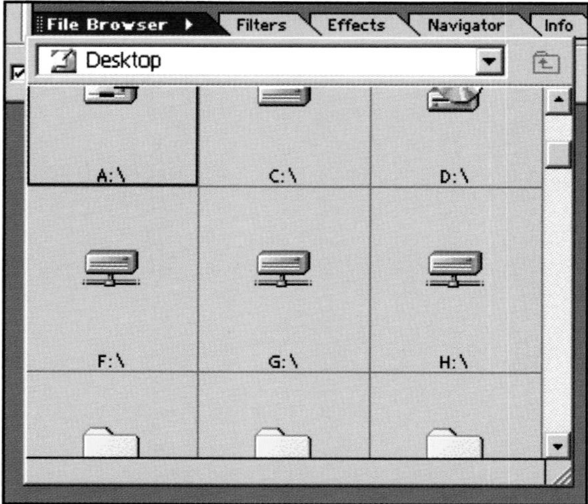

3. Now find an image on your computer to work with. It can be anything – for this quick tutorial it doesn't matter. I'm going to use an image from my Christmas vacation that I shot a couple of years ago. You can use it too if you like, it's on the CD and it's in the `Chapter01` folder called `giraffe`.

Take note of the way the File Browser navigates through your files and folders – double-clicking on folders opens them to reveal the subsequent folders and files, and the full path of the location is shown at the top of the File Browser palette. You can jump backwards using this menu, or go back one folder at a time using the folder icon to the right of it. When you do get to a folder with images in it, Elements will display image previews (known as **thumbnails**) for you in the File

Browser. Open the image by double-clicking the preview. Also, bear in mind that you can resize the File Browser palette using the bottom right handle – this comes in handy when browsing through a folder with several images.

4. Now that we have an image open, let's crop it a little to frame the subject better. From the Toolbar located at the left of your screen, choose the Crop tool (or as a shortcut, just hit C).

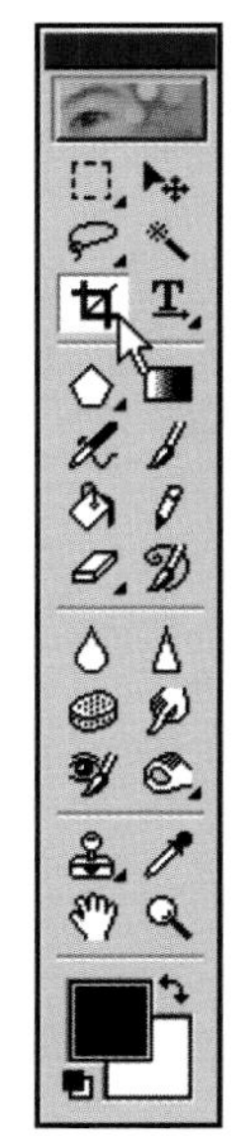

5. Move over to your image and use the Crop tool to click and drag a selection onto your image.

It doesn't have to be perfect at first, because you can use any of the eight little square handles around the edges of the selection to adjust it accordingly.

6. Simply click and drag on a handle to adjust the size of the crop area. I want to crop this image to focus more on the subject, the Lego giraffe, and eliminate some of the uninteresting background.

Notice how the area outside of the Crop tool's selection is darkened. This is how Photoshop Elements shows you what area is going to be cropped out and allows you to better judge how the resulting image will look.

You can change the settings of the crop display too, using the Options bar. You can specify whether or not to show the cropped area as darkened by checking or unchecking **Shield cropped area**, and you can change the color and transparency of the darkened area to your liking also in the options bar. Use whatever is comfortable for you – the default setting works fine for me.

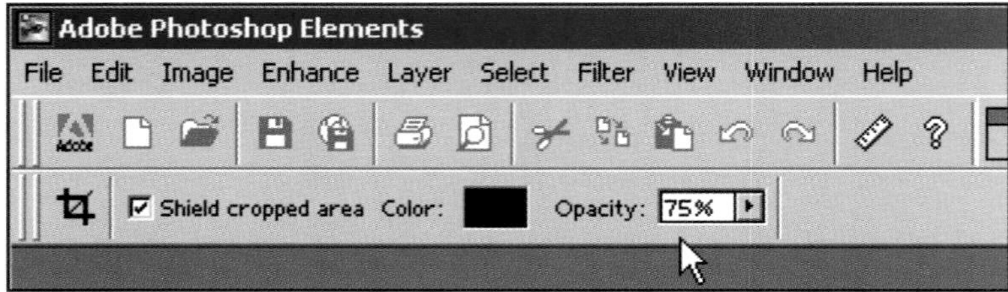

Once you get your crop selection where you want it, you can either hit ENTER/RETURN to apply the crop, or you can click the check box at the right hand side of the Options bar.

Remember, you can always use **Edit > Undo Crop** if you aren't happy with the results. We now have our image cropped to our liking and we'reready to apply a stylized frame.

7. We're now going to add a frame to our image in one simple step using one of Photoshop Elements' built-in effects. Click on the **Effects** tab at the top of your screen to open the Effects palette.

This palette contains lots of different **Effects**, which are actually a bundle of simple Photoshop steps contained in one action. They are powerful tools for applying stylistic variations to your images, and very handy at this early stage for doing some cool-looking things without our having to worry too much about the specifics. We'll cover more of these effects later – for now we'll just look at the **Frames** effects.

8. From the drop-down menu directly underneath the Effects tab, choose Frames.

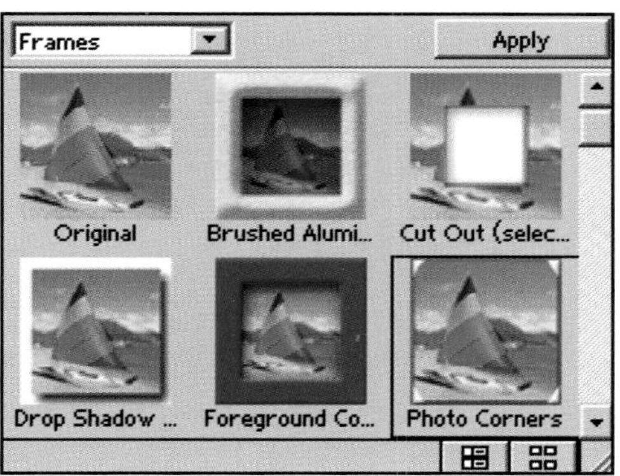

9. For this image let's use the **Photo Corners** effect. As you can tell from the preview, this will give the photo the effect of being placed in a photo album.

10. To apply this effect, you have three simple methods to choose from. You could click on the preview, and then drag it on to your image; this method is known as **drag and drop**. Alternatively you could double-click the preview or, finally, you could click it once and then click the **Apply** button in the upper right corner of the palette. Whichever method you choose, sit back and watch as your photo automatically goes through the steps of creating our selected effect.

11. When the process is done, a pop up will appear asking **Do you wish to keep this Effect?** If you like the way it looks, click **Yes** and we're done! If not, click **No** and your image will revert back to its previous state and you can try another effect. You can also check the **Don't show again** box if you want to bypass this question every time, but I like to be able to see how my image will look before I choose.

Okay, so that was easy enough, we've started to get to grips with the Elements interface, now close the image through **File > Close**. You probably don't want to save the changes you've made to the image, so click **No** when you get prompted with this question. Now we'll move on to the next section.

File types

Photoshop Elements allows you to save your images in several different file formats. The format you choose will vary depending on the nature of your project. For instance images destined for the web will need to be compressed to make them faster to download, so you'd opt for an efficient file type such as a **JPEG**. However, if you plan to print your images then it is important to maintain high quality images, which means opting for a larger file format, such as a **TIF**. We'll discuss all of the different file types later in the book, and we'll look at which settings are appropriate for your needs.

To get a sense of the different file formats available in Photoshop Elements we'll return to our giraffe image from the first Quick Task and save it in various formats.

QUICK TASK: SAVING A FILE

1. Using the File Browser palette, select and open the `giraffe.jpg` image again.

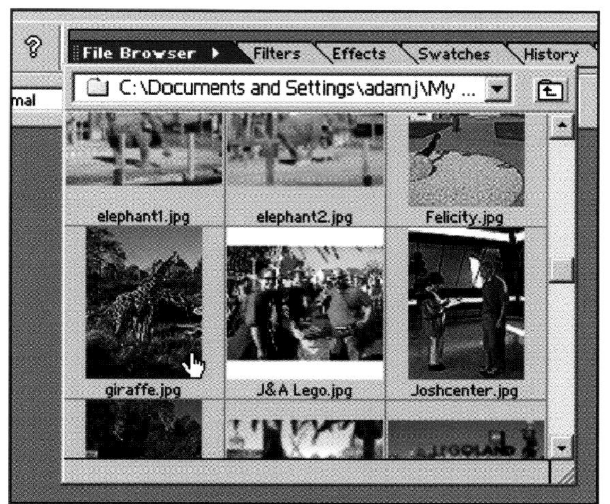

2. When the file opens, select **File > Save As** from the main menu and take a look at the dialog that comes up.

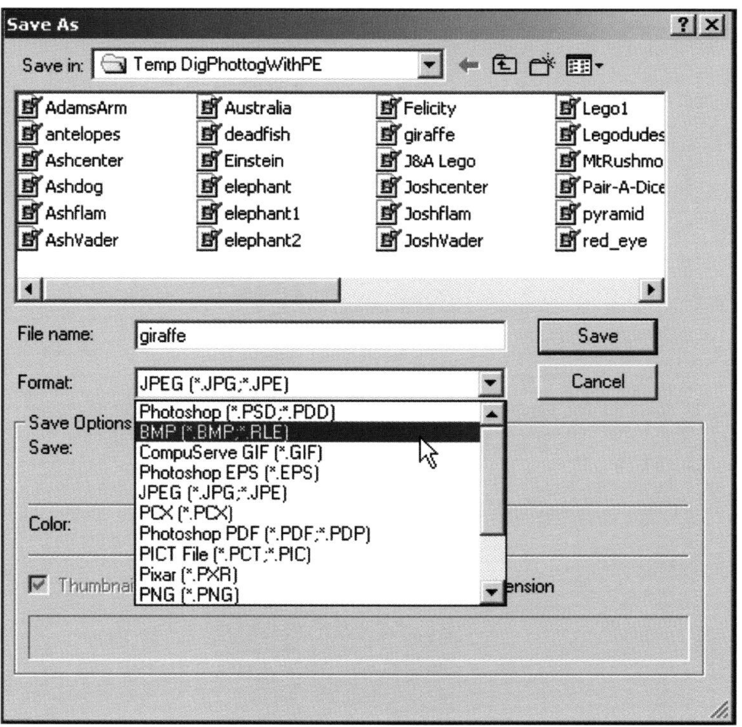

3. In the **Save Options** field you can see the various formats in which you can save the image. Notice that the format at the top of the list, the default setting, is **Photoshop (*.PSD, *.PDD)** – this will become important once we start working with layers, as it is the only format that allows us to save our document with the layers preserved.

4. Create a new folder on your hard drive named File Types, then return to the Save As dialog and select the second choice in the Save Options list; **BMP**.

5. In the **File name** field call this file `giraffe1`, and click the **Save** button, and you have now saved the giraffe image as a BMP, a Windows Bitmap file. Congratulations!

6. Repeat this Save As procedure three more times, saving in the **CompuServe GIF**, **JPEG**, and **PNG** file formats. These are the most commonly used Photoshop file types; use the default settings for each one, and also make sure that each time you start by opening the original `giraffe` document, and change the names of the files to `giraffe2` and so on for the rest of the files.

7. Once you've finished, let's go back to the File Browser and find the File Types folder you created on your desktop. Once you've found it, you should see the previews of the four images we just created using Save As. To open all four at the same time, hold down SHIFT and click each one. With all four selected hit ENTER and they will all open on screen together.

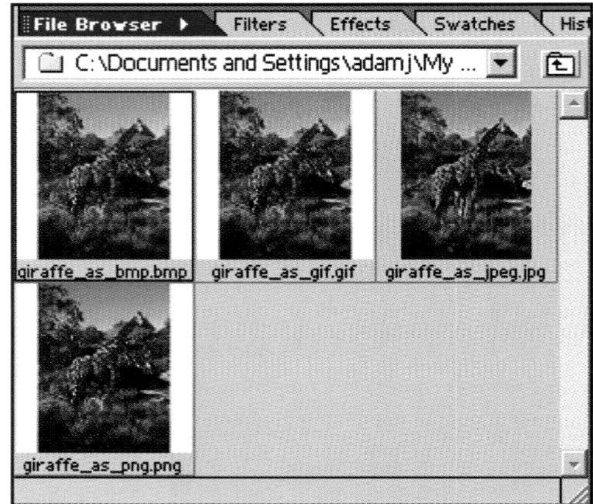

8. You now have four canvasses on screen, and we want to arrange them so that we can compare the different file formats (They're stacked on top of each other right now, but if you move each one around you can see that we have four open). Let's zoom in close to each image to get a close look at how our files ended up looking.

9. With `giraffe1.bmp` as the active document, choose the **Zoom** tool from the Toolbar and click on the canvas until it is four times its original size. You can check how far "zoomed" in you are by looking at the little box in the bottom left hand corner of the canvas, we want this to be at 400%. Drag the edge of the canvas to fill your screen so you can see as much of it as possible.

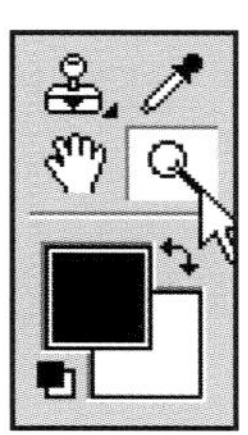

400%

You can also zoom using the keyboard no matter what tool you are using by hitting Ctrl/Cmd ++ to zoom in; and Ctrl/Cmd+– to zoom out.

10. Repeat this for each document so each one is at 400% and fills the screen. With the screen full, you can switch between documents using the Window menu from the main menu.

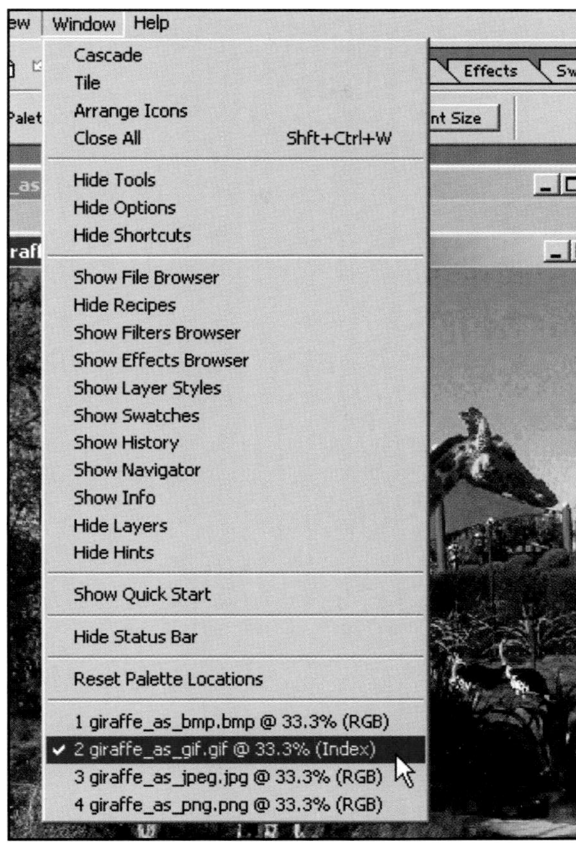

11. Now, return to the Toolbar and choose the **Hand** tool, this allows you to pull the canvas around when you are zoomed in close, although it is not actually moving the image's position on the canvas. To confirm this, notice how the scroll bars move as you drag with the Hand tool. Also, the Hand tool does nothing when your image is fully viewable on your monitor. Let's drag the giraffe's face into the center of the canvas of each file so we can compare each file format.

You can activate the Hand tool, even if you are using another tool, by using the spacebar. Although there are few exceptions to this shortcut – for instance it doesn't work when you are using the Type tool.

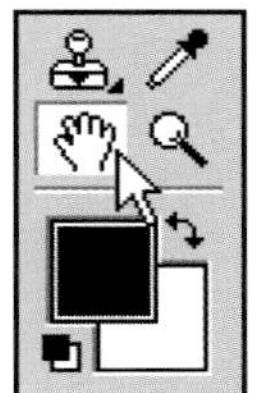

12. Now, a quick way to switch between documents that is useful in our situation is to use the shortcut Ctrl + Tab. (PC only). Use this shortcut to quickly bring each document to the front, and notice any differences that immediately stand out. Have any of the images altered in any way?

You should have noticed that the image saved in CompuServe GIF format, mostly known just as GIF, suffered a significant change, while the other three remained largely the same. There are small differences in the compression caused by the JPG, BMP, and PNG formats, but the GIF format was the most noticeable because it restricts the image to 256 colors. The GIF format is best used for images with broad flat colors like line drawings and logos. We'll cover appropriate file formats for certain types of projects later in the book, but for now just be aware that you have several options, and that the PSD is the only one that saves layers.

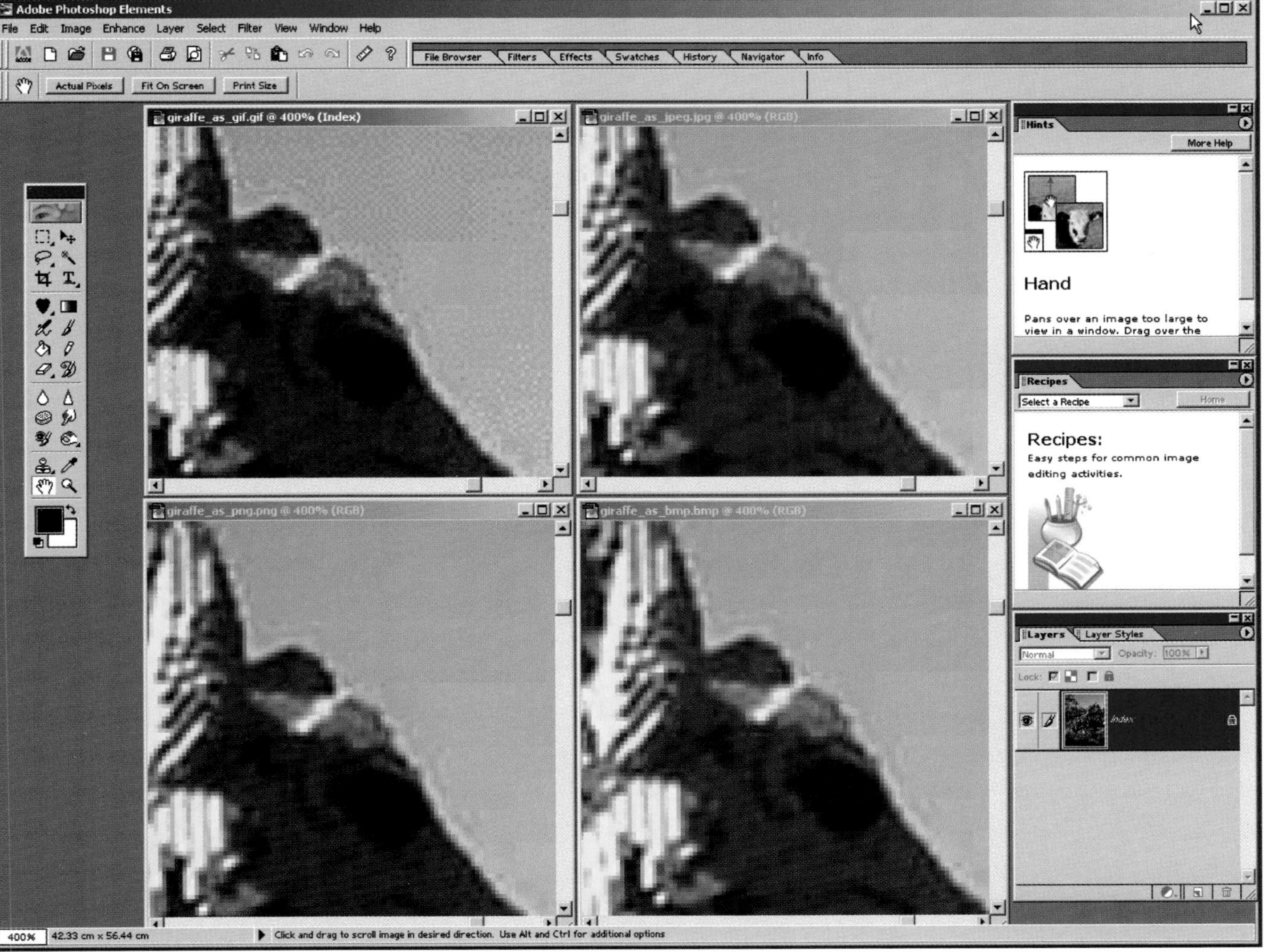
Adobe Photoshop Elements
File Edit Image Enhance Layer Select Filter View Window Help
File Browser Filters Effects Swatches History Navigator Info
Actual Pixels Fit On Screen Print Size
giraffe_as_gif.gif @ 400% (Index)
giraffe_as_jpeg.jpg @ 400% (RGB)
giraffe_as_png.png @ 400% (RGB)
giraffe_as_bmp.bmp @ 400% (RGB)
Hints
More Help
Hand
Pans over an image too large to view in a window. Drag over the
Recipes
Select a Recipe
Home
Recipes:
Easy steps for common image editing activities.
Layers Layer Styles
Normal
Opacity: 100%
Lock:
Index
400%
42.33 cm x 56.44 cm
Click and drag to scroll image in desired direction. Use Alt and Ctrl for additional options

Importing Photographs

Let's spend a few minutes and go over how you actually get the images you shoot with your digital camera into Photoshop Elements. Earlier we opened an image that already existed on your hard drive – the process of getting files from your camera is very similar.

Depending on the type of camera you have, there are a few ways in which you might connect to your computer. The two main options are either to remove the storage media from your camera and place it in the appropriate drive or reader, or to connect your camera directly to your computer using a cable.

Removable Media

Some cameras store photos on a floppy disk, which you would obviously just place in your floppy drive. Others store photos on memory cards, in which case you would insert it in the reader that you purchased for the particular memory card used by your camera.

Connecting Directly

If you don't have a drive to read your storage media, then you must connect directly to your computer. Most cameras connect via serial or USB cable, but either way you have to set your camera to the correct mode for transferring the data on the card to the computer through the cable. Also, ensure that you have installed the right software so that your computer recognizes your camera as an external device.

Moving files

So now you should be able to see the storage card of your camera on your computer, regardless of how you have it connected. The next step is getting the images off your storage card and onto your computer. Every camera is different, and if you have problems you should consult your camera's manual, but in broad terms you need to find the folder on your storage card that contains all your images, and simply copy it to a location on your hard drive. There are so many different ways to get images off of your camera and questions about what to do with them after that I think a few basic pointers are in order.

- Create a directory on your computer where you keep all of your digital pictures. This may seem obvious, but it is very important to have all of your photos well organized. Keep them in clearly labeled folders so that when it's time to dig up some older shots it's not a headache.
- Keep in mind that once you get a sizeable amount of digital pictures in your archive, you may have to explore different options for backing them up, to free up valuable room on your hard drive. Burning them onto CDs is an excellent option if you have a CD burner, purchasing an external hard drive is a legitimate and relatively inexpensive solution, and taking advantage of a ZIP drive or other high capacity removable storage also works well.
- Never work off of your camera's media card. If you've ever done this you've probably noticed how much slower the performance is in whatever image editor you use. Media cards are really only meant for recording and transferring images, and will only hinder your performance if used otherwise.

By now, you're getting comfortable with the process of getting your photos into PS Elements. You've had a chance to tinker with some of the tool and effects, and familiarized yourself with the various menus and palettes, and how they work together. In the next chapter we'll take a closer look at our digital laboratory and start correcting some common photographic problem areas.

2 Quick Fixes

Exploring our new digital laboratory

Sometimes photography can feel like a bit of a gamble: you take a beautiful roll of film, encapsulating some perfect moments, and when you excitedly pick up your developed pictures you are left feeling utterly disappointed.

When shooting with traditional cameras, there's nothing more frustrating than getting photos back from the lab and finding all sorts of problems. The dream roll of shots you took in Hawaii is discolored, over-exposed, *under*-exposed, and you look like a red-eyed demon in half the shots.

Digital photos, however, allow you the freedom to make those crucial adjustments with relative ease. Photoshop Elements has several built-in tools that allow you to swiftly make corrections to those less-than-perfect shots.

What's not always easy, however, is being able to determine which of your photos need to be adjusted without going through the whole, time-consuming business of opening each one individually on your computer. You may have noticed a recent trend among high street photo developing services to include an extra exposure or two with your photos, which shows your whole roll of film in small thumbnails. These are useful for getting a quick glance at your developed roll without having to shuffle through the whole stack of photos. This is called a contact sheet, it's a very useful tool in photography, and Photoshop Elements has the capability to create these from your digital photos.

So why would you want to create a contact sheet? For one, contact sheets are great for identifying the shots that need correcting, as mentioned before. Also, you can use contact sheets to catalogue groups of images, which becomes important as your collection of digital images grows.

QUICK TASK: SAVING A FILE

Let's take a look at just how easy it is to create a custom contact sheet from a group of your images. Before we start, make sure you have a nice sized group of photos to work with – a contact sheet with four photos defeats the purpose. These images will either be on your camera or already exist on your hard drive. If they are on your camera, go ahead and download them to your computer and copy them to their own folder, as we did in Chapter 1.

1. In Photoshop Elements, go to **File > Automate > Contact Sheet II**.

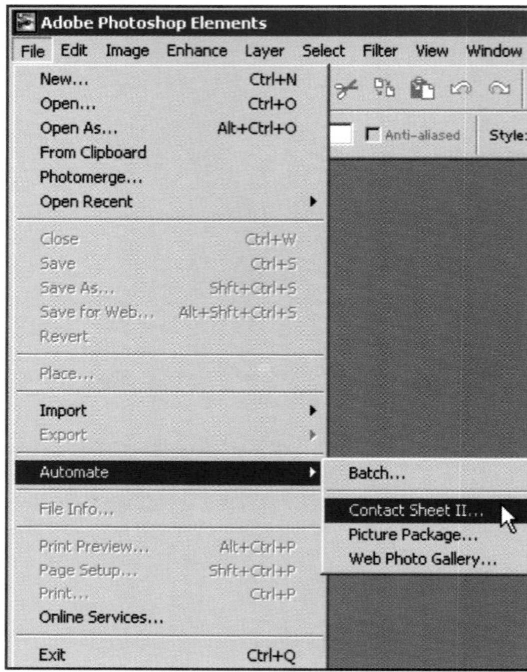

Take a look at the dialogue you are presented with:

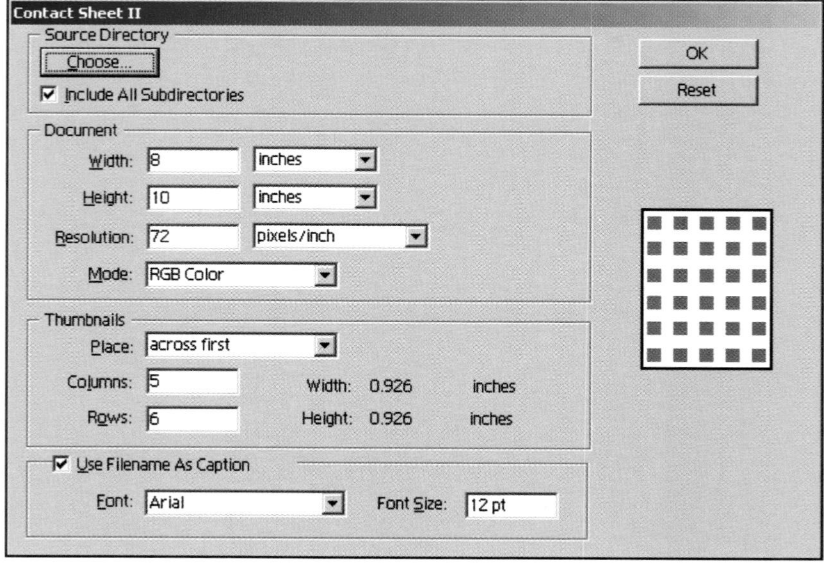

Notice that the first thing we have to do is locate the source folder of our images. Keep in mind that your photos may be in a different format than mine – most digital cameras save images in JPEG or TIFF format.

3. Click **Choose** and if you have subfolders of images within your selected folder that you want to include, make sure that you check the **Include All Subfolders** checkbox. We'll now be asked to find our folder of images that we just prepared – I'm going to use some images from my Christmas trip a couple of years ago.

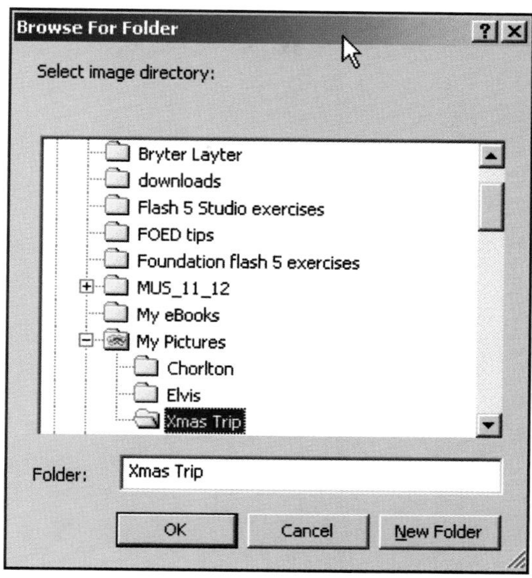

4. With our folder selected, we can now start customizing the contact sheet to our liking. The first thing we'll set up is the document size. I'm going to leave mine at the default settings since we'll only be viewing the contact sheet on-screen.

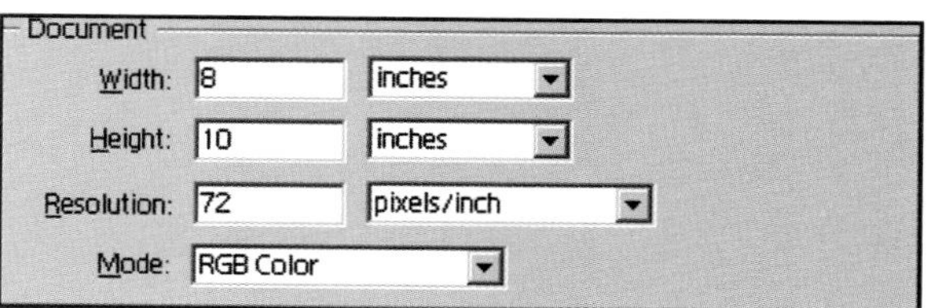

If, however, you intend to print your contact sheet you'll need to set the resolution to at least 150, but ideally 300. Note that you are unlikely ever to need a resolution greater than 300. This book, for example, has pictures saved at a resolution of 300. Changing the resolution will not affect the print size, it will only affect the pixel size, and hence the quality of your image. Before printing you'd also need to adjust the width and height to the size of the bounds of your printer.

5. Next let's look at the **Thumbnails** options. Here you can specify how many rows and columns you want on each sheet. As you adjust the amount of rows and columns, the preview of the layout on the right updates accordingly, as does the readout of the size that the thumbnails will be. You can also specify how you want the thumbnails to be ordered using the **Place** popup menu – **across first** or **down first**.

6. Choose a setting that best suits the amount of images you have and the size of thumbnail that you want. If you have 30 images but want a bigger thumbnail so you can get a better sense of the actual image, try changing the settings to 3 columns by 5 rows.

It's okay if your images take up two contact sheets. However, if you want to fit all of your images on to one sheet to make archiving easier, then make sure you set the columns and rows so all your images will fit. I'm going to change my settings to 5 by 7, so I can fit all 31 of my images on a single sheet; it's simply a matter of multiplying the columns by the rows.

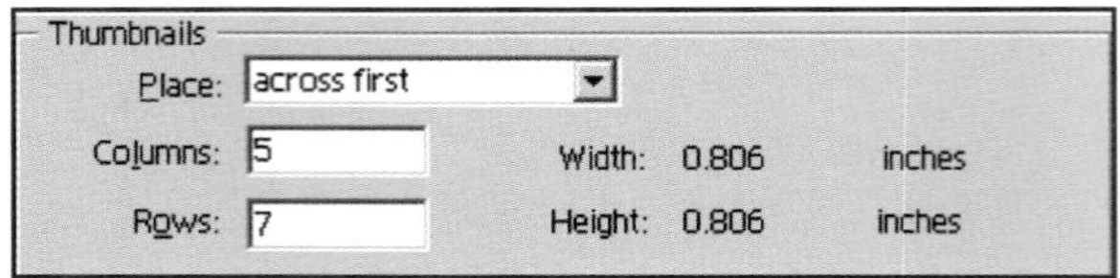

7. Finally, you can choose whether or not you'd like to have the file's name as a caption underneath each image. This is very useful for referencing archived photos, since the names that your camera will create for your images are generally pretty nondescript. Let's select this option. Choose a font and font size that you think will look nice. I'm going to use Arial at 11 pt size. Clear and simple!

8. With all of our contact sheet options set up and ready to roll, let's go ahead and click OK and watch what happens. It will probably take a little while, especially if you have a lot of large images. When it's finished, go ahead and save the file in the same folder as the source images – call it `Contact_Sheet.psd`.

You can now take a look at your contact sheet and decide which images need some tidying up. If the thumbnails are too small for you to see any basic problems, try creating another sheet with bigger thumbnails or a higher resolution. Keep in mind that with a contact sheet, we're trying to catch the obvious imperfections that jump out right away – things like exposure and color problems. We'll get into the more intricate fixes later in the book.

Another thing to look for in your contact sheets is consistent problems – for example you might have an entire sheet where the shots are too dark, which might indicate that you need to adjust the settings of your camera. You can save yourself a lot of work by using your contact sheets as a measuring stick for your camera's performance.

As a side note, it's also a good idea to make sure that your monitor is properly calibrated – if every single one of your photos looks odd then the chances are it's your monitor's settings and not your camera's. Consult the manual for your monitor and operating system for calibration procedure.

Correcting the basic problems

Quick fixes

Now we've covered a method for determining which photos in a group may need correcting, let's spend some time working on a few images that have some of these basic problems we talked about. Photoshop Elements makes fixing these problems a snap, while also allowing for fine-tuning as well.

Auto Levels and Auto Contrast

In looking at my group of images, there are a few that appear to need some tweaking. The first one we'll pick out is the shot of the Taj Majal. You can find this image on the CD – it's called `Taj_Majal.jpg`.

Here we have a shot suffering from low contrast and washed out colors. In Photoshop Elements, you can use the **Auto Contrast** and **Auto Levels** commands from the **Enhance** menu to quickly correct this problem.

So what's the idea behind these commands?

- **Auto Contrast** takes the overall contrast of the image, which in this case is low, and automatically adjusts the lightest colors of the image to white, and the darkest to black. In essence, this darkens the shadows, and lightens the highlights.

- **Auto Levels** is similar to Auto Contrast in that it finds the lightest and darkest values of an image, but in this case, instead of adjusting them to white and black, it proportionally adjusts the pixels in between these two values. Also, with Auto Levels you may notice color shifts while with Auto Contrast this won't happen.

Although with most images Auto Contrast and Auto Levels yield similar results, it is important to know how they differ – let's see how they affect our shot here.

1. Go to **Enhance > Auto Levels** (SHIFT +CTRL/CMD+L) and let's try this command first.

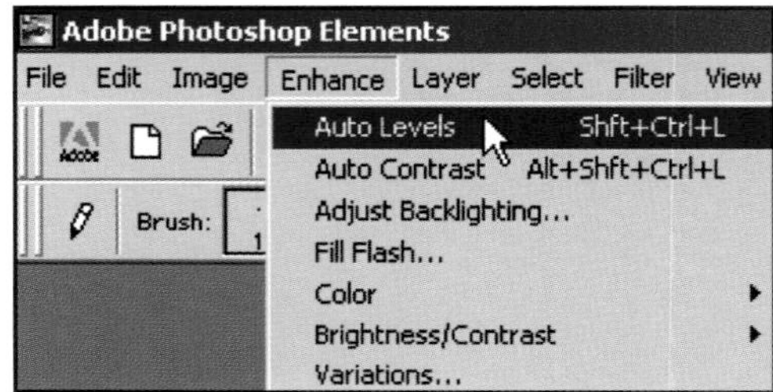

Here's the result. We now have good contrast and didn't experience any negative color shifting that sometimes happens with Levels.

2. Go to **Edit > Undo Auto Levels** (ALT/OPTION+CTRL/CMD+Z) and let's apply Auto Contrast to see if it affects our original image any differently than Auto Levels. On the menu, it's right under Auto Levels at **Enhance > Auto Contrast**. You can see the result overleaf.

It looks pretty close to the results of the Auto Levels, doesn't it? When adjusting your own images, I suggest always trying them both out and determining which one yields better results. Most of the time, though, they'll be pretty similar.

3. Now let's see how we can use the same Auto commands to fix an image that has too much contrast and is generally too dark. We'll also see with this image how the two commands can give us different results. Open the image `Mt_Rushmore.jpg` from the CD.

This shot is a bit dark – it was shot outside with natural light so it should appear much brighter and have better contrast. Let's give it a spin with the same Auto Levels and Auto Contrast commands that we used on the last image and see what it does for us.

4. Go ahead and repeat the procedure we used on the first image; first apply Auto Levels. **Enhance > Auto Levels** (SHIFT +CTRL/CMD +L).

5. Then Undo this, (ALT/OPTION +Z) and got to Auto Contrast. **Enhance > Auto Contrast** (ALT/OPTION +SHIFT +CTRL/CMD +L).

Do you notice the change in color? The sky appears the same, but the color of the mountain changes. Here we can see the color shift I was talking about earlier. The brownish tone of the mountain in the original color was slightly altered by Auto Levels while it remained the same after Auto Contrast. So why would we ever want to use Auto Levels, then, if it could possibly cause color shifting? Well, not all color shifting is bad. You may find that by applying Auto Levels you end up with a more appealing image.

These quick, one-shot fixes are valuable tools that can save you a lot of time. But what happens when the results of Auto Levels and Auto Contrast don't quite do the job? Sometimes an image requires a greater degree of accuracy, and Auto commands just aren't enough. Let's look at the options that are open to you in these instances.

Fine tuning

The **Enhance** menu also includes a versatile set of tools to give you even more control over your images. Let's continue working with the Auto Contrast version of the Mount Rushmore image and see if we can use the additional features of the enhance menu to make finer adjustments.

Let's open up the Enhance menu and experiment with the features of the **Color** submenu on our Rushmore image.

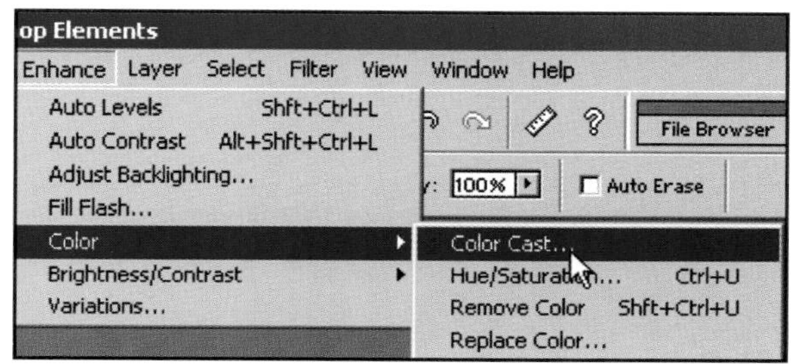

Color Cast

1. Let's start out with **Color Cast**. Select it and take a look at the window that comes up.

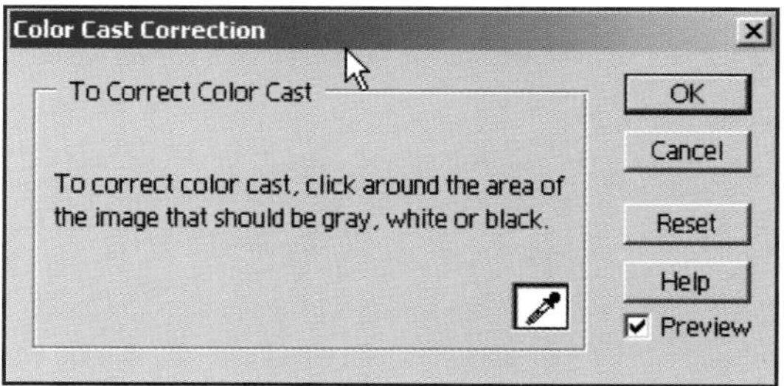

Seems pretty simple, doesn't it? Color Cast is a very general tool for balancing the overall mix of colors in an image, but it can often yield unwanted results.

2. With the Color Cast dialog open click an area of your image with the eyedropper that should be gray, white, or black. Try clicking some areas of our photo and notice what happens.

Because we have no true gray, black or white areas we end up with unsatisfactory results: At best we'll get some small color shifting in the mountain tone, and at worst we'll get a disgusting blue tone cast over our entire image.

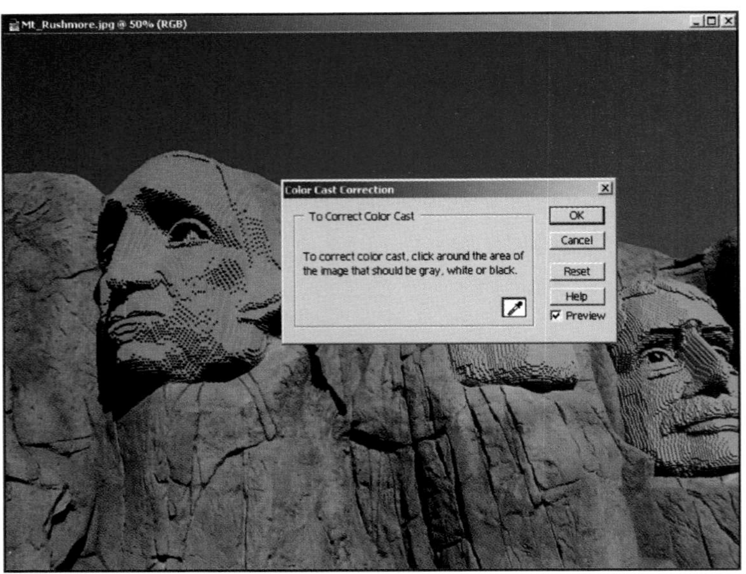

3. Click Cancel, we won't apply Color Cast to our image.

I would recommend using this tool sparingly – it's useful for images that have obvious color balance problems, but for images that already have a decent color balance it doesn't have much of an effect. Make sure you follow the instructions carefully and only click in an area that should be gray, black or white. (Unless you are deliberately aiming for a more surreal effect!)

Hue/Saturation

The **Hue/Saturation** option is a powerful and versatile tool for fine-tuning our images. Select this now and let's have a look at the window that comes up.

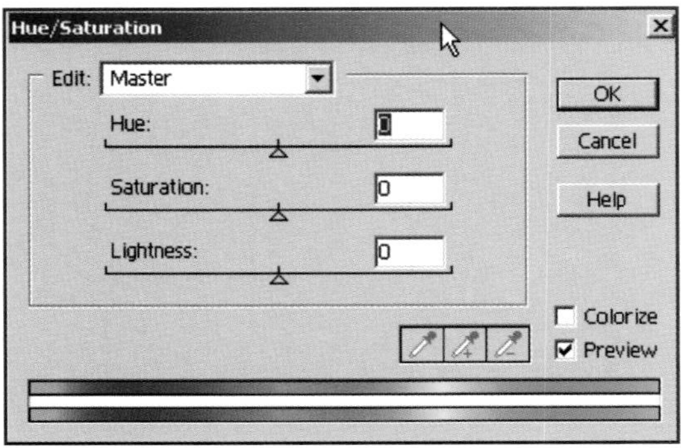

The Hue/Saturation tool allows you to adjust not only the **Hue** and **Saturation** but also the **Lightness** of an image. We can also work on specific color channels as well as the entire image, by going to the **Edit** field at the top of the window, where we can choose which channel to edit.

1. Still using the Mount Rushmore image, ensure that the Preview box is checked, and drag the **Hue** slider in either direction. Notice what happens to our image. The overall hue of the image is affected since we have Master selected in the Edit. You can see how this would be a lot more useful than the Color Cast tool.

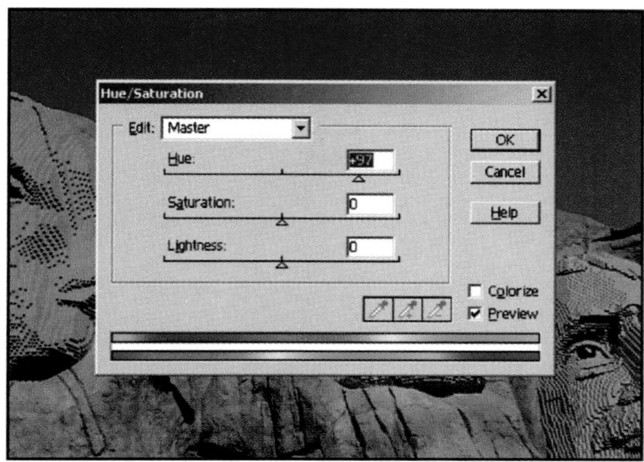

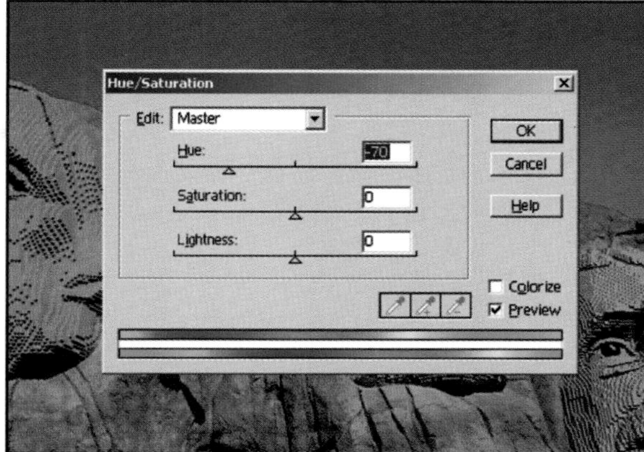

2. Suppose we wanted to change the hue of just the sky? Select **Blues** from the **Edit** drop down menu. Now drag the sliders and notice what happens. You can also use the eyedropper tool to select specific colors from the image that you want to affect.

In the Edit drop down, notice that there are also Reds, Yellows, Greens, Cyans, Blues, and Magentas to choose from.

- Reds, Greens, and Blues (RGB) are for screen adjustments.
- Cyans, Magentas, and Yellows (CMYK) are for print color adjustments.

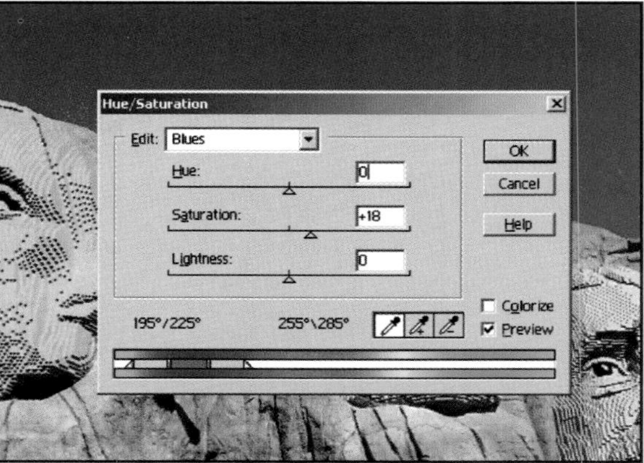

3. Next is the **Saturation** slider. Set the Hue back to 0 and the Edit popup back to Master. Drag the Saturation slider in both directions to get a sense of what it does. If you need to spice up or tone down the colors in an image, the Saturation tool is very effective – although be careful that you don't crank the saturation of your image up beyond printing capabilities.

4. We can get nice, deep color in this particular image when we bump up the Saturation to around 20. Remember, the Saturation settings can also be applied to a specific color channel.

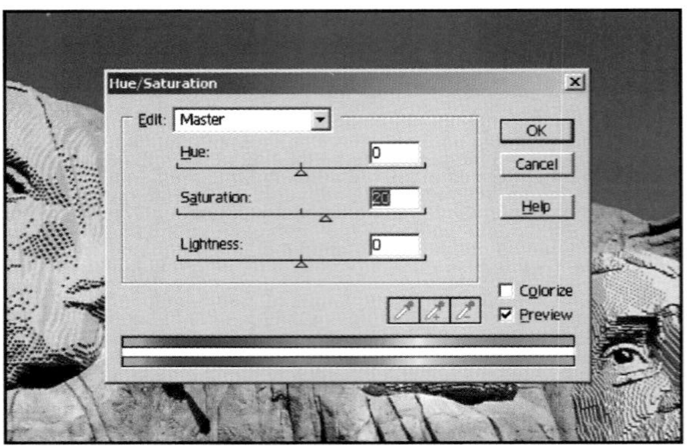

5. Next let's look at the **Lightness** slider. The important thing to understand about the Lightness slider is that it has no effect on the contrast of an image. Lightness simply lightens or darkens the image or specific channel as a whole – relative to the entire composition – it won't make any adjustments to the contrast. Drag the slider around to get a sense of how it affects our image. Again, though, if there were a specific color that you wanted to lighten/darken, you would use the Edit popup menu to select it and then adjust with the slider. Try selecting Blues and lightening the sky.

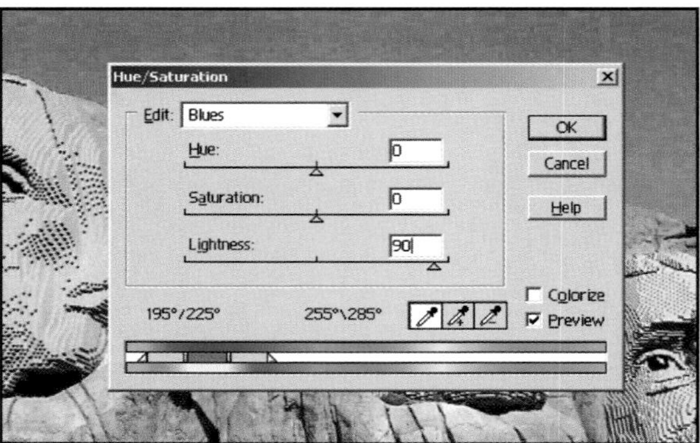

6. Finally, if you're curious about the **Colorize** checkbox let's look at what that can do for us. Set all the sliders back to 0, set the Edit field back to Master, and check the colorize box. We instantly have a monotone effect, based on the foreground color of the toolbar. Drag the Hue slider and notice how the color tone shifts. Also try adjusting the Saturation slider for more/less color.

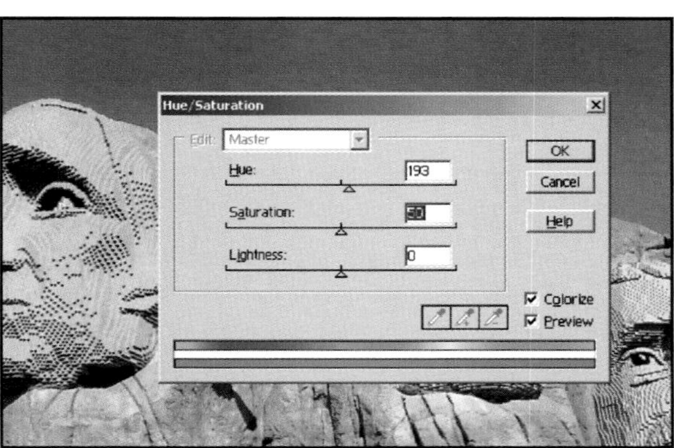

Remove color

Moving on down the **Enhance > Color** submenu we have the **Remove Color** command. This has the effect of removing all the color from an image to make it appear black and white.

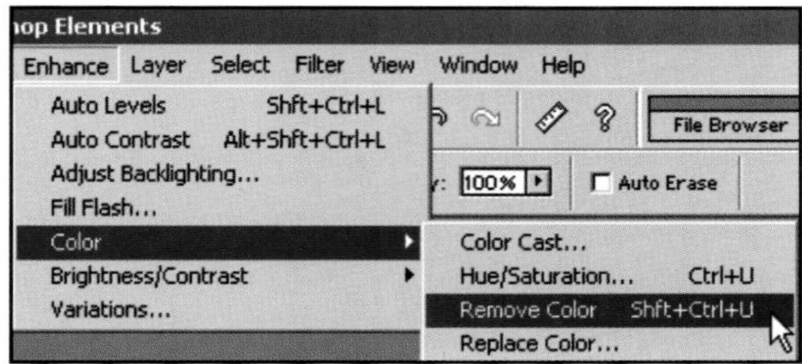

What it actually does is set the color saturation to –100. In this way it retains all the color information at an impossibly low saturation, rather than throwing it all away. You continue to work in **RGB** color mode, which will come in handy if you want to later add color to your image. Had you simply changed the mode to **Grayscale** you wouldn't be able to add any color effects, because all color information would have been binned.

Replace color

Last of all on the Color submenu we have **Replace Color**. This command works in a similar way to changing the hue of certain channels using the Hue/Saturation command. Let's open up the Replace Color command and have a look at its features.

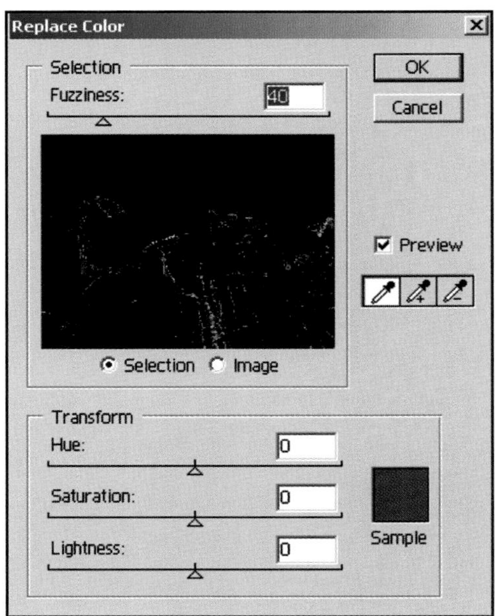

Does the bottom of the window look familiar? It's the same sliders we saw in the Hue/Saturation window. What makes this command different is that you can be more specific and have more control over the color you select to change.

1. Let's use the eyedropper to choose our sky. Click on our main image anywhere in the sky and notice how the Replace Color window changes. The selection preview should now have the sky highlighted, showing a white gradation to represent it.

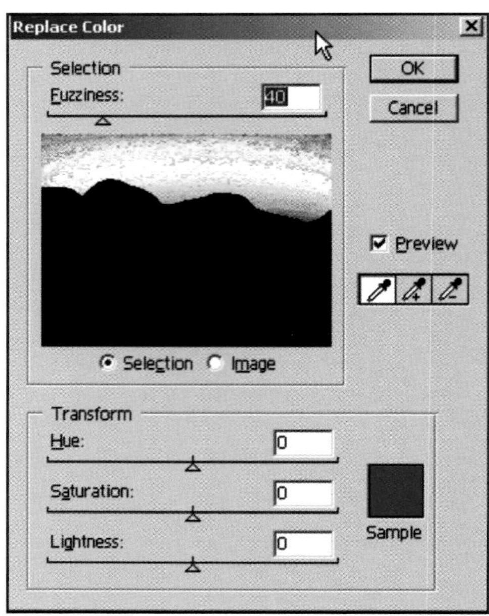

2. Well, we want to select more of the sky so lets adjust the selection by sliding the **Fuzziness** control to the right. Notice how the white fills in to a more solid selection. Don't go too far to the right or the selection will start to creep into the mountains.

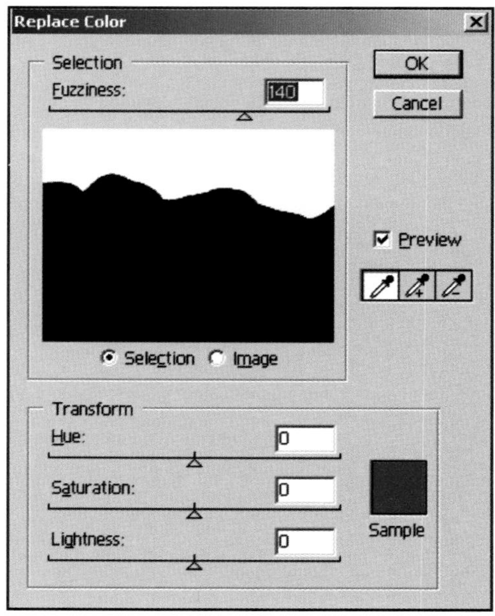

With a nice, solid selection we're now free to make adjustments to the sky using the Hue, Saturation, and Lightness sliders just as we did before. Experiment with these sliders and notice how the sky's color changes, but the rest of the picture is not affected.

Brightness/Contrast

With the Color menu rounded out let's move to the Brightness/Contrast submenu and take a look at its commands. If you find that the Auto Levels or Auto Contrast commands just aren't giving you the results you were looking for, it is here that you would do your fine-tuning.

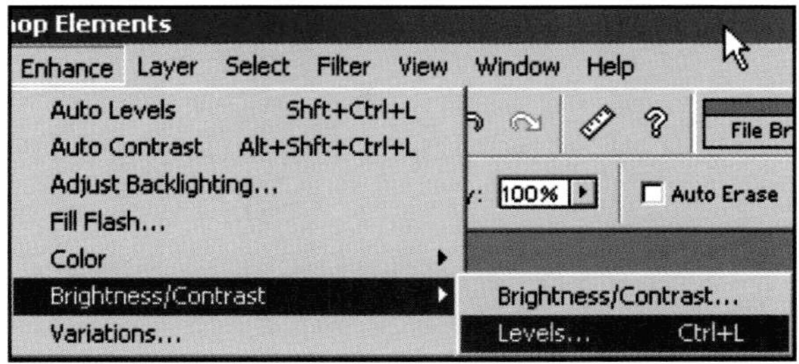

1. To compare these commands with the Auto commands, let's open up the original uncorrected Taj Majal image again.

Photoshop® Elements has a nifty option to help us locate recently used documents. Go to File > Open Recent, and you'll be able to locate your document more easily.

2. Select **Enhance > Brightness/Contrast > Brightness/Contrast**. Let's experiment with the settings of this command.

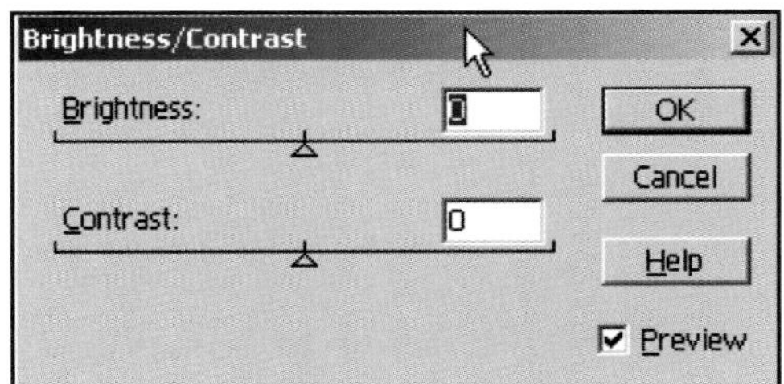

This window is pretty self-explanatory – sliding the **Brightness** to the left increases the image's brightness and to the right decreases it. I suggest adjusting the **Contrast** first, however – once you get a Contrast setting you're happy with, then go ahead and adjust the Brightness. Use the Preview checkbox to toggle between the adjusted and original image.

What's really important here is to realize that you have more control than simply trusting the outcome of the Auto Contrast command.

3. Here, my setting are Brightness = -5 and Contrast = +37, and the image looks drastically better. Hit Cancel; we don't want to actually apply these settings.

Levels

Now let's take a look at the **Levels** command: **Enhance > Brightness/Contrast > Levels.**

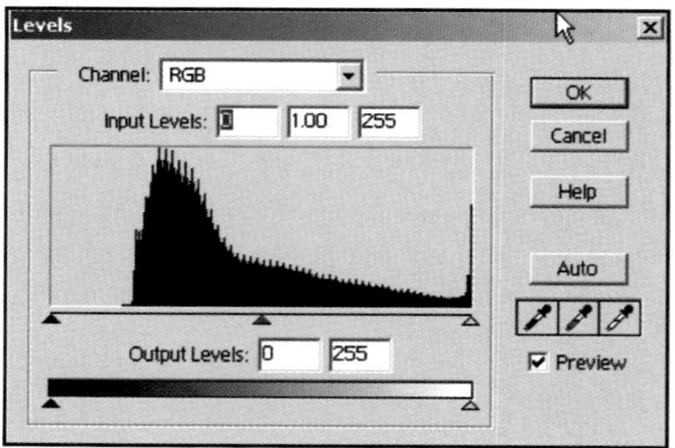

In the Levels dialog box you will see a Histogram; a visual guide that gives you command over an image's key tones. The three sliders of the Histogram represent the **shadows**, **midtones**, and **highlights** in the image, and are accordingly marked by color. The simplest way to adjust an image using the histogram is to first move the shadow and highlight sliders to the first group of pixels on either end of the scale. In other words, fill in the gaps. As you can see in our histogram above, there is a gap on the left side that we should move the shadow slider to.

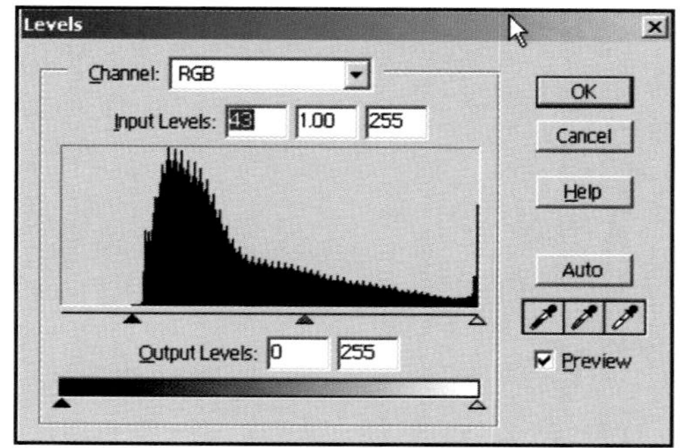

The highlight slider on the right can go without adjustment, since no gap appears on that end. Now, with the shadow and highlight point set, we can adjust the midtone slider to increase or decrease the intensity of the middle range tones. Slide it to either side and notice how the image changes – the shadows and highlights should remain at their settings while the middle ranges adjust to the slider's position. The middle range usually won't need much correction, but it's always helpful to experiment with the settings just to compare different results.

Did you notice the **Auto** button in this window? If for some reason you just can't get the right settings, Auto will apply the settings that Auto Levels would use, and bail you out. Keep in mind, however, that this should be a last resort – as mentioned before Auto Levels settings don't always yield the best results. So although the Levels command may look complex, it's really just a matter of getting used to interpreting the Histogram and determining where to place the sliders. Cancel the Levels window and let's move on to the final command on the Enhance menu.

Variations

The **Variations** command is what you might call the Jack-of-All-Trades tool when it comes to color and tonal correction. It is excellent for images with basic problems but shouldn't be used for precise adjustments. The **Variations** options adjust color balance, contrast, and saturation in an easy to use thumbnail-based interface that allows you to compare your working image with the original image side-by-side.

Select **Enhance > Variations** and let's take a look at the interface.

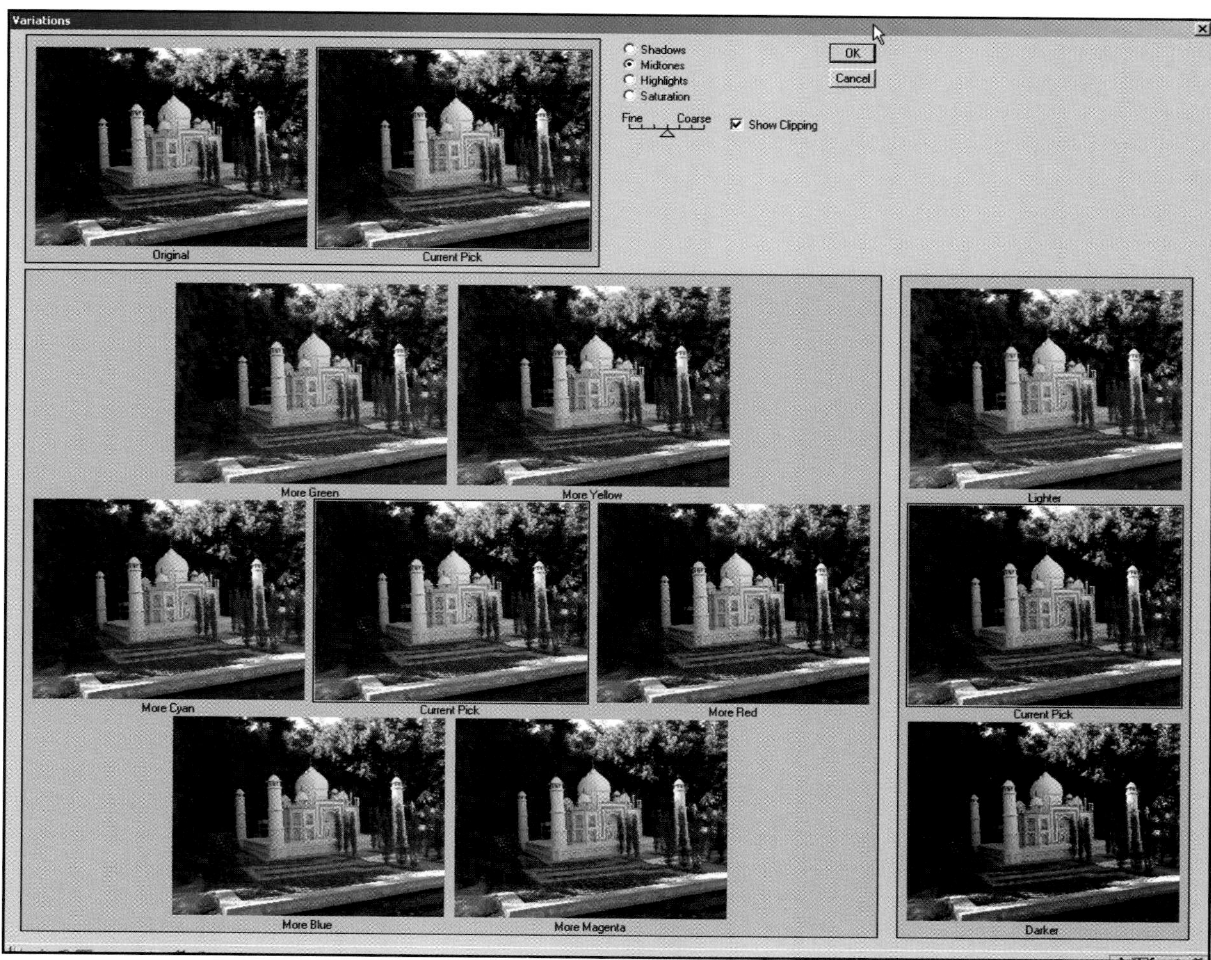

At the very top is where we'll compare our adjustments to the original image. If at any time you want to reset to the original image, click on the Original thumbnail. Next we have the **Shadows**, **Midtones**, **Highlights**, and **Saturation** radio buttons. Use these to select which tones of the image you would like to adjust, or if you want to change the saturation of the colors. The **Fine/Coarse** slider adjusts the severity of the adjustments. The checkbox next to the Fine/Coarse slider, **Show Clipping**, indicates values that have been clipped from the image. If checked it will display parts of a thumbnail as neon if the adjustment will cause the same parts of the current pick to become pure black or pure white. This helps you to avoid unwanted color shifts.

In other words, you click the visually represented adjustments to add them to your image until you reach the desired final adjustment. The center thumbnail always represents the current state, and, as mentioned at the beginning, can always be reset at the top by clicking the Original icon. Try experimenting with the Variations interface as it takes some getting used to. With a little practice you'll realize how effective a tool it can be for quick fixes.

Red eye removal

Finally, to wrap up this chapter, let's look at the **Red Eye Brush** tool (Y). This has to fall into the category of frequent photo problems. We're going to be working on the image `red_eye.jpg` from the CD, so go ahead and open it up now.

Notice the severity of the red eyes in this image. Let's use the Red Eye Brush to get rid of it. Select the Red Eye Brush from the toolbar, and notice the settings that come up in the options bar.

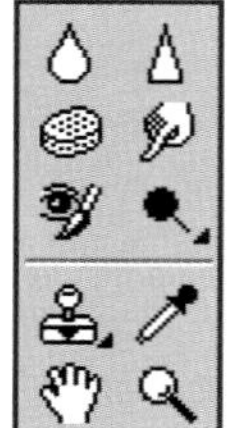

In a nutshell, this is how the tool works: you select the color of the red eye, select the color you want to replace it with, and then brush over the area of the red eye, and it will be replaced with the selected color. Let's try it out.

1. First use the **Zoom** tool, to zoom right into the eye on our left.

2. We want the eye to fill the whole canvas, so with the Zoom tool selected, click and drag across the area you want to select (as if you were creating a rectangular marquee).

3. Now, reselect the Red Eye Brush, and choose a good size to work with; I've chosen a 13 pixel soft brush.

4. Set the **Sampling** drop down to **Current Color**.

5. Now click on the color swatch next to the **Current** field on the Options bar, and use the eyedropper to select an average red tone of the red eye.

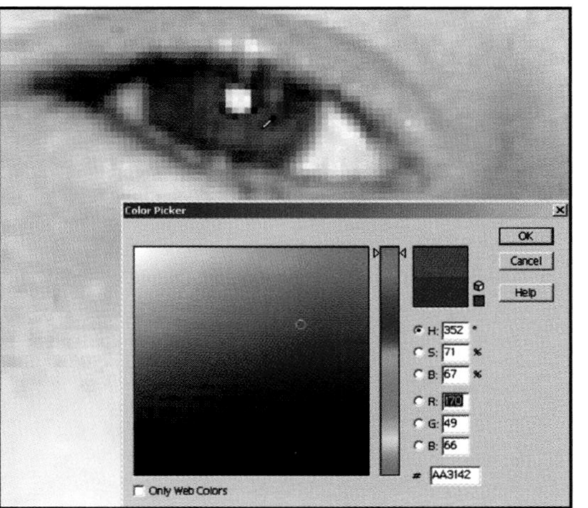

6. Next, select the **Replacement** color swatch; you are going to choose a color to replace the red eye with. Use the eyedropper to grab a color from the actual eye as a reference then darken it up.

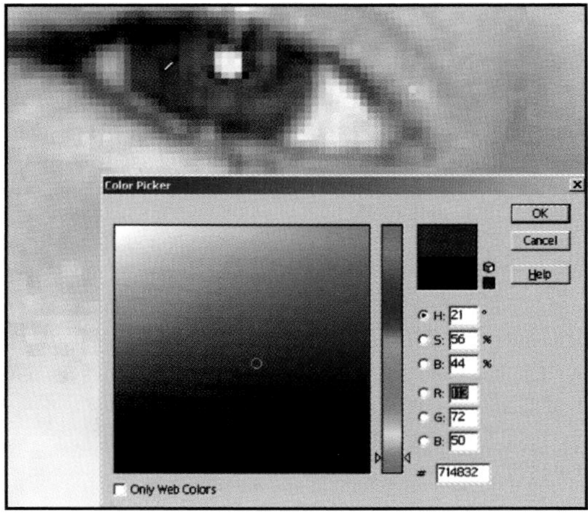

7. The **Tolerance** controls how similar the pixels surrounding our selected color must be in order to be replaced. Set the Tolerance to 40%.

So here is our options bar before we get ready to apply the brush:

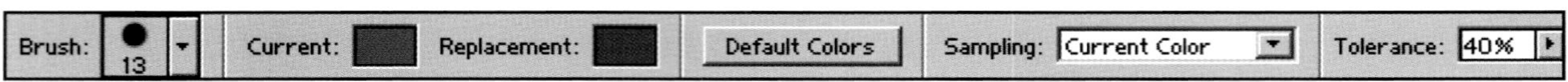

Now, it's as simple as taking our brush and painting over the red eye, and if our settings are correct, the redness in the eye will be replaced by the darker color we selected.

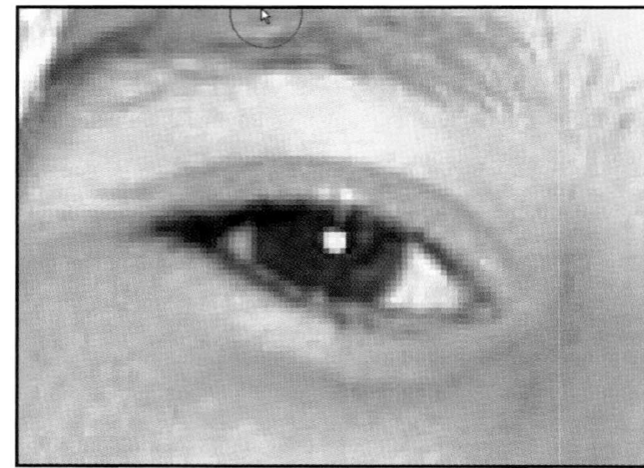

If you run into problems here, try adjusting the tolerance or using a different sized brush. It might take a couple runs to get the settings right on your system. Once you get comfortable with this tool it's a snap to fix all your red-eye pictures.

Conclusion

We've had a look at quite a lot of new things in this chapter – hopefully you're beginning to realize the flexibility of digital photographs and that Photoshop Elements provides several options for correcting your not-so-perfect images. Don't be discouraged if you struggle with color and tonal corrections at first – these are powerful tools that require a lot of work to get a handle on. Through practice you'll get comfortable with certain techniques and develop your own manner of solving problems.

3 Selections and Layers

So that's what Digital can do...

In the previous chapters we've spent some time familiarizing ourselves with some of the more standard procedures of photo editing: cropping, color correcting, tonal correcting, and red eye removal. It's one thing to take the images you've shot and correct the color and tone to make it a better looking image, but we'll see this chapter how we also have a powerful set of tools in Photoshop Elements for selecting, moving, and altering the composition of our photos as well.

We'll also introduce the concept of layers in this chapter: this is another key feature of photo editing that gives you the freedom to combine several elements into one composition and keep them all independently editable of each other. Layers are also useful for correcting images without destroying the original.

Selection tools

Before we get started, let's take a moment to cover the functionality of the basic selection tools that we'll be using to manipulate some images. In Photoshop Elements selections are defined by a dotted line, sometimes referred to as "marching ants". When you create a selection, any effects or adjustments applied to an image, or a layer, will only be applied to the area of the image, or selected layer, inside the selection. So let's look at some of the different ways that we can create selections.

We need an image to play with, so open up `Mt_Rushmore.jpg` from the CD.

The Marquee tool

The Marquee tool lets you define both rectangular and circular selections. To create your selection, click and drag on the canvas, and release when you have the desired area selected. By holding down SHIFT while selecting, you can constrain the selection to a perfect square or perfect circle. Be sure to release the SHIFT key only **after** your selection has been made. You can also move your selection while still defining it, by pressing the spacebar. This is useful if you start selecting a certain area, and then realize that you actually want to define a separate part of the image.

Let's try out all of these on our image to see how they work.

1. Select the **Rectangular Marquee** tool from the Toolbar.

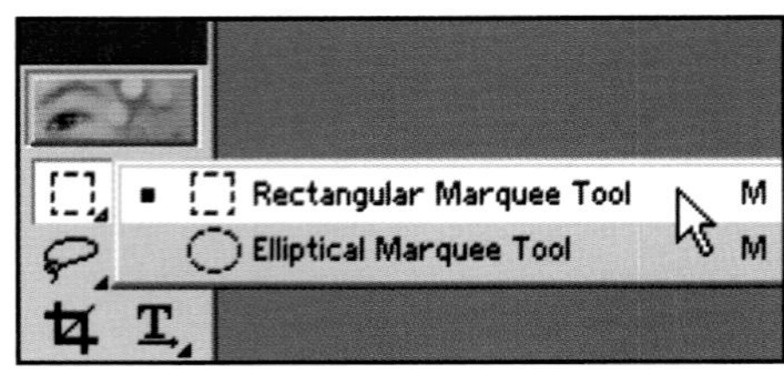

2. On `Mt_Rushmore.jpg`, click and drag anywhere on the canvas to start defining a selection, but don't release yet. Notice how the point that you click will be in one of the corners of the selection, depending on where you click

3. While you're defining your selection, press SHIFT and notice how the selection stays in a perfect square shape as you drag.

4. Release SHIFT and try pressing ALT/OPTION – now the point where you clicked is the center of the selection.

5. Now, let go of ALT/OPTION and press the SPACEBAR. You can now keep the current size and shape of the selection and move it on the canvas.

6. You can also use the SHIFT and/or ALT/OPTION and SPACEBAR together to keep your desired shape while moving the selection on the canvas. Experiment with all of these shortcuts to get a good sense of how they work together.

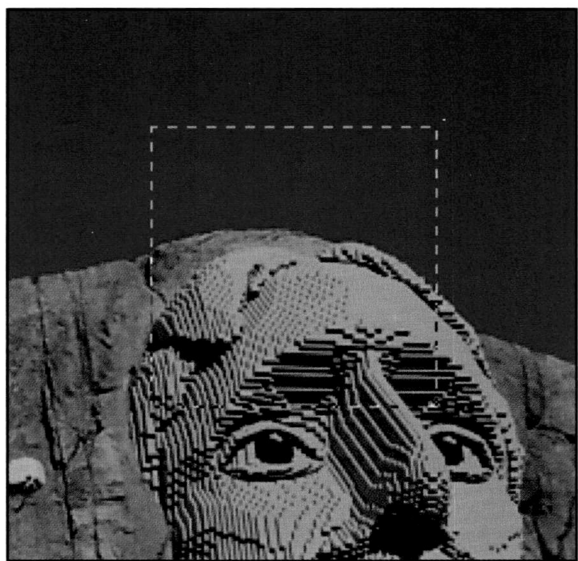

You can add, subtract, or intersect your selections by using the selection buttons in the Options bar. Let's take these buttons as they appear, from left to right:

- **New selection** lets you define a new area. This is the one we will choose for now.
- **Add to selection** means that you can make a new selection and add it to the one you have already made.

- **Subtract from selection** allows you to select an area and remove it from the selection you have already made.
- **Intersect with selection** allows you to select a section of your existing defined area.

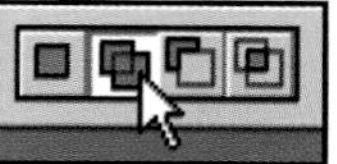

7. Now, just so we can see how the selection only allows the area inside of it to be affected by any adjustments, go to **Enhance > Auto Levels** and see what happens.

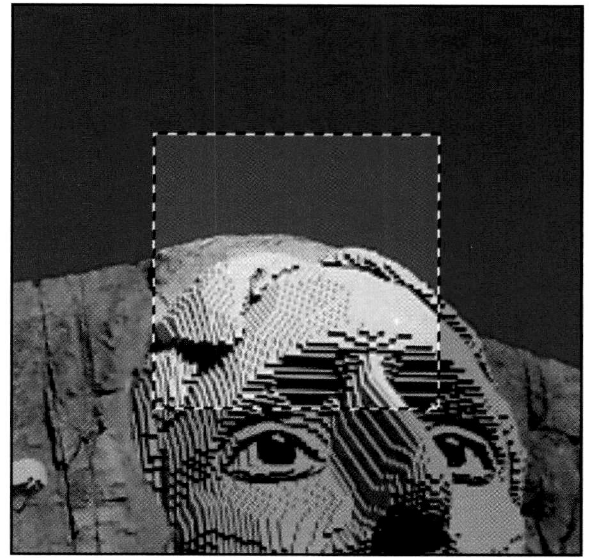

Even after you have defined your selection area, you can move it around by clicking inside of it and dragging without affecting the image. Try doing this now.

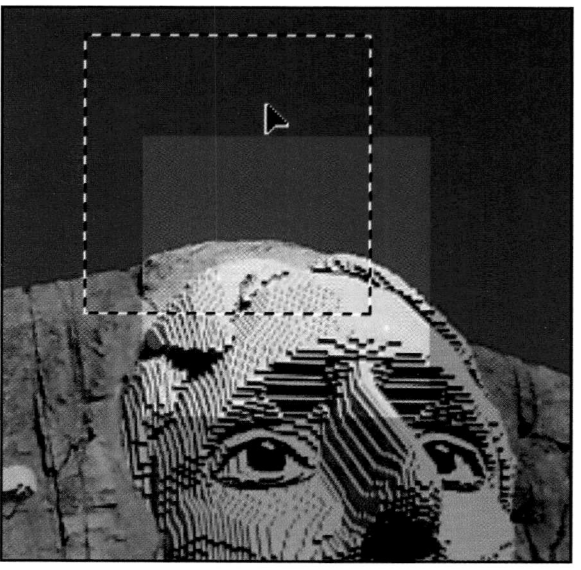

This is not to be confused with selecting the **Move** tool and then altering the selection, which will actually move the pixels inside the selection with it. (Notice how the move cursor changes to show scissors when you put it inside the selection.)

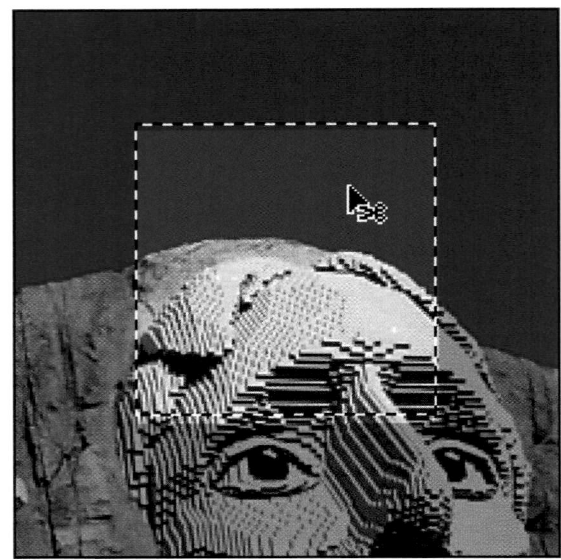

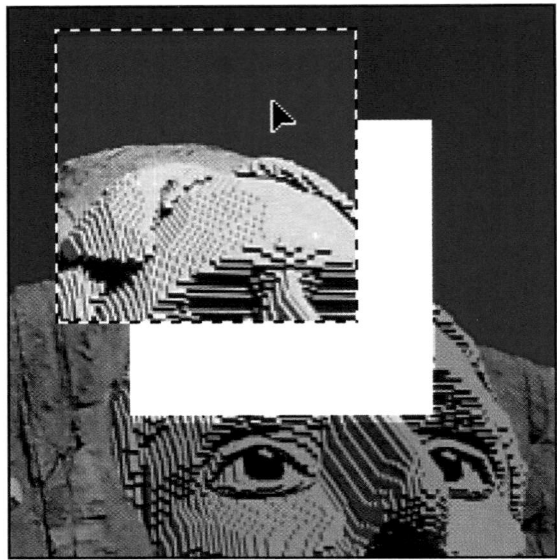

To deselect an area, either click on the canvas anywhere outside of the selected area or use the shortcut CTRL/CMD + D.

To invert a selection, that is to choose everything else, apart from your selection, go to **Select > Inverse**, or use the shortcut, SHIFT+CTRL/CMD + I.

8. Now let's choose the **Elliptical Marquee** tool from the Toolbar. Notice how it behaves much like the Rectangular Marquee tool.

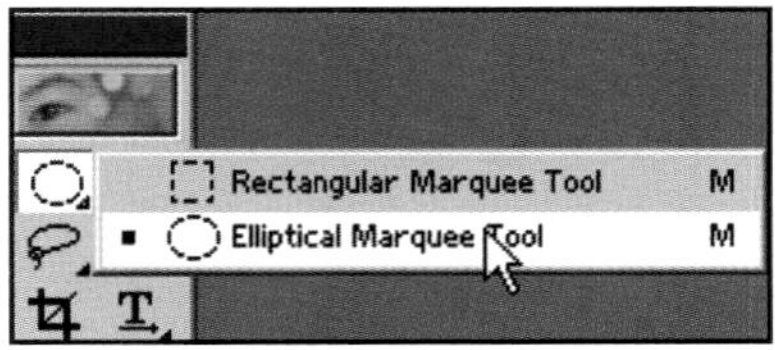

Experiment with the Elliptical Marquee tool, using the SHIFT, SPACEBAR, ALT and OPTION shortcuts, and notice how similar it is to the Rectangular Marquee tool.

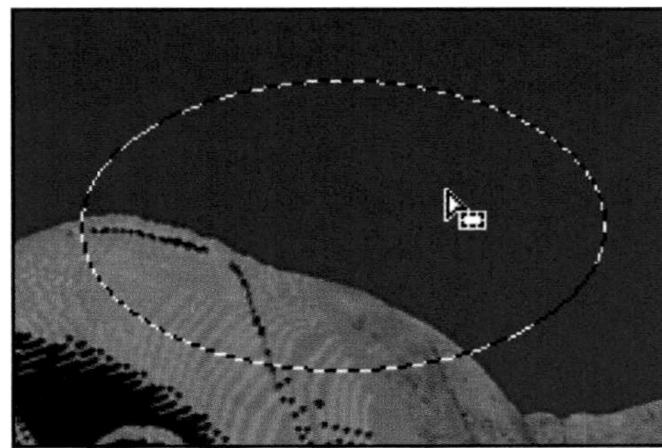

The Lasso tool

Rectangular and elliptical selections are fine for making basic shape selections, but what happens when we need to make more complex selections? This is where the Lasso tool comes in, which gives us complete freedom to make a selection of any shape. There are three different lasso tools – the basic **Lasso Tool**, the **Polygonal Lasso Tool**, and the **Magnetic Lasso Tool**. Let's see how each one of these works.

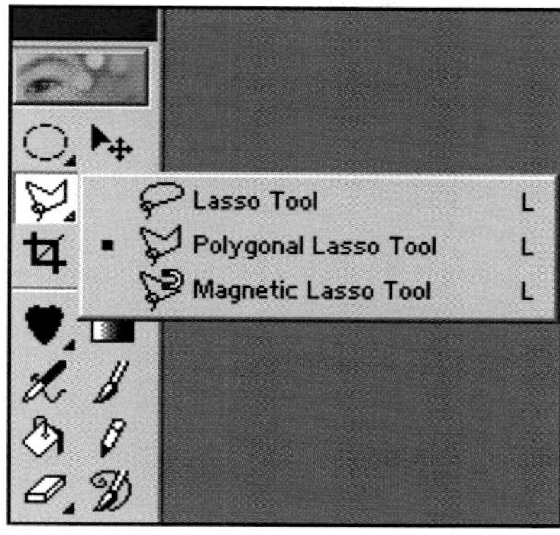

1. First, it really helps to be able to see your image up close while drawing a selection, so zoom in to the image using the Zoom tool, which is found in the bottom right hand corner of the toolbar.

2. Select the **Lasso** tool from the toolbar. This tool allows you to draw a selection on the canvas as if you were drawing with a pencil – in any freehand shape you like. Pick another area of `Mt_Rushmore.jpg` and try drawing a selection with the Lasso tool. Make sure that when drawing the selection you end up where you started to complete the selection. I've used the tool to draw a selection around the left head in the image.

You can switch from freehand to straight-edged selections, by holding down Alt/Option while using the regular Lasso tool. Click where segments should begin and end.

So, how did you get on with drawing using the regular Lasso tool? Tricky isn't it? As you probably discovered, the regular Lasso tool isn't very precise – unless you have a super steady hand your selection will almost always end up a little off. For a more exact selection, I prefer using the **Polygonal Lasso** tool.

3. Deselect your previous selection, (CTRL/CMD+D) and choose the **Polygonal Lasso** tool. Let's try making the same selection around the leftmost head, but this time we'll see how the Polygonal Lasso can offer more accuracy. The way this tool works is that you just click from point to point until you return to your starting point, you will then see the cursor turns into a little circle to indicate that you have reached the starting point, and that you're about to close the selection off. To close the selection off from anywhere further away, simply double click, and Photoshop Elements will close it by taking the shortest route back to your starting point.

If you make a mistake along the way, use the Delete key to step back.

Notice how much easier it is to draw with the Polygonal Lasso tool? We'll be using this tool again later in the chapter.

The last lasso tool is the **Magnetic Lasso** tool, this snaps to defined areas in an image, based on their color. You can adjust the settings for this tool in the options bar.

4. Select the Magnetic Lasso tool, and notice how the Options bar changes to show new settings.

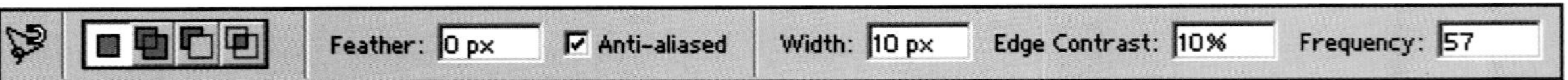

The Magnetic Lasso tool is best used for selecting areas that are already well defined, as the tool will search for the strongest area of an image as you drag it along. If there is no natural edge to snap to then the results may be unpredictable. However, we can adjust the settings of the tool to accommodate the nature of the area we want to select.

- The **Width** setting dictates how wide an area the tool will look in when trying to detect edges.
- The **Edge Contrast** setting tells the lasso how much contrast to look for.
- The **Frequency** setting determines how often the lasso places an anchor point.

5. Try tracing the edge of the figure's face to see how this tool functions.

Keep a few things in mind when using the Magnetic Lasso:

- The first time you click you set the first anchor point, and from there you can either release and drag, or keep the mouse pressed and drag.
- You can also use the DELETE key here to remove anchor points and step back. Or you can move the cursor back along the selection until you reach the point where things went wrong.
- If the lasso goes off on its own little mission, then you can click to create your own points.
- To switch temporarily to the regular Lasso tool whilst using the Magnetic Lasso tool, hold down ALT/OPTION and drag with the mouse.
- To temporarily activate the Polygonal Lasso, hold down ALT/OPTION and click.
- Remember, if you should want to end the selection before you've reached the starting point, then you can always double-click to achieve this.

So how did your selection turn out? It probably worked great along the top of the head where there is good contrast with the sky, but along the inside it was probably a little erratic. This tool works best on an image with an object against a solid background.

The Magic Wand tool

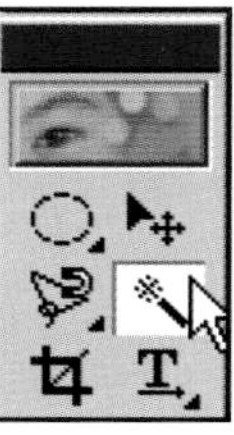

To round out the selection tools, let's look at how the **Magic Wand** tool allows us to select similar groups of pixels depending on the settings we define.

1. Select the **Magic Wand** tool and take a look at the Options bar.

- **Tolerance** specifies how strict or liberal the color range is for the wand. A higher tolerance will select more color; if you enter a lower value then this will select colors similar to the pixel where you clicked.

- The **Anti-aliased** checkbox allows the selection to have smooth edges. Anti-aliasing is the process of displaying the smooth edges in graphics accurately by softening the difference between edge pixels and the background. The term is most often associated with type – you've probably seen Aliased type on the web, recognizable by its noticeably jagged edges (often called "jaggies"). Anti-aliased type has smooth edges and blends seamlessly with its background.

- The **Contiguous** checkbox keeps only adjacent pixels within the same color range selected.

- If you are working with layers the **Use All Layers** checkbox will consider all the layers when defining the selection.

2. Let's try using the Magic Wand tool with its default settings to select the sky. Go ahead and click anywhere in the sky and see what kind of selection we get.

3. Not bad! Just to get sense of how a different setting would look, Deselect the selection, set the Tolerance to 4 and click on the sky again.

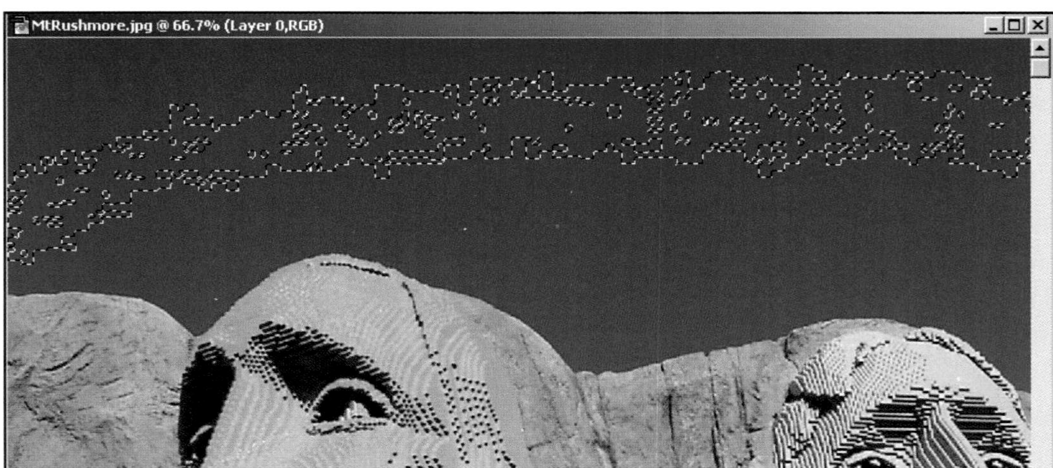

Ugh! Since we set the Tolerance to be stricter, it included less colors and as a result we have a jagged selection. So always be sure to experiment with the settings when you are trying to get a certain area selected – if you need a smaller selection, try making the Tolerance value lower, and if you need a wider selection then set it to a higher level.

Hopefully you're beginning to get comfortable working with selections, as we'll be using them in a tutorial along with layers.

CREATING A PHOTO COLLAGE

We're going to use some of the images that I worked with earlier, when creating a contact sheet to make a simple photo collage. We'll use some of the selection tools I just introduced along with layers to arrange several images on one canvas. We'll see how working with layers allows us to individually move or alter each piece of the composition without affecting the other parts of the composition.

Introduction to layers

Before we get started let's make sure you're clear on the concept of layers. Imagine layers as acetate (transparent plastic) sheets stacked on top of each other. Each sheet can contain an image or other element that can be moved on its own without affecting the others. Adjustments and effects can also be applied to this sheet, or layer, without affecting the others. Also, the order of the sheets can be rearranged at any time so that one could appear on top of or underneath another. Each sheet can also be set to a certain visibility, or **Opacity**, to fade it back if desired. All of these settings will be applied through the **Layers** palette, which you'll become familiar with through the course of the tutorial.

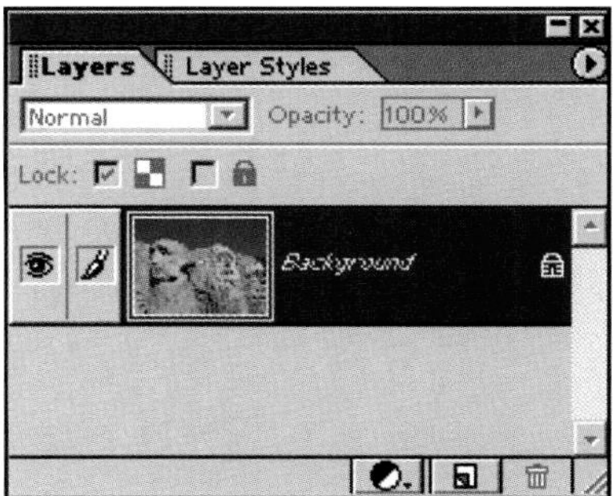

So with that in mind let's get started! Here's basically what we're going to do in this tutorial:

- We'll create a new, blank canvas that we will end up moving our selected images on to.
- Then we'll open up our photos, and create various types of selections around the sections to bring over on to the blank canvas.
- Next, we'll move the selected parts of each photo over to the blank canvas, each one being on its own layer.
- Finally, we'll arrange each layer so that we have a final composition of photos for our collage.

1. Create a new canvas by selecting **File > New** or by typing CTRL/CMD+N. Give your new document the following settings, pictured below. This will give us a horizontal canvas with a white background.

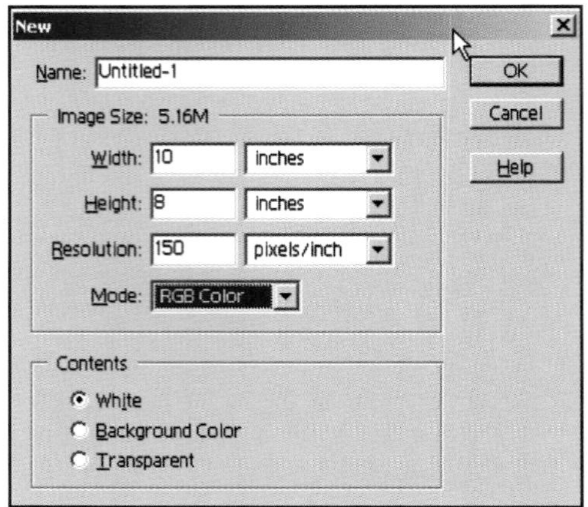

With the resolution at 150 our final image will be high enough quality to print – anything less than 150 and pixels usually start to become visible, and as a result the image looks less sharp.

Preparing the photos

Leave the new document open for now; we'll come back to it after we have our images prepared. Let's take a look at the images that we want to use for our collage. We'll open up the contact sheet I created earlier, and use it to help us pick out some photos for the collage. Open up `ContactSheet.psd` from the CD.

2. I think we'll make a collage of photos from my trip to LegoLand, so I'll choose several photos from that part of the contact sheet. Let's use `Australia.jpg`, `Einstein.jpg`, `Elephant.jpg`, `Legodudes.jpg`, and `MtRushmore.jpg`. These can all be found on the CD. Close the contact sheet now that we have our images selected.

3. Open up `Australia.jpg` and we'll start out with a basic collage technique. Select the Rectangular Marquee tool and drag a selection around the building in the photo, as I've done in the image below.

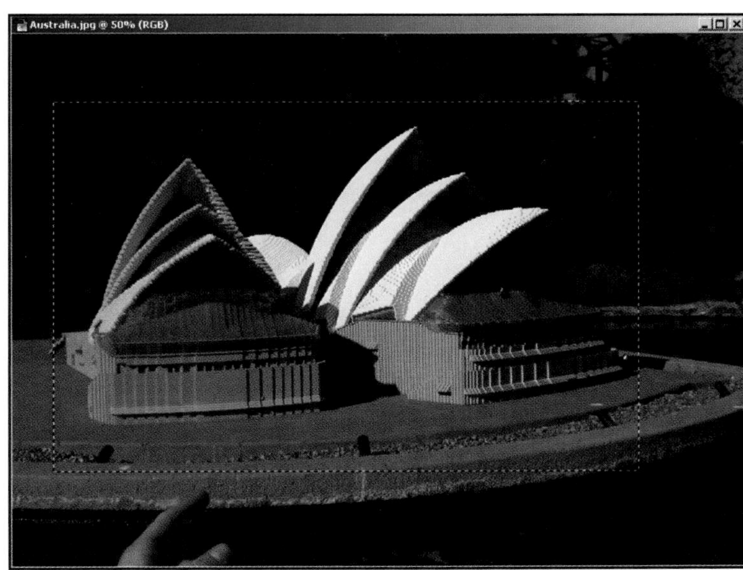

Now, we could simply take the area we've selected and use the Move tool to drag it into our blank canvas that we previously created, but that wouldn't be very exciting. Instead, we'll apply a feathered effect to the selection so that it will blend better with our final composition.

4. To feather a selection, choose **Select > Feather**, or click ALT/OPTION+CTRL/CMD+D. For our image we'll enter a **Feather Radius value** of 25. But this depends on the extent to which you want your edges to be softened. Also, bear in mind that the extent to which an image will appear be feathered depends on the resolution. With a higher resolution, you'll need to a higher feather radius to get a noticeable effect – it's just a question of there being more pixels to process!

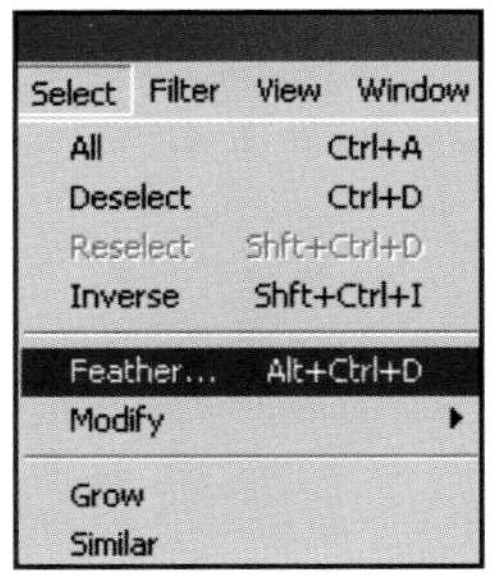

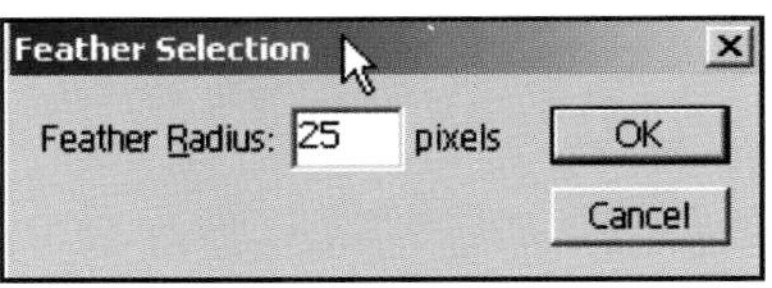

Notice how our selection now appears rounded on the edges to reflect the softening caused by the feathering.

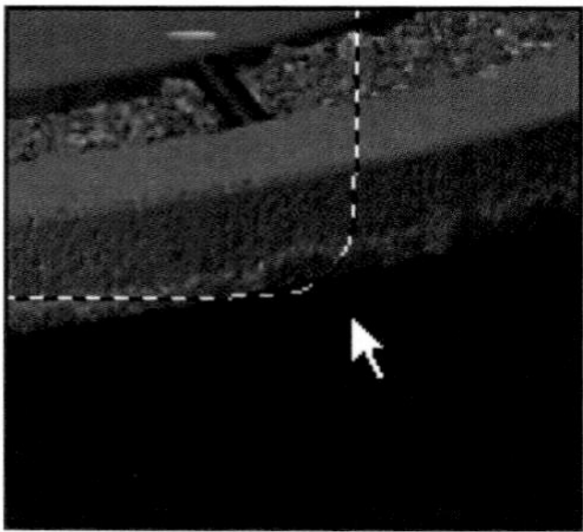

Now we can choose the Move Tool from the toolbar and move the part of the image inside of our selection over to our blank canvas.

5. First, reduce `Australia.jpg` to 25% by adjusting the scale box in the bottom left hand corner, so that you can see more of our blank canvas.

6. Now, choose the Move Tool, click inside of the selection, and drag into the blank canvas we created.

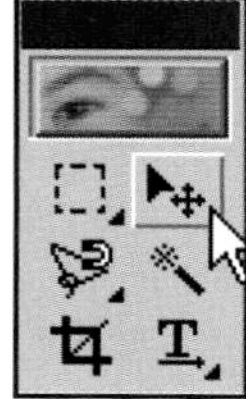

That was pretty easy, wasn't it? Have a look in the **Layers** palette; notice how our feathered image now resides on its own layer – anytime we drag a selection over from another document it is automatically placed on its own layer. (If you cannot see the Layers palette, go to **Window > Show Layers** to open it).

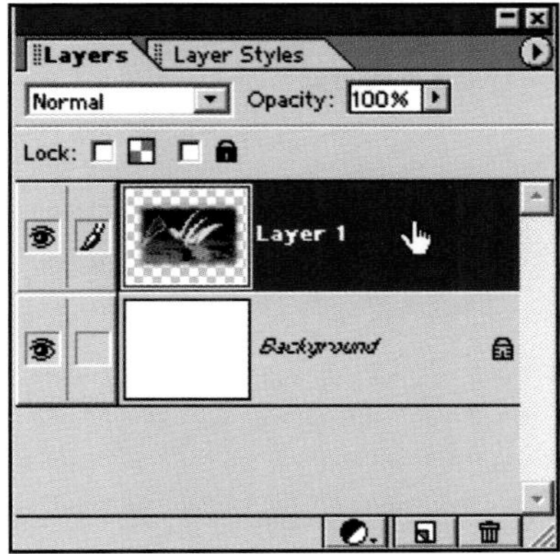

7. Before we forget, let's save our document. Name it `Collage.psd` and save it to your hard drive. Notice the extension: PSD – this denotes a Photoshop file, which is the only format we can save in and still preserve the separate layers of our document.

8. For the sake of keeping things organized, let's change the name of the layer we just created from the default "Layer 1". To do this, you can either right/Ctrl-click the layer name in the **Layers** palette to bring up a drop down menu, or double-click, on the layer name to open up the **Layer Properties** dialog. We'll call this layer, "Opera House", so type this in as the new name in the window that comes up.

I would encourage making this a habit when you work – the thumbnails in the layers palette can be helpful but it's easier on the eyes to not have to squint every time to see what layer you're on.

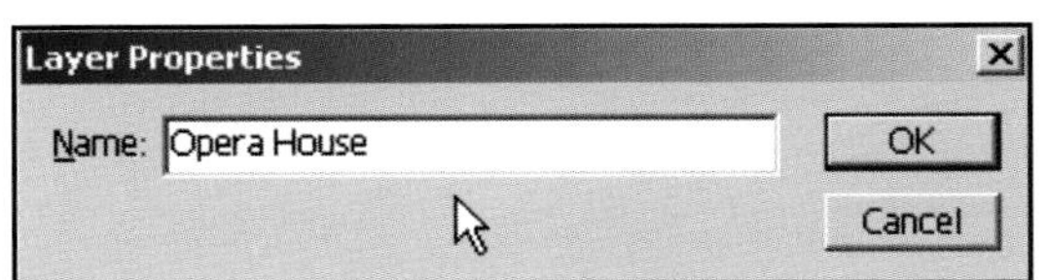

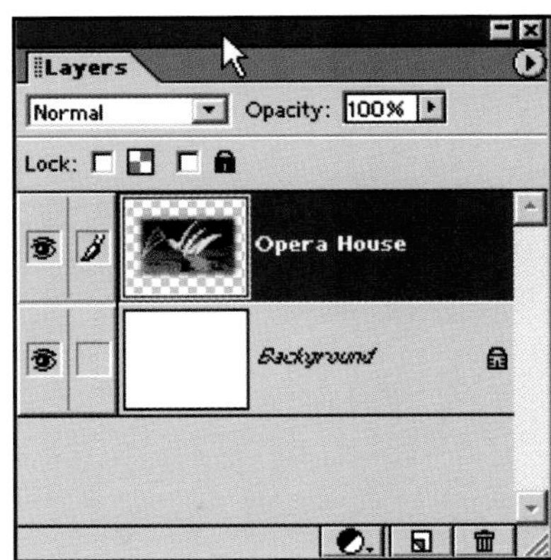

Don't worry that the image takes up a lot of the canvas; we'll adjust that later. Let's move on to preparing our second image.

9. Close `Australia.jpg` since we're done with it, but do not save any changes you have made, and open up `Einstein.jpg`.

10. For this image, since the main figure is sort of rounded, let's use the Elliptical Marquee tool to create a selection. Click and drag a selection around Einstein's Lego head as in the shot below. Don't worry if it seems too close.

11. Just like we did before, choose **Select > Feather** but this time enter a setting of 50 so we can see the difference from the previous image when we had it set to 25.

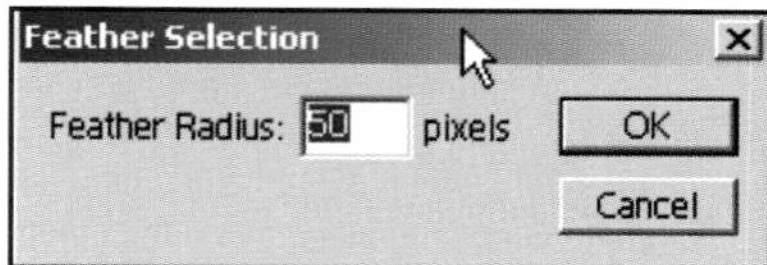

12. Again, like the first time select the Move tool and drag our selection over to `Collage.psd` and once again, our selection is placed onto a new layer.

13. Double-click the new layer thumbnail in the Layers palette, and rename it Einstein in the Layer Properties dialog box. Notice how the Einstein layer interacts with the Opera House layer – like two sheets of acetate. Again, the new image is taking up a lot of the canvas but leave it for now, we'll fix it later.

14. Go back to `Einstein.jpg` and close it – we're ready to move on to the next image.

15. Open up `Elephant.jpg` – this time we're going to use the Lasso tool to "cut out" the elephant. With `Elephant.jpg` opened, select the Polygonal Lasso tool. We're going to use it to draw an outline around the edges of the elephant.

16. To make things easier, zoom in to around 300% and start drawing from the elephant's back. Keep clicking all the way around the elephant until you reach the beginning of the selection, which will finish it. This may take a little while, but stick with it and remember that you can use delete to back up as you are clicking.

17. Once you have the entire elephant selected, add a small amount of feathering so that the elephant doesn't appear jagged on the edges due to our polygonal selection. Choose **Select > Feather** and enter a setting of 2 pixels.

18. When you're done, select the Move tool and drag the selection over to `Collage.psd`. You might have to zoom back out in `Elephant.jpg` first so you can see it.

19. So on `Collage.psd`, we now have another layer – go ahead and double-click this new layer and name it Elephant in the Layer Properties dialog box.

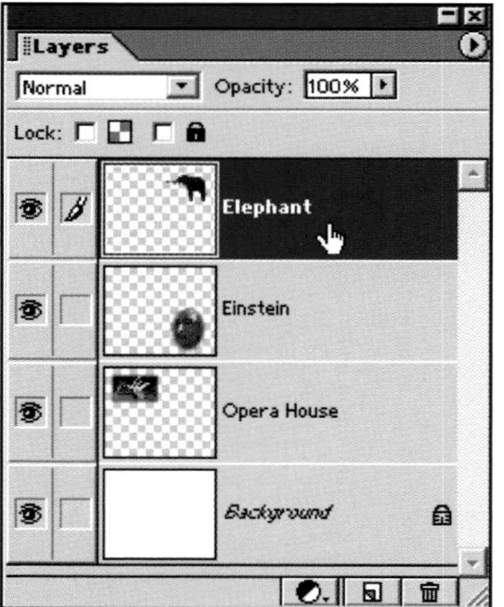

20. Now close `Elephant.jpg`, and open up `Legodudes.jpg`. We'll use this image to try out the Magnetic Lasso tool again. This tool should work really well here, as we have an image with a nice clean background all the way around our main object.

21. Let's use the Magnetic Lasso tool to cut out the Lego dudes and the blocks they are climbing on. Select the Magnetic Lasso tool, but before we start, let's adjust the settings in the options bar to make the tool a little more precise. Use the settings pictured below. I narrowed the Width, and increased the Edge Contrast, and the Frequency, all to force the tool to make a better selection.

22. With the settings ready to go, click once to start the selection. Then continue all the way around, letting the Magnetic Lasso tool continually snap to the edges. If you mess up, use DELETE to back up and try again. Also, hold the SPACEBAR (temporary Hand tool) to scroll the canvas around if you are zoomed in.

23. When our selection is complete, use feather again to give it a soft edge, this time set it to 1 pixel. Now select the Move tool and drag it over to `Collage.psd`. Rename the new layer Legodudes.

24. Finally, let's assemble the last piece of our collage. Close `Legodudes.jpg`. Open up `MtRushmore.jpg` – we're not going to use a selection for this image, so just drag the entire image over to `Collage.psd`. When you've moved it over, name the new layer Mt. Rushmore. Then go back to `MtRushmore.jpg` and close it.

So now we have `Collage.psd` with a white background layer, and five layers that we added to it. It looks like a mess right now, so let's go about cleaning it up.

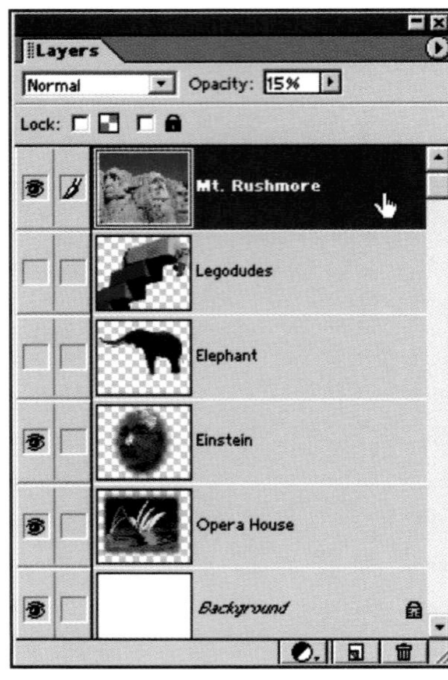

1. To start, let's use the Mount Rushmore image we just dragged over as the background image. Go to the Layers palette, and see how at the moment it's on top of all the other layers. We can quickly change that by clicking and dragging it just above the Background layer in the Layers palette. Notice how the cursor changes to a closed hand when you press the mouse.

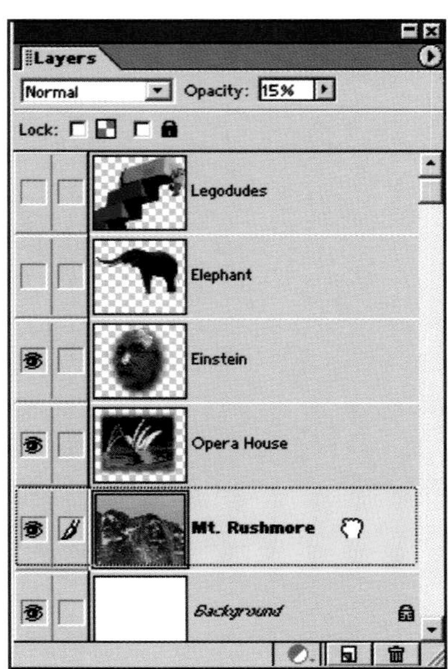

2. This should be the exact size of the canvas, but you might not have it lined up to the edges. If not, select the Move tool and drag it until it lines up to the edges, it should snap to an edge when it gets close.

3. With it correctly positioned, let's tone it down a bit so it doesn't take away from the other images. To do this, let's change the opacity to 15%. This is done using the Opacity slider at the top of the Layers palette, you can either type it in, or use the slider.

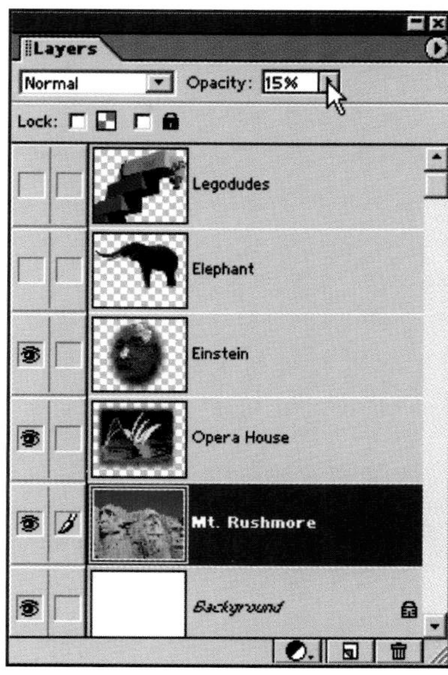

4. After you have set the opacity, hide all of the other layers in the palette except for the background by clicking the eye next to each one, so that we can get a good look at our faded back image of Mount Rushmore.

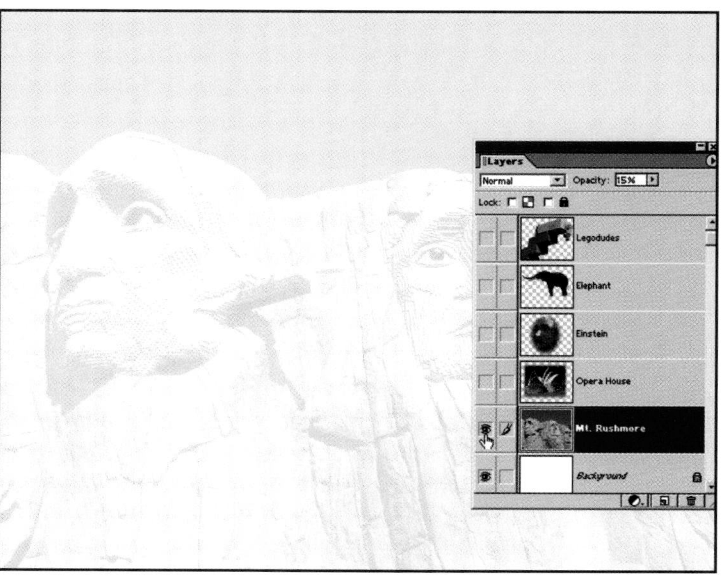

5. Now we can go to work arranging the other layers, one by one. Show the Legodudes layer by clicking the empty box where the eye was in the Layers palette. Let's arrange this image so that it appears to be coming out of the bottom left corner of the canvas.

We have two problems, firstly the image is too big, and also, it needs to be moved. We can solve both of these problems using the **Transform** tool.

6. Select the Legodudes layer by clicking on it in the Layers palette. Be really careful here that you have selected the correct layer, as it can be so frustrating to make an adjustment, and then realize that all along you have been working on the **wrong** layer!

7. Go to **Image > Transform > Free Transform**, or the shortcut CTRL/CMD+T. The layer should now have a box with a set of handles around it.

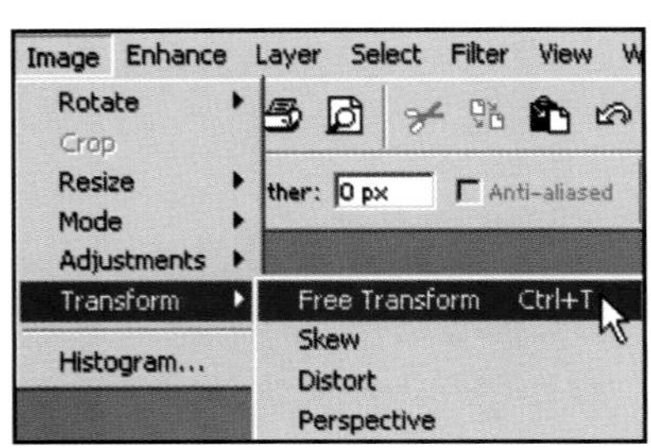

8. With the Free Transform tool, we can move, scale, and rotate the image. When the cursor is anywhere inside the boundaries of the box, it can be moved. Move the layer down into the bottom left corner of the canvas. It should snap to it when it gets close. See the eight little squares around the edges of the Free Transform box? They are used to scale the layer. Grab the upper right square and drag down and to the left to scale down the image. Hold down SHIFT to maintain the proportions of the image.

9. Scale the image to about a quarter of the canvas, and hit ENTER to apply the Free Transform. If the bottom left of the layer doesn't bleed off of the canvas, use the arrow keys with the Move tool selected to nudge it off.

10. Next, let's show the Elephant layer, and make sure it is the active layer, (remember the active layer is the one that is highlighted in the Layers palette). Using the Move tool, move it into the upper right corner of the canvas.

11. Let's also use the Free Transform tool again to scale it down in order to make room for the other layers. Remember to hold down SHIFT to keep the proportions.

12. Let's now scale down the remaining two layers. Show the Einstein layer in the Layer palette, and make it the active layer, by clicking on it in the Layers palette. Use Free Transform to scale it down and move it to the bottom right of the composition.

13. Then use the Eraser tool, sized 100 pixels at 60% opacity, to gently remove some of Einstein's background, particularly the blue sky.

14. Let's finish off the piece by showing the Opera House layer and moving it into the upper left corner, then scaling it to fit.

Here's the final composition. It's not exactly a beautiful work of art, but through its creation we have learnt a whole raft of useful techniques, including making selections, feathering them for softer edges, manipulating layers, and adjusting images using the free transform option. Why not practice these techniques by making some collages of your own? In the next chapter we'll move on to personalizing your photos even further, by adding text and geometric shapes to your work.

4 Drawing tools

A professional look made easier

In the previous couple of chapters we've covered a good many of the basics for editing and correcting your images, and we've even used multiple images to create a composition through the use of layers. Up to this point, though, everything we've created has only involved the use of our original photography, with no additional elements.

This is only half the story. Another reason that Photoshop Elements is such a versatile program is that it offers a host of tools allowing you to add features to your photos. You can apply text, shapes, airbrushing, painting, and there are a multitude of options for customizing these features. In this chapter we'll spend a little time introducing these tools and their options, and then go through a tutorial in which we create a mock magazine page layout to implement them.

Drawing and painting

Photoshop Elements offers a great set of drawing and painting tools for customizing your photos. These tools can be used to create original art from scratch, or to add to existing photos. Conveniently, these tools all reside in the same area on the toolbar – right underneath the moving and selecting tools.

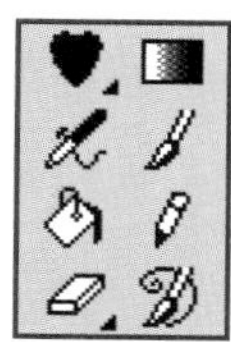

To get a sense of how these tools work by themselves, let's work on a blank canvas for now. Go ahead and create a new document, make it 5 x 3 inches, with a resolution of 150 dpi. The mode should be RGB, and set the contents to white.

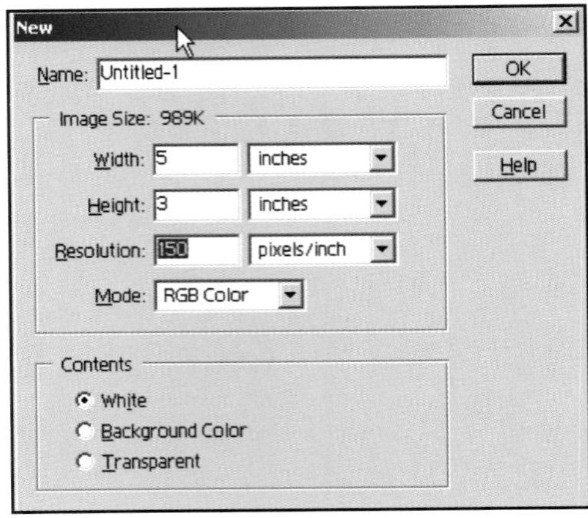

Airbrush tool

The **Airbrush** tool simulates the behavior of a traditional airbrush, applying smooth, gradual tones of a selected color. The Airbrush tool can be used for touching up photographs, and is very popular amongst magazine designers for making those supermodels' nicotine-stained teeth pure white, or hiding those bloodshot eyes! We'll have a go at something like this in the tutorial, but for now let's select the tool and see how it works on the canvas.

1. Select the Airbrush tool and pick any color using the **Color Picker** (bring up this window by clicking on the foreground color square at the bottom of the Toolbar) – I'm going to use red, with a **hexadecimal** color value #F31313.

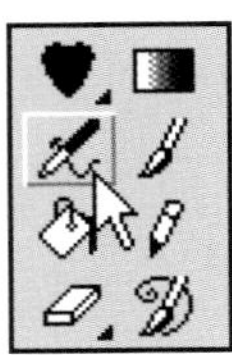

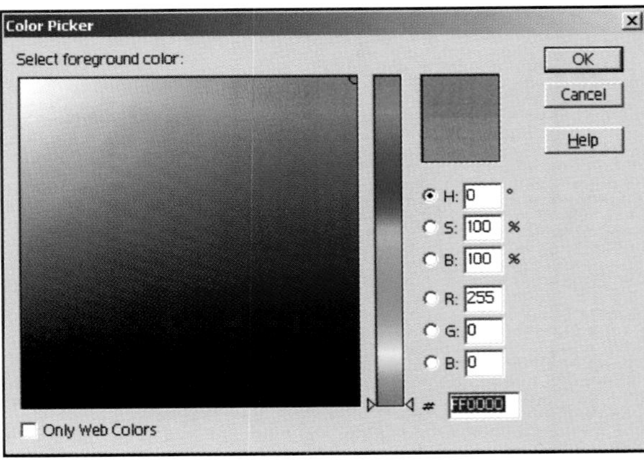

2. Before we start airbrushing, we'll choose a suitable brush from the options bar. I'm going to use the 100 pixel soft brush in Normal Mode at 100%. Since a lot of the brush settings are similar for the different drawing tools, we'll get into customizing them later.

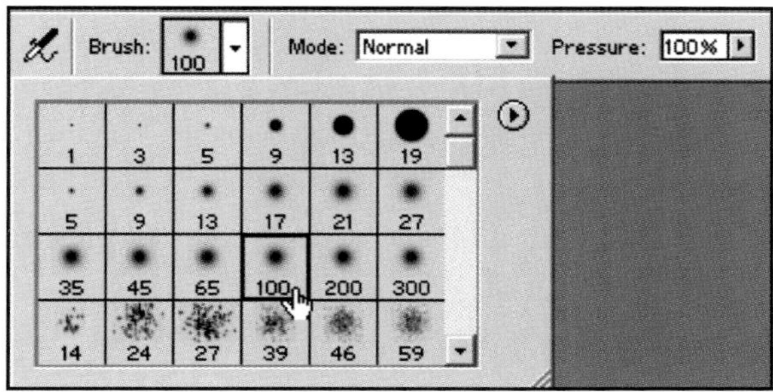

3. So let's start throwing some paint around – click and drag on the canvas to start painting with the Airbrush tool. Notice how it behaves – we simulate applying pressure by holding the mouse down. Try holding it in one place and notice how the paint just builds up. We'll see later how this tool can be used to make subtle changes to our images by adjusting the options.

Paintbrush tool

Now, let's switch over to the Airbrush tool's neighbor, the **Paintbrush** tool.

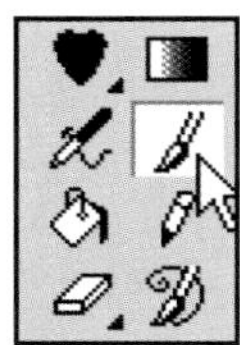

1. We'll use the same settings that we had for the Airbrush tool – 100 pixel soft brush set to Normal and 100%.

2. Lay some paint down with this brush, and see how it differs from the Airbrush tool. It's a small difference, but try to notice how the Paintbrush tool paints an even stroke no matter how much "pressure" you apply. Again, we imitate pressure by holding the mouse down in place, just as we did with the Airbrush tool, to build up paint.

On the next page, we can see two brush strokes; the left one made by the Airbrush, and the right made by the Paintbrush tool. Both were made with a 100-pixel brush with the same settings, and both were held down for the same period of time. As you can see, the Airbrush tool, responds much more sensitively to the pressure applied. It is due to the tool's sensitive nature that we will use it extensively throughout this chapter.

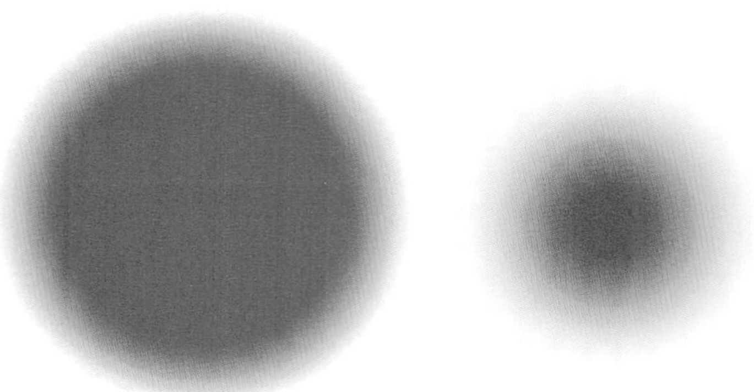

We'll now moving on to look at some other painting tools so to clear our canvas got to **Select > All** and then go to **Edit > Clear**.

The Paint Bucket tool

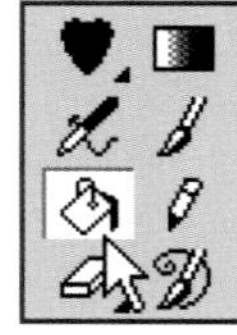

The **Paint Bucket** tool is handy for filling selections and layers with a solid color. It works like most photo editors – with a color chosen (in this case, the foreground color) you simply click in the area that you would like to fill.

Let's try it out by changing the color of our canvas background to blue. First, we have to select a shade of blue as our foreground color. As we did before, click on the foreground color square at the bottom of the toolbar to bring up the Color Picker. Choose any shade of blue. Use the vertical slider to adjust the range of colors to choose from.

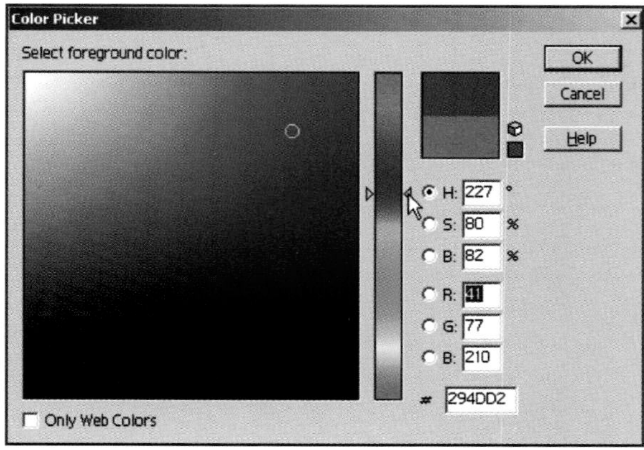

With the Paint Bucket tool selected, click anywhere on the canvas and watch the background fill with the blue. If you want to only fill a specific area then create a selection, using any of the techniques covered in Chapter 3, and then click inside it with the Paint Bucket tool. We'll cover this in more detail later in the tutorial.

The Pencil tool

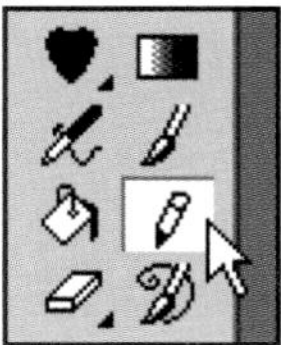

The pencil is used for drawing hard-edged lines. Select the **Pencil** tool and take a look at the Brushes that come up in the options bar. Notice how there are no soft-edged brushes to choose from, like there were with the Airbrush and Paintbrush tools.

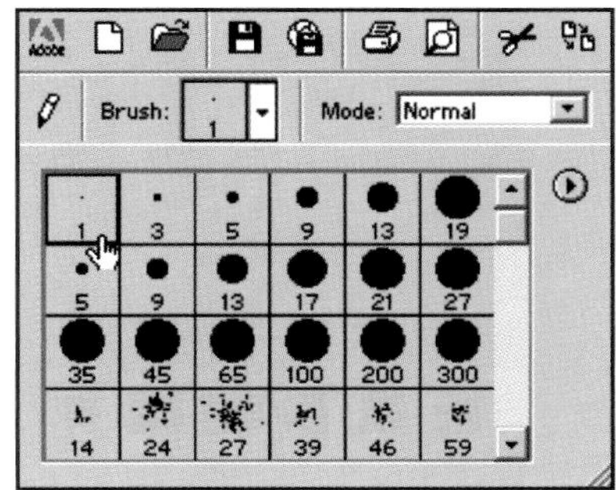

Let's select the 1 pixel brush and choose any color (don't use the same color that you used with the Paint Bucket tool). Draw some freehand lines on the canvas; you'll see that there's a much harder no-nonsense feel to the pencil. It has a very literal response to your mouse movements. It's great for precision, but doesn't suffer shoddy mousemanship!

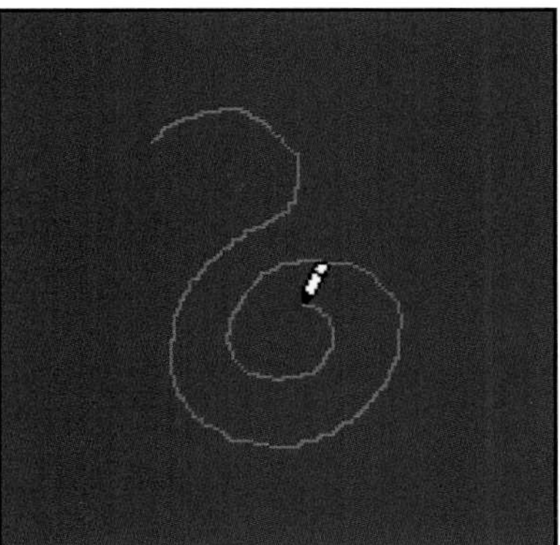

Gradient tool

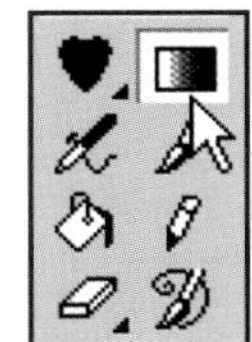

Wouldn't it be a shame if we could only create solid-colored objects? Don't mock – it was once the case! The **Gradient** tool, however, allows us to create gradual color blends using either built-in gradient fills, or our own customized fills. Choose the Gradient tool, and then let's take a look at the options bar to see the choices available to us.

1. Click on the gradient preview to bring up the **Gradient Editor**.

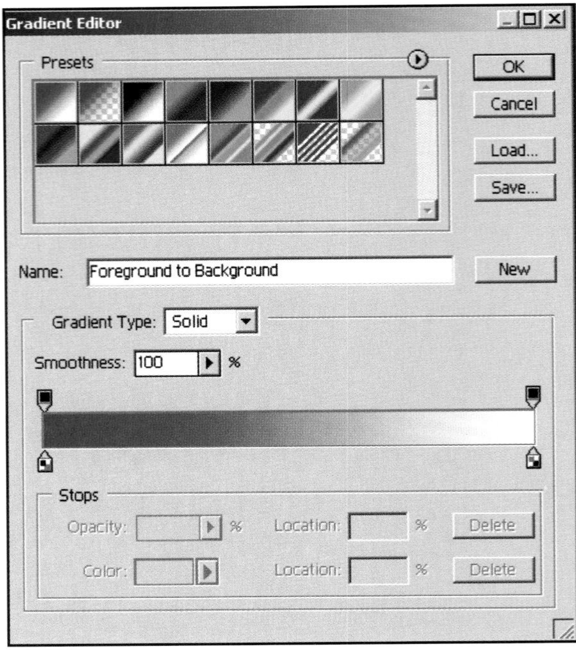

At the top of the Gradient Editor we have a bunch of **Presets**, (default gradients) to choose from. For more choice, click on the arrow at the top right of the Presets and you will be presented with a list of even more groups of default gradients.

2. Select a few just to see how many more are available. To restore the originals select **Reset Gradients**.

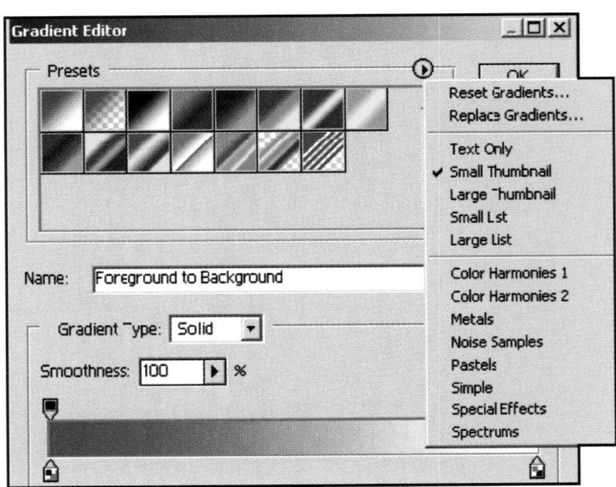

3. Click on a couple of the fills, and notice how the bottom of the editor changes to show the settings of each Preset. In the screenshot opposite I've clicked on the Copper gradient, you can see the bottom of the editor change to reflect this gradient's settings.

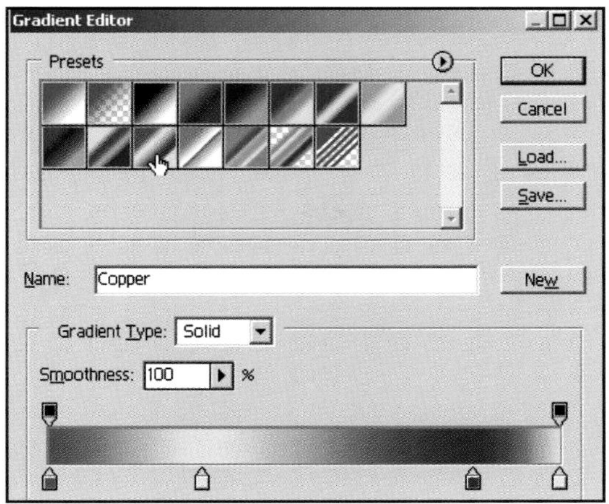

That's where a lot of people stop with the Gradient tool, but it's a crime to do so. It's really quite versatile if you're looking to create your own gradients. You can do this in the Gradient Editor. Let's take a quick look at how:

- The four tabs at the top and bottom of the slider are called **Stops** – the stops set points on the slider where **color** and **opacity** are defined. (Opacity refers to how opaque an image is; low opacity would mean that a picture would be see-through).

- The top of the slider is for opacity stops, and the bottom is for color stops. So in my example below, which is a blue to white gradient, the top two opacity stops are both at 100%, and the bottom two color stops are blue (on the left) and white (on the right).

- To see and adjust the settings of each stop, click on it and notice the settings that appear at the bottom of the editor. You can tell which stop has been selected at any given moment, as the arrow at the top of the tab will be black.

- When you click on a stop a diamond will appear at the midpoint between two colors or gradients. You can adjust the midpoint to set the point at which two opacities/colors are blending together in equal measure.

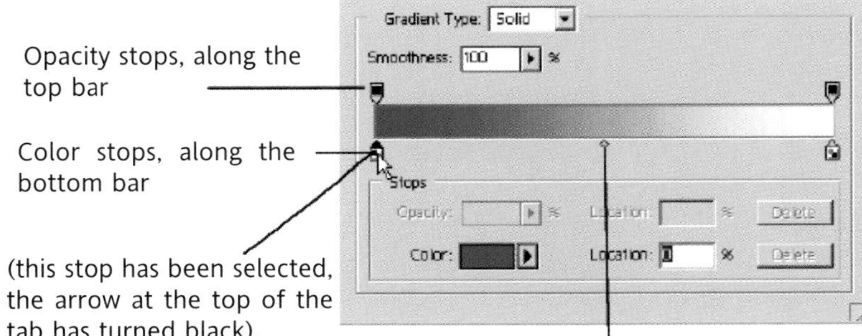

This diamond indicates the midpoint between two colors. At this point, both colors are mixed together in equal proportions

4. So, if you wanted to change the color of the blue stop, either double click on the stop, or click in the blue color swatch at the bottom of the Gradient Editor and select a new color – it's that easy.

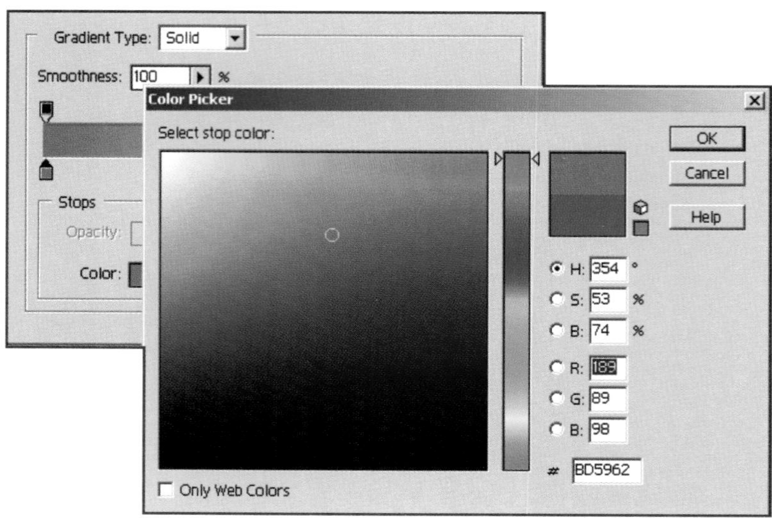

5. Alternatively, we might want to have the blue fade to transparent. To do this we would click on the top right opacity stop and change its settings to 0% Opacity.

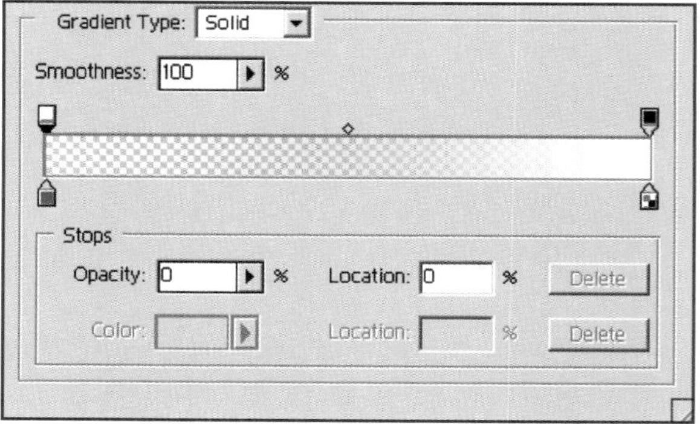

We are not limited to just two color or opacity stops in our custom gradients. To add another stop, simply click an empty area along the top or bottom of the slider, and a new stop will be created. By default this new stop will be filled with the color of the last stop selected.

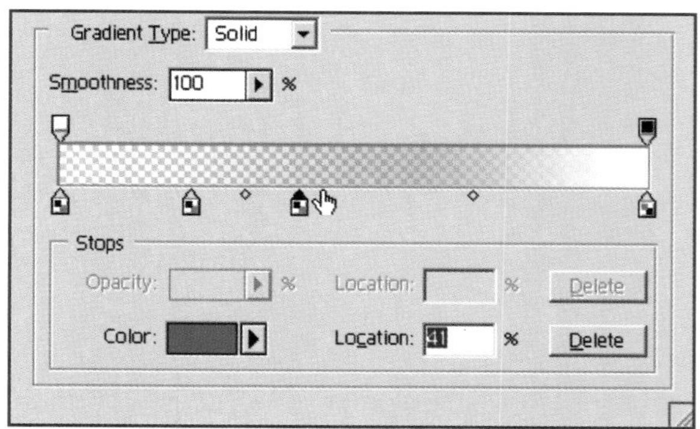

Of course, if you wanted to add a new color, just like before you could either double click on the stop itself, or go down to the color picker at the bottom of the window.

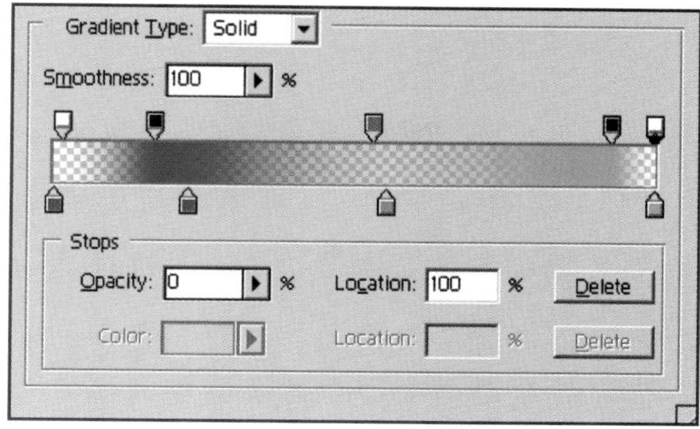

If you create a gradient and would like to save it for future use, it's easy. Simply enter a name in the Gradient Editor Name field and click New to add it to the current set of fills.

Let's apply some gradients using the different types of available styles.

4. Select a gradient fill from the Gradient Editor or create your own, then close the editor. Now we must choose which type of gradient we would like to use from the options bar. From left to right we can choose from – **Linear**, **Radial**, **Angle**, **Reflected**, or **Diamond**.

5. Choose the Linear for now; it's the first one.

6. To draw a gradient on our canvas, click and hold to set the starting point, and drag to set the angle. When the angle and length of the gradient is how you would like it to be, release the mouse to apply the gradient. Here's a gradient I made with a purple to orange fill, and linear style:

Try experimenting with the different styles of gradients to see how they look, and also try dragging the gradients in different directions, and at various lengths across the canvas.

Here are the same settings as before but with a Radial style applied.

Just as with the Paint Bucket, you can use the Gradient tool to fill any selection, as well as the entire canvas.

Eraser tool

The **Eraser** tool isn't really a painting or drawing tool, but is so often used in conjunction with these tools that it deserves to be covered here. In behavior, the Eraser handles a lot like the airbrush.

The Eraser works best when working with layers – if you use the Eraser on a canvas with no layers (just a background), the background color set in the toolbar will show through, if working on a single layer canvas then transparency will show through. I'm sure you can imagine how the basic Eraser works – but there are two other Erasers tucked away in the toolbar that perform quite differently. Let's look at these briefly, the first being the **Background Eraser** tool.

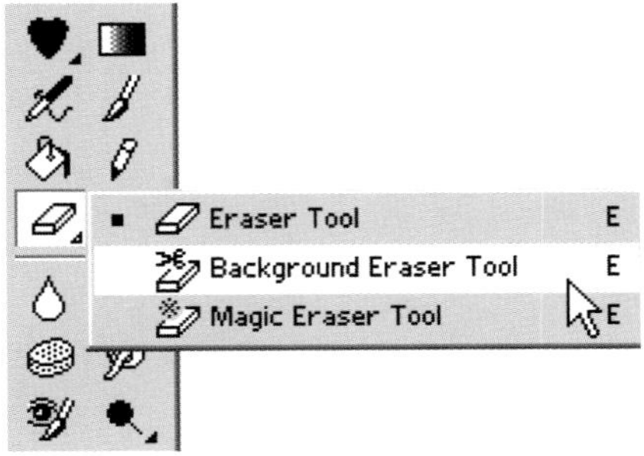

The way this tool works is that it erases the background pixels around an object on a layer to reveal transparency – try to relate it to the Magnetic Lasso tool, in that it tries to define the edges of an object and separate it from its background. While the Magnetic Lasso takes this difference in object and background, and draws a selection, the Background Eraser uses the difference to remove the background. Its settings can be adjusted using the **Tolerance** value.

1. To test out how it works, let's quickly open up the `Legodudes.jpg` image from the last chapter. First, double-click the background layer, to ensure that transparent pixels will show through when we erase. Now, choose the Background Eraser tool with a 100 pixel or so brush. Set the limits to **Discontiguous**, and make the tolerance fairly low, around 5%. Now erase the sky around the central figures.

Notice how even though the brush touches the main figures it only erases the sky? You might notice that the settings could be changed for the better, though, as some of the blue sky is still visible on the edges of the blocks. This could be fixed by adjusting the Tolerance.

Now let's take a look at the **Magic Eraser** tool.

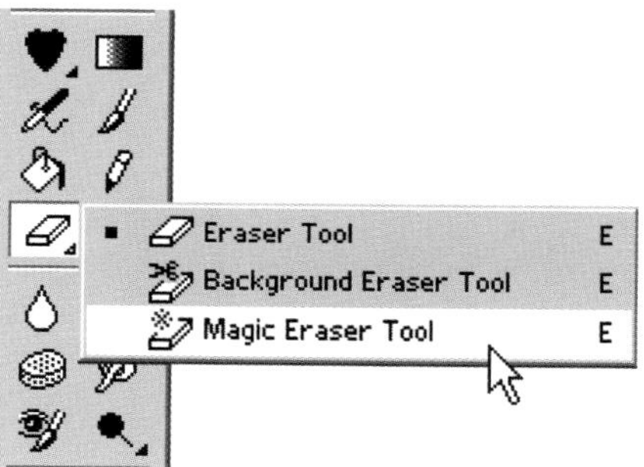

2. The Magic Eraser will automatically erase all similar adjacent pixels to the one you click on. It works well for erasing solid fields of color – try clicking on the edge of the blue block in `Legodudes.jpg` and see what happens.

This completes our overview of the tools that we'll use during this chapter. Before we jump into the tutorial, I'd also like to introduce the brush options and the **Text** tool, which you'll most likely be using a lot with your digital images.

Brush options

Most of the drawing and painting tools in Photoshop Elements use a common set of brushes with settings that can be easily modified. The program also comes with custom made brushes that simulate spatter, chalk, stars, and so on. Let's take a look at these and how to customize the settings.

1. Select the Airbrush tool and take a look at the brushes tray in the options bar.

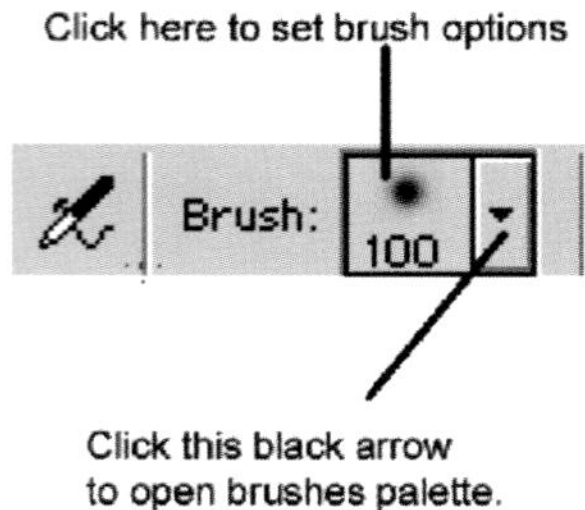

2. Click on the thumbnail of the brush and the window that pops up will allow you to set your own brush options. Here you can adjust the settings of the brush, and save it as a new brush if you want. The **Diameter** specifies the pixel width of the brush; the **Hardness** sets the hardness of the edge of the brush, and the **Spacing** sets the amount of space between marks as you drag a brush.

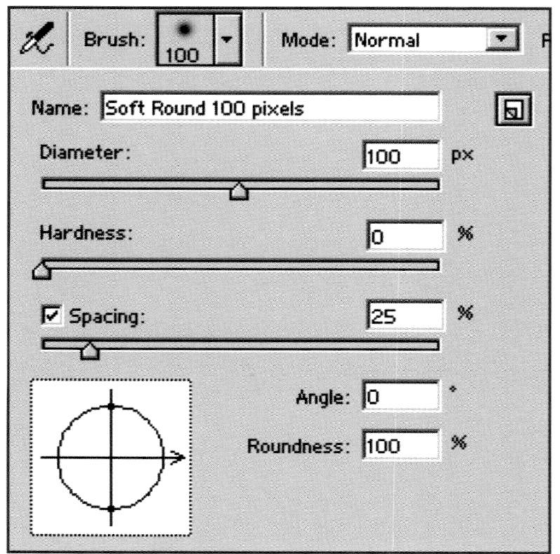

You can also change the **Angle** and **Roundness** to create non-circular brushes for calligraphic effects. Once you've set new brush options, you can save them as a new brush. To do this, simply click the page icon in the upper right corner of the window, and it will be added to the brushes tray. Try experimenting with different settings and see what kind of various brushes you can create.

You might also notice that there are several custom brushes in the brushes well – try experimenting with these. You can also load other sets of custom brushes, just as we did with the Gradient Editor.

3. Click on the arrow in the upper right corner to show a list of brush sets to load.

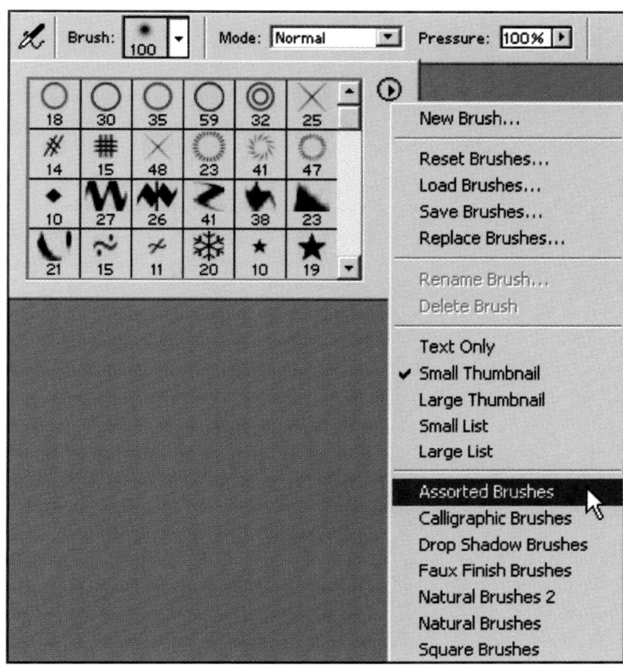

4. To restore the original set of brushes click on **Reset Brushes** from the same menu.

Type tool

One of the great benefits of using Photoshop Elements is that you can create and edit type directly on the canvas, so you can always see how it will affect the layout.

1. If you still have `Legodudes.jpg` open, undo all the changes we made to it – if you closed it then open it back up so we can apply some text to it.Click on the **Type** tool and have a look at the options bar.

The options bar lets us set the font, font size, alignment, color, direction, and warping. For now, we'll cover the basics and get into the more advanced effects later in the book.

2. Choose a nice, clear font, set it to around 100 pts and the color to white, and type "Legodudes" on the canvas.

3. When you're done typing press ENTER, notice how the type is now on its own layer, you can now use the Move tool to adjust its position on the canvas.

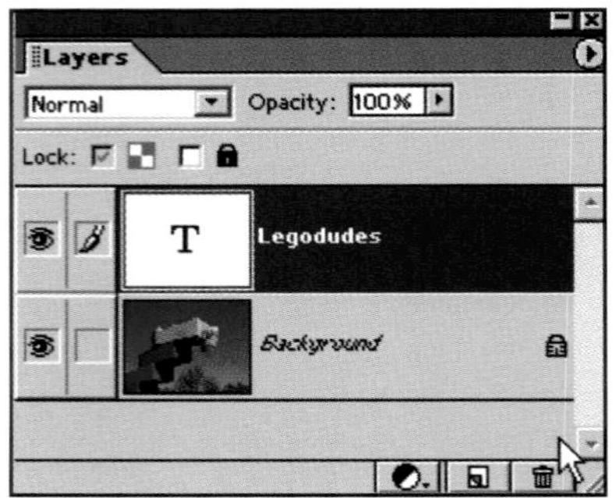

The best part is that if you wish to edit the text at any time all you have to do is select the Type tool and highlight the text or double-click the "T" icon in the Layers palette to highlight all the text. That's the basic functionality of type in Photoshop Elements – it's really easy to learn because it behaves in the same way as most text editors, or word processors.

MAGAZINE LAYOUT

Let's take some of the things we've learned in this chapter as well as the previous few, and create a funky 60s style retro magazine layout. We'll take a photo of a model and first touch up some moles on her face, then cut her out of the background to prepare it for the layout. We'll then create some geometric shapes to add visual elements, as well as some text with the type tool to complete our mock magazine layout.

Preparing the photo dimensions

1. Let's open up `retro_ad_model.jpg` prepare it for the final layout.

2. The first thing we want to do is change the image size and resolution of the photo to match the settings that we want for the final layout. Currently, the image is 16.667 x 22.222 inches, at a resolution of 72 dpi. You can check this by going to **Image > Resize > Image Size**.

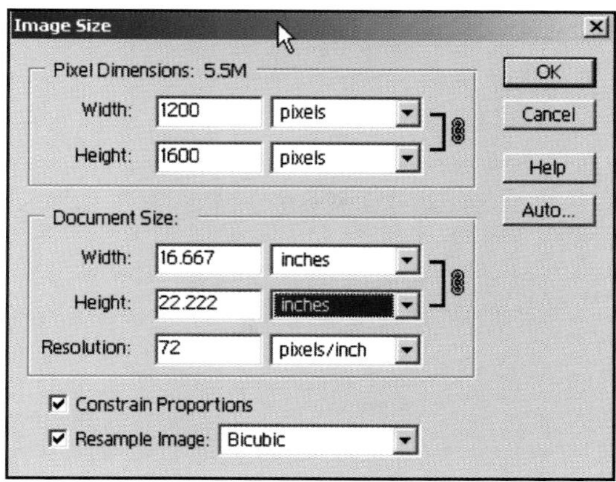

3. We want the final layout to be 8.5 x 11 inches, so we're going to have to do some adjusting here. In the **Document Size** area, change the Width setting to 8.5. Notice that the Height automatically changes to 11.33 inches. That's because we have checked the **Constrain Proportions** checkbox, which will always keep any adjustments to the document size proportionate to the original size.

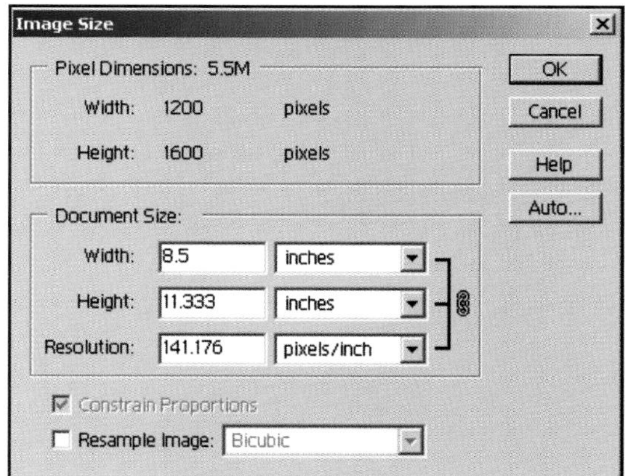

4. Leave the dimensions as it is, because if we uncheck the Constrain Proportions box, and set the height to 11, the image will be slightly distorted to fit the new canvas size. Also uncheck the Resample Image box – the resolution will now reflect our alterations to the picture size without incurring any of the fuzziness we would have got by resampling.

5. The problem we now have is that we want to change our document from 11.33 inches high to 11 inches high, but we don't want to alter the dimensions of the image. We could use the Crop tool, but in order to be precise we'll use the **Canvas Size** command. Using Canvas Size changes the size of the canvas without altering the proportions of the image.

6. Go to **Image > Resize > Canvas Size.** Set the height to 11 inches. Notice how we can also set the **Anchor** for the resize.

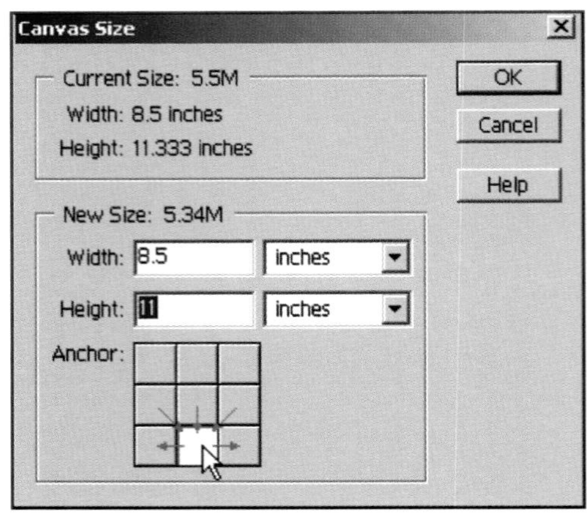

7. The **Anchor** sets the point, from where the canvas resize is applied. This will depend on your image – in our case, since we don't want to trim any of the model, we'll anchor the bottom, which means the top will be trimmed by 0.33 inches.

8. To set the anchor at the bottom, click in the bottom middle square, then click OK. When the alert pops up telling you that your new canvas size will be smaller than the current canvas size and clipping will occur, click **Proceed**.

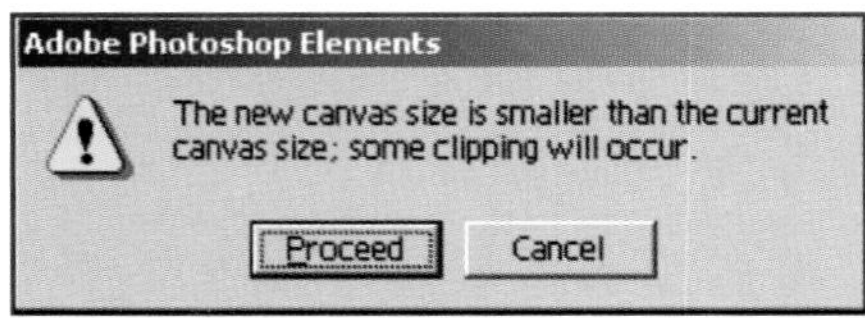

9. We now have our document set to its final working size, go to **File > Save As** and name it `retro_layout.psd`. It is important to save it as a PSD – Photoshop file – because later we'll be using layers, and a JPEG file will not support layers, it will compress them.

Preparing the model

How many pictures have you taken where you wished you didn't have to see those unsightly blemishes, or perhaps an ugly scar? With a little help from the **Eyedropper** tool, and Airbrush tool, these can easily be covered up. Let's remove a couple of moles from our model's face to test out this technique.

1. Zoom in to the model's cheek so that you can clearly see the two moles.

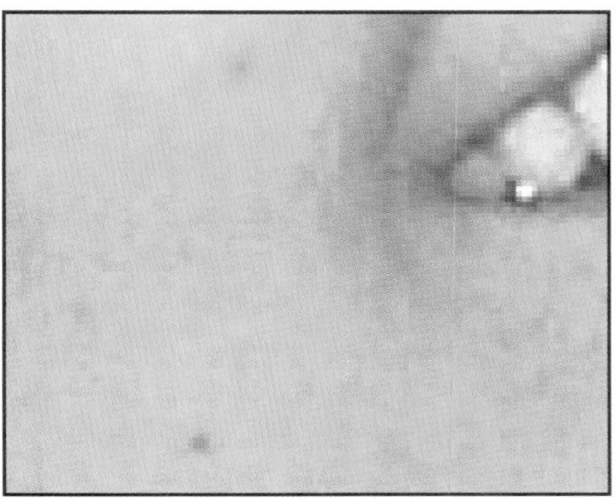

2. Select the Eyedropper from the toolbar, which allows us to sample colors from our document.

3. In the options bar, note the **Sample Size** option. Sample Size sets the area that the Eyedropper samples from – in most cases you can use the **Point Sample** setting, which samples exact pixels, but when sampling from skin tones it is often better to use the **3 by 3** or **5 by 5 Average**. Let's set our Sample Size to **5 by 5 Average**.

The reason why I suggest using the **5 by 5 Average** Eyedropper sampler when sampling skin tones is that in most cases, especially with low to mid-range consumer digital cameras, any given area of skin tone is defined by several different shades of a color on a pixel-by-pixel basis (you can really notice this when zooming in close). The danger in using the default Point Sample is that you may pick up a single color that when applied to an airbrush may not blend as well as if you took a 5x5 or 3x3 sample, which more accurately represents the overall tone of the general area of skin.

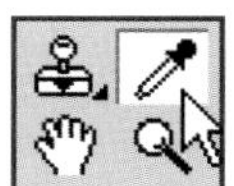

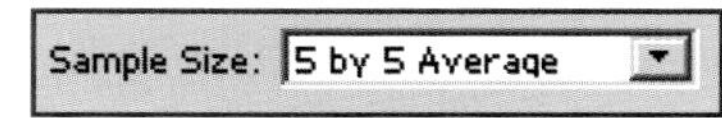

4. Let's cover up the top mole first. Use the Eyedropper to click an area near the mole, and notice how that color is now set as the foreground color on the toolbar.

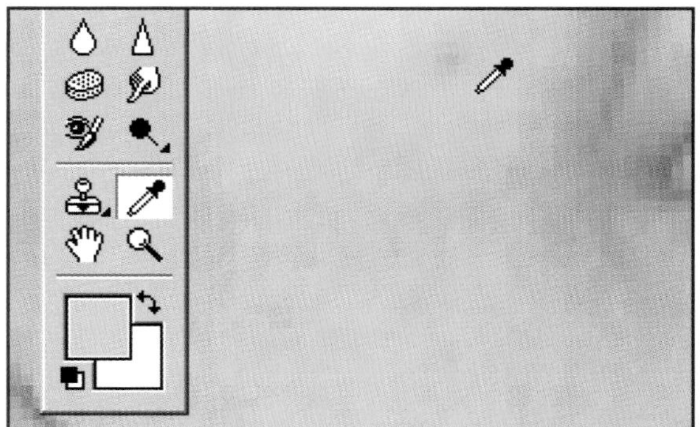

5. Now we'll switch over to the Airbrush tool and use it to paint over the mole.

6. First, go to **Layer** > **New**, or click CTRL/CMD+ SHIFT + N to create a new layer. Name this layer, Adjustment. Having this adjustment layer means that you avoid working on the original image, so should you make a mistake it will be easier to remedy.

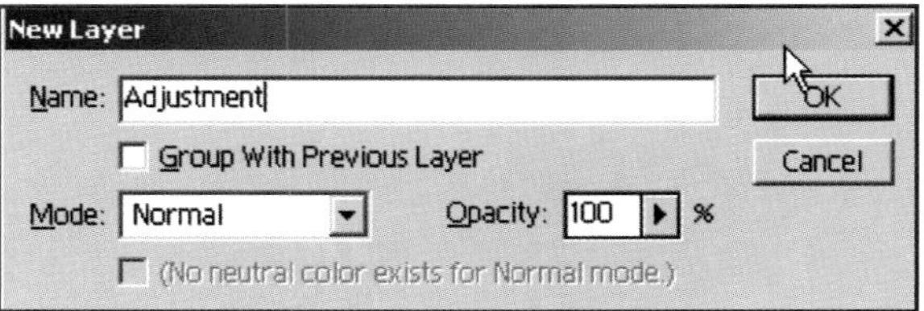

7. Select a soft brush from the Airbrush options at a size that is just a little larger than the mole – that way we can cover it in just one click. I'm using a 17 pixel soft brush. Now click on the mole once with the Airbrush tool and the mole will be covered! It should be perfectly blended now – if not try **Stepping Backward** (CTRL/CMD+Z) and use the Eyedropper to select a different shade of skin tone that will match better.

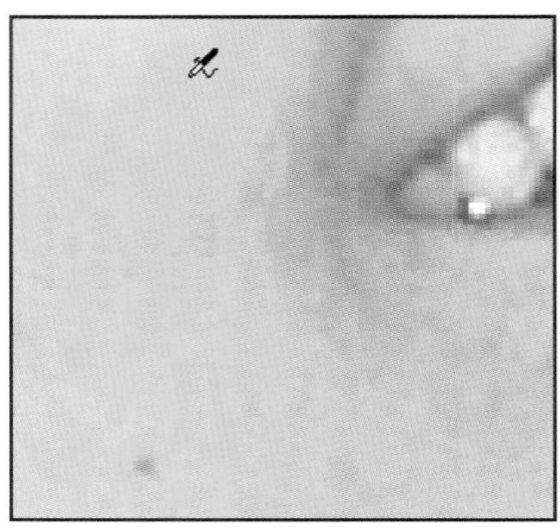

8. Use the same method to cover the other mole, too – make sure you use the Eyedropper again to select a new color since the bottom mole is a different color to the skin tone.

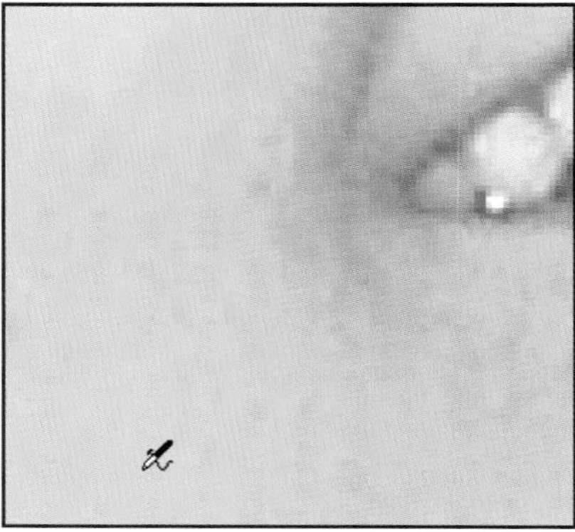

9. Zoom back out a little so you can see all of the model's face, see if you can tell that she used to have two moles on her face. You shouldn't be able to!

10. When you are happy with your Photoshop makeover, merge the adjustment layer with the Model layer, so that they become one and the same layer. To do this, click on the arrow in the top right hand corner of the Layers palette, this will bring up the layers menu. Select **Merge Down**, and you'll be left with just the Model layer.

Cutting out the model

We want to have the model on her own layer in order to be able to place some objects behind her, so we'll have to cut her out of her background. Think back to Chapter 3, when we covered the different ways of creating selections. What would be the best way to create a selection around our model? There are a couple of different ways we could go about it: We could use the Polygonal or Magnetic Lasso tool to manually draw a selection around her, which would probably take a while. Or we could also use the Magic Wand tool since we have a fairly uniform background. Let's try the Magic Wand, since it could potentially save us a lot of time.

1. First we need to change the background layer to a regular layer. This is because, as a background layer it is locked by default (see the little padlock icon in the Layers palette) so we can't make any adjustments to it. Change this layer over now by double-clicking on it in the Layers palette. When the **New Layer** dialog box comes up, name it Model.

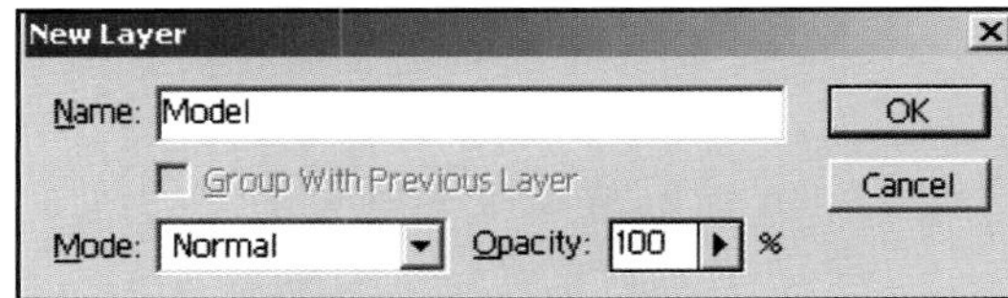

2. Choose the Magic Wand tool from the toolbar, leave its default settings in the options bar and click anywhere in the white upper area of the background. Notice the selection that is created. (If your selection is not like this, it could be that the Tolerance setting is not at the default level of 32).

3. Not exactly what we wanted, but don't give up yet. Don't forget that we can add to our selections using the **Add to selection** button in the options bar. Click this button, and then click in the undefined part of the

background to the left of the model. (Another way to add to a selection is to hold SHIFT and click in the area that you want to include).

4. Keep clicking the unselected areas on both sides of the model until the entire background is selected. This is what's nice about the Add to selection feature – it's not a one-time shot, you can use it as much as needed to complete a selection.

5. Cutting out the background is now simply a matter of hitting DELETE, but before we do this we need to add a little bit of feathering to the selection so the edges of the model aren't too hard.

6. Choose **Select > Feather**, enter 1 for the setting and click OK.

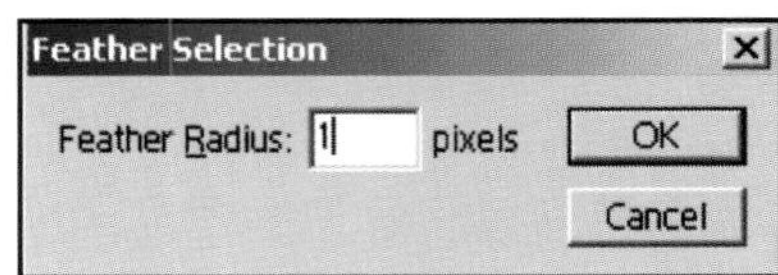

6. Now we can click DELETE to get rid of the background, and click CTRL/CMD+ D to deselect.

7. We now have the model on her own layer, and free of the background. Let's add a new layer behind her so we don't have to look at the checkerboard pattern. In the Layers palette, create a new layer by clicking the **New Layer** icon.

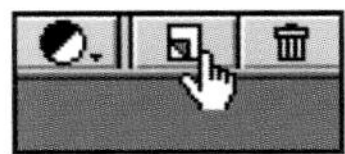

8. Rename the new layer White Background by double-clicking on it in the Layers palette to bring up the Layer Properties dialogue. Click and drag the new layer to move it below the Model layer in the Layers palette then use the Paint Bucket to fill the layer with white.

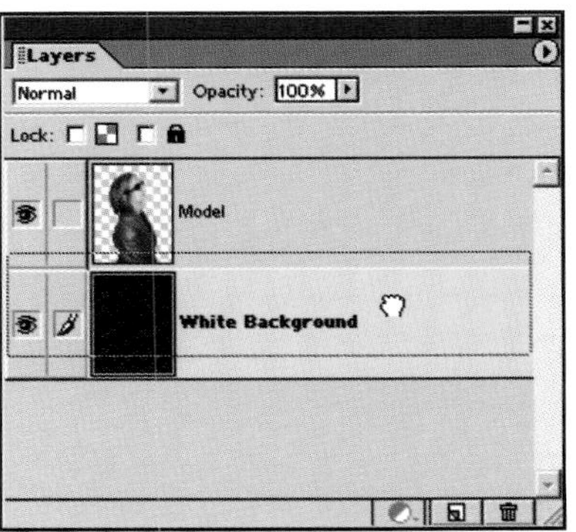

Sizing up the model

At this point our model is almost ready for the final layout. I think she takes up way too much of the canvas, especially as we want to add other elements to the layout. So let's use the **Transform** command to scale her down and make room for the rest of our composition.

1. Make sure you have the Model layer selected in the Layers palette; remember this will be the highlighted layer. Now click **Image > Transform > Free Transform**, or use the shortcut CTRL/CMD+T.

2. Grab the upper right corner of the transform box and drag it down and to the left, to scale the model down. Be sure to also hold down SHIFT so that we keep the same proportions. Scale her down so that she is about three-quarters of the height of the canvas. Before you hit ENTER, also move the model to the left of the canvas, by clicking and dragging inside of the transform box. Hold down SHIFT now, too, so that you move her on a straight line (in this case keeping her at the bottom of the image).

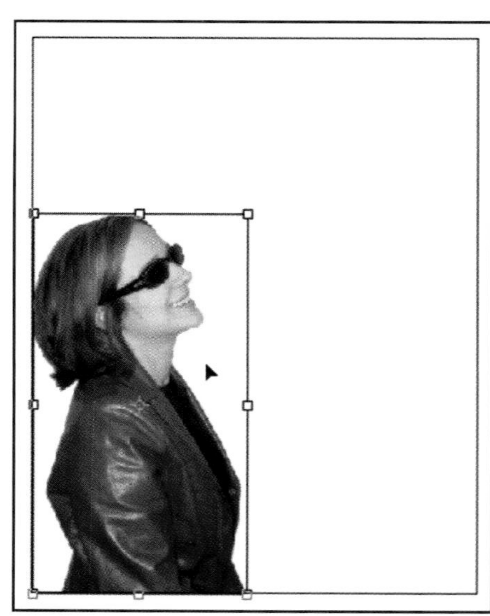

Adding graphic elements

We're now ready to start adding some elements of retro style to our layout. We're going to add some strips of funky color to give our layout a dynamic, vibrant feel.

1. Click CTRL/CMD+ N to create a new layer. (This is my preferred method of doing this but of course you can also click on the Create a new layer icon, or go via the Layer menu). Name this layer Funky Colors, and move it in between the background and Model layers.

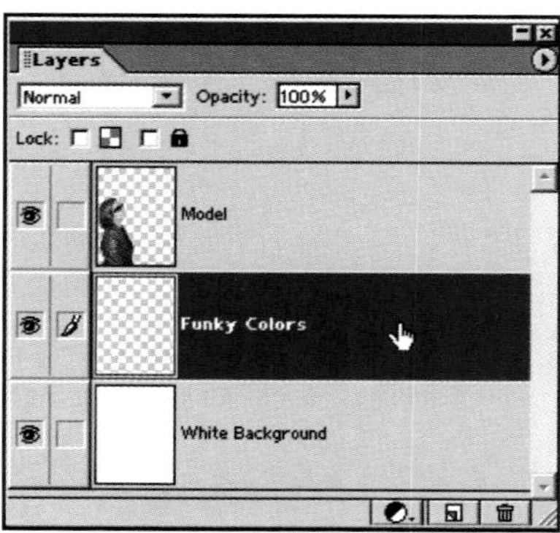

2. Now we'll create some selections to fill with color. Select the Polygonal Lasso, and click at four points of the canvas to draw an irregularly shaped rectangle as I've done below.

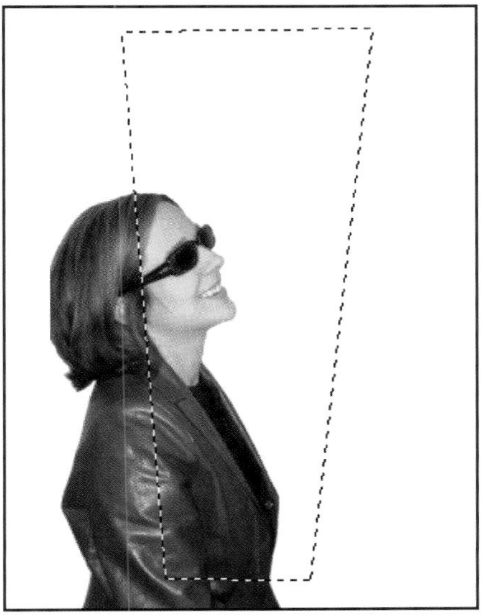

3. Now click on the foreground color square on the toolbar to bring up the Color Picker. Choose a bright green color (I've used R:0 G:255 B:0), or whatever you prefer here. Use the Paint Bucket to fill the selection with the green color, then CTRL/CMD+ D to deselect.

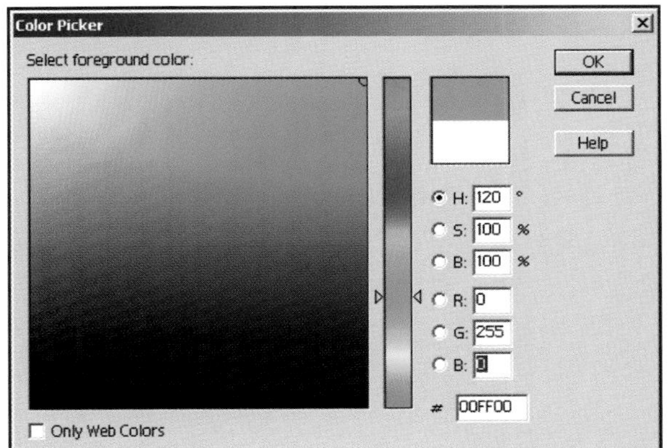

4. Create a new layer, and call it Type Background, make sure that this layer is between the Model layer and the Funky Colors layer in the Layers palette.

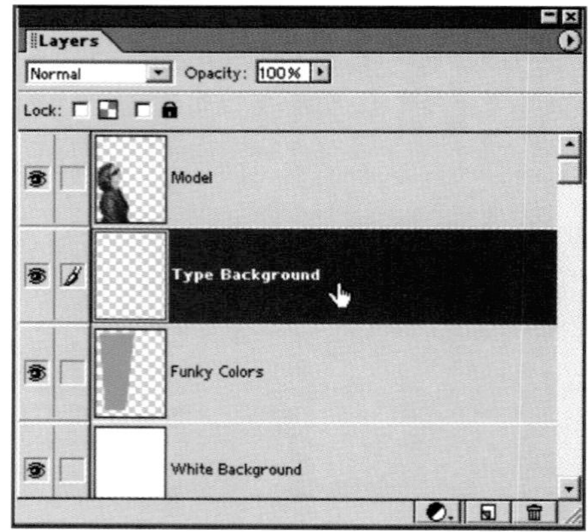

On this layer we'll make two more areas of funky color, again using the Polygonal Lasso and the Color Picker. Use the colors R:227 G:0 B:107 for the magenta color and R:238 G:185 B:0 for the yellow.

5. We've now introduced some graphic elements to spice up our layout. As you've probably guessed, the last two elements we added will now be used as the background for our type treatments.

Adding type to the layout

With our graphic elements in place, let's now begin laying down some type to complete our layout.

1. Select the Type tool, and before you begin typing set the color in the options bar to white. Choose a fun font and type in all capitals the word "FASHION" in the top area of color. Adjust the font size so that the word fills up a good portion of the space – about 72pt.

2. Now use the same font and all capitals again to type the word "QUEEN" over the second area of type background color.

3. Before we move on, let's change the opacity of the Funky Colors layer. It's a bit too bold and competes with the title too much. Select the Funky Colors layer in the Layers palette and set the opacity to 25%. Much better, a lot easier on the eye.

4. To round out our layout, let's add some more type. We'll list some of the model's clothing items, and their prices, to the empty white area in our layout, using some of the same colors that are reflected in the Type background.

5. Select the Type tool again, and use the same font that you used for the title, but don't type in all caps this time.

6. Set the type color in the options bar to the same magenta color in the title, it's best to use the Eyedropper tool while you have the Color Picker window open, so that you aren't still typing in white, and change the type size to a smaller size, around 20 pts or so. Type the word "Sunglasses" and click ENTER.

7. Now, use the Type tool again to create a fake product number underneath the word "Sunglasses", something like "Item #200987". Change the type color to black in the options bar. Using the type tool again, type the price underneath the Item # – make up a price like "$12.00" or something. Use the yellow color from the header for this type.

8. You're probably wondering why we don't just enter all of this type into one type layer. Unfortunately, Photoshop Elements doesn't allow you to control the line-height of your type, known as leading, so in order to be able to control this we must enter each line of type separately.

9. Continue to enter a couple more garment titles along with item numbers and prices – I'm going to create entries for the leather jacket and t-shirt.

10. When you're done entering all of your "product info" type you may find that you want to move the position of the writing. In order to move the type as one coherent block you can group these type layers together by clicking next to the eye icon in the Layers palette. You'll see the chain link icon appear, which indicates that two or more layers are linked together.

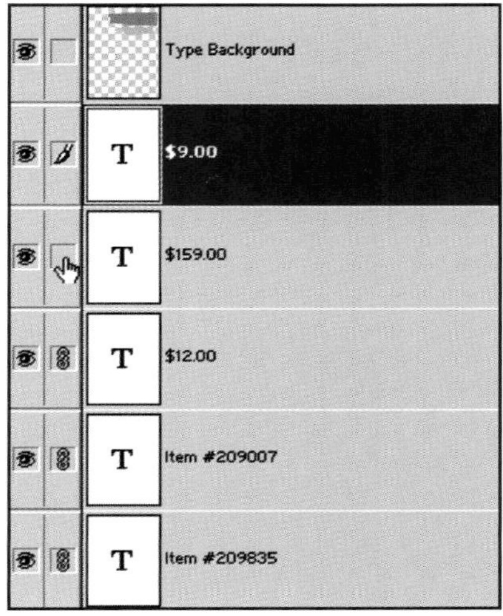

11. Here is the final layout:

So we've learnt the first steps of magazine layout. But there are plenty of other potential pitfalls, for example this ink spill (on the file `retro-ad-model2.jpg`). You could try the airbrush as before, but the gradient stops it being a viable option.

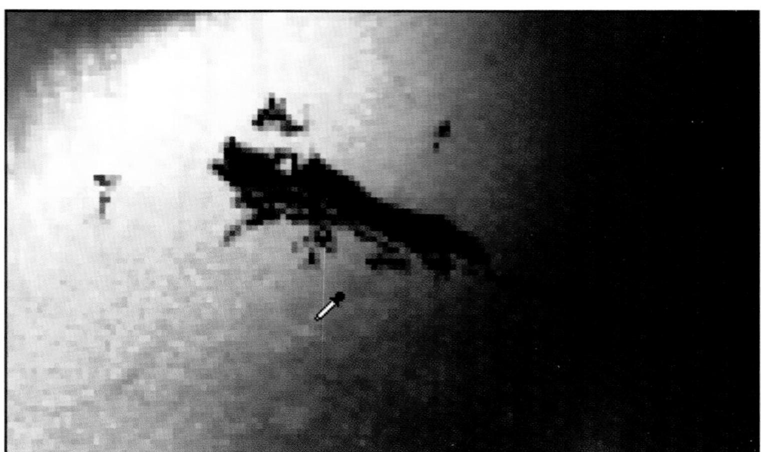

This image has much more contrast, and the ink we are trying to cover up isn't on a continuous tone of skin, so the Eyedropper tool and Airbrush aren't much help. There must be a better way to solve this problem, and indeed there is, which leads us into Chapter 5, where we will introduce more advanced tools for solving these problems.

5 Advanced imaging tools

So, we've just seen how to get rid of simple blemishes on photographs using the Color picker and the Airbrush tool. We've seen the effect of digital makeup – now if only it were as simple in real life! But, as we saw with the last example, some blemishes cannot be covered up so easily; on these occasions we need to use more advanced tools to achieve satisfactory results.

In order to solve the problem that we encountered at the end of the chapter we'll enlist the help of some powerful touch-up tools: We'll start with the **Clone Stamp** tool. After we've mastered this, we'll refine the process with the following tools: **Burn**, **Dodge**, **Blur**, and **Sharpen**.

Clone Stamp tool

Imagine instead of painting with a color, you could paint with the picture itself – if you took a photograph and covered it with a thin layer of sand, then stuck your finger in the sand and dragged it around a bit, you would reveal a finger-wide line of the image: wherever you move your finger, the image is revealed. Now imagine painting in this way using the photograph itself as the paint!

The Clone Stamp tool is used to select a part of an image that is unblemished, and paint over any marks using the untarnished section as paint. This takes a bit of getting used to, but once mastered, is an invaluable tool. To put it another way, we're acting like surgeons here, grafting a piece of healthy skin which we got from one place on the body over some damaged piece in another area. Once it's healed no one would guess that there had ever been any damage there.

What does this mean to us as photographers? Isn't it amazing the number of times we take what we think is the perfect shot, only to discover some small quirk, either with the film, the developing or that some pesky moth flew into frame? With digital tools, we're able to circumvent these problems, and even (as we'll see later) give the image a life and purity it never had to begin with.

Have a look at the image from the end of the previous section, entitled: `highcontrast.jpg`. Can you remember why we found it hard to correct this image?

To recap: the problem that we were having with this image was that because of the lighting, the skin tone changes too much to simply use one color to fix this. Enter: the Clone Stamp tool. Remember, the Clone Stamp tool works in the following way: you select the area you want to copy, then when you start drawing, that area is used as the paint for your starting point. Often with this tool, you'll find it necessary to sample the unblemished (parent) area more than once. Let's jump right in and see this point in action.

Quick task: Removing the spot

1. We're going to start off with a quick exercise to get you familiar with how this tool works before we go any further with our `highcontrast` image. So open up the image: `chapter 5 - clone tool sphere exercise.psd`.

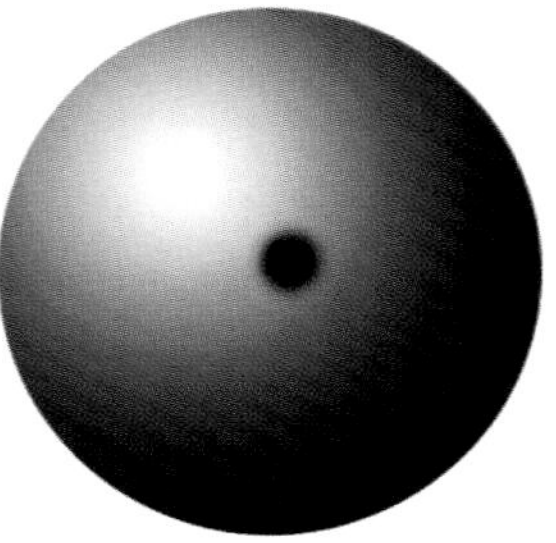

2. If it's not already open, you can bring up the Layers palette by clicking on the tab in the Palette well. I like to have this palette open all the time: click, hold and drag the Layers palette tab onto the main work area. This will dislodge the palette from the palette well, and leave it on your main work area. If you want to put it back, all you need to do is close it by clicking on the tiny **x** in the top right corner of the palette (if you're using a PC) or a square in the top left hand corner (If you're working on a Mac).

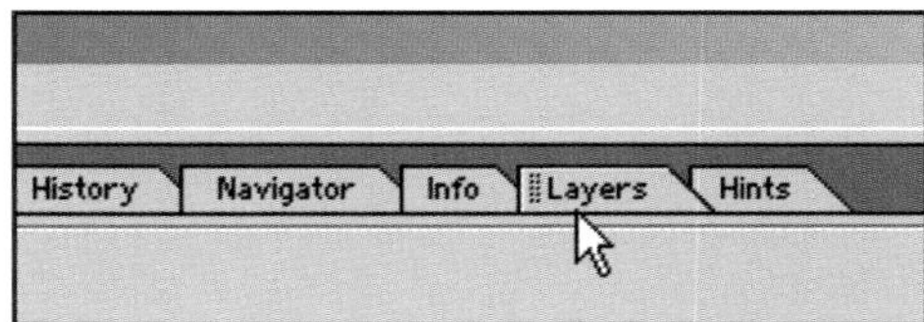

3. Make a copy of the background layer by clicking on the little arrow in the top right hand corner of the layers palette. This will open a drop down menu; now select **Duplicate Layer** to create an identical layer to the background layer. As you'll see later this isn't the only method of duplicating layers, but what's nice about using this technique is that you'll get prompted to name the new layer before creating it. Let's call it *spotfree*.

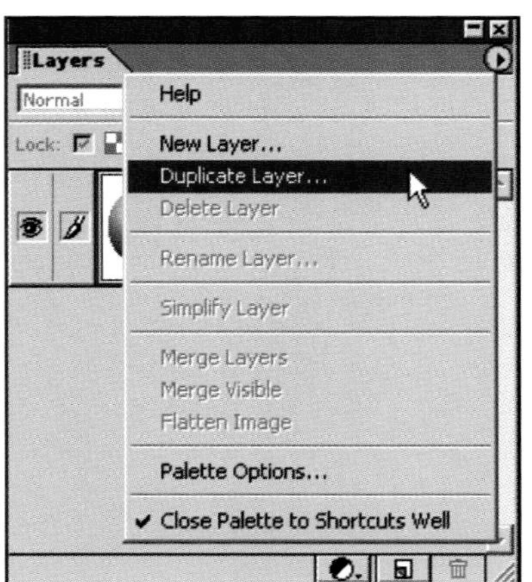

So, why did we do this? Well, we are about to alter our original image, but it is good practice to preserve the original image not only in case you should need it at a later date, but also as a point of reference. Often when retouching we get so engrossed in what we're doing that we go too far, and the image becomes unrealistic and untruthful. We're trying to tamper with the image in such a way that it is not noticeable; having the original image around is useful.

Now we know we're not tampering with the original layer we can feel free to mess with the spotfree layer. Notice the little eye to the left of the picture on the spot free layer. By clicking on this eye you can alternately show and hide that particular layer. If you try this now you might notice that absolutely nothing happens. The reason for this of course is that you have an identical layer below, so hiding the layer simply shows you the same image!

4. From your toolbox, select the Clone tool.

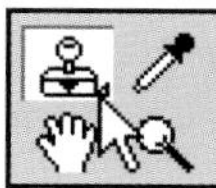

5. Notice that your cursor changes to a tiny picture of a rubber stamp. This will probably get in our way, as we are doing fairly fine retouching. Let's change the cursor to a more precise one Click on the **Preferences** tab at the bottom of the **Edit** menu. This will pop out a whole list of preferences that you can change about the way Adobe Photoshop Elements looks and functions. Click on **Display & Cursors**.

6. This brings up a tiny dialog box showing your current settings for the way the display and cursors behave. In the **Other Cursors** section, on the right hand side of the palette, click on the **Precise** button. This sets our cursor to a tiny crosshair (you can also use Caps Lock to toggle the crosshairs). While we're at it, let's change the **Painting Cursors** to **Brush Size** – it's important when using the clone stamp that you know how much of the unblemished area you're sampling at any time.

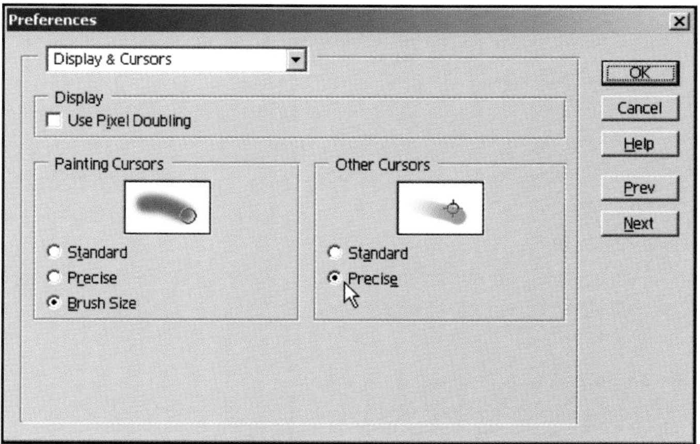

7. Clicking OK closes the dialog box and takes us back to our exercise. Before we start (and I wish I'd listened to my own advice here many times) we must check to see if we're working on the correct layer. We want to be working on spotfree, and not our original – the background. The active layer is always the highlighted one, to activate a layer click on its name in the layers palette.

You'll notice that the sphere we wish to remove the spot from has fairly fine gradation. We're going to have to be careful about the way we retouch the dark spot out of it. It is preferable therefore to drop the opacity of the brush. Reducing the opacity of the brush basically means we are using less paint – we are watering it down a bit. This effectively means we'll be able to blend the unblemished paint with the blemished. Why is this useful? Well, as you'll see in the sphere example – the change in color from white to black is extremely fine. We're going to pick an unblemished area to paste over the awful black spot. Chances are though, we're not going to pick from an area that is exactly the same color as where the spot is. Because of this, we're using a lower opacity brush so that the unblemished doesn't just splodge on top of the blemish – it mixes together. Let's try it now.

8. We're going to use a diffuse edged brush of size 17 which we select from the brush selector on the options bar.

9. Set the brush opacity of the brush on the options bar to 15%, and make sure that the **Aligned** box is checked.

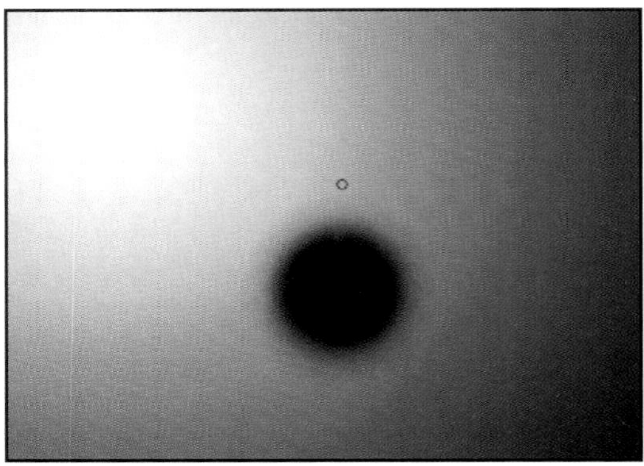

As suggested by its name, the Aligned option ensures that your selected area will align itself to your Clone Stamp. When you move the stamp, the "paint" area will move accordingly. In other words, the offset is the same for each stroke.

A little cross shows you exactly where the stamp is taking paint from, it samples the paint from this area, and applies it to wherever you move the Clone Stamp tool.

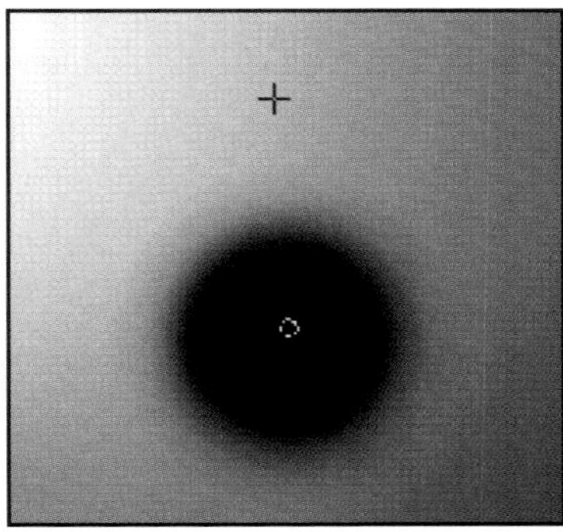

So if we decided that we wanted to graft some paint from the top left area of the sphere and then paste this over the black blemish we would hold down the ALT/OPTION key and click on this top left area, then click on the blemished area. This would take the top left area as a reference point and paint whatever we clicked on ontop of the blemish. If we now clicked 5 cms to the right if the blemish, the tool would take paint from 5 cms to the right of where we originally drew paint from and paste it at that point.

If we were retouching a picture of a simple band of gradated color, as in the picture below, it would be fairly easy to do the retouch.

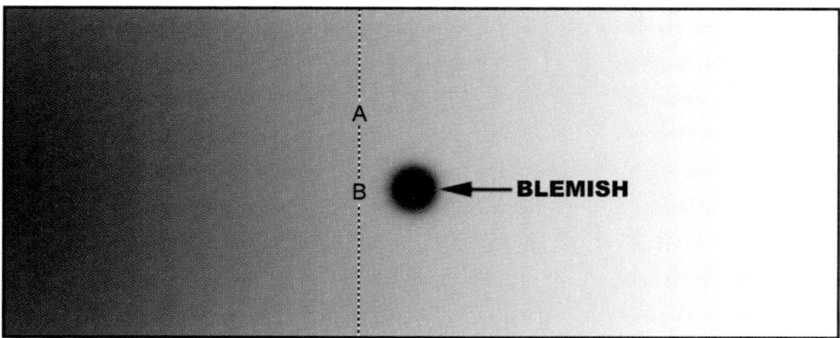

We would simply pick color from point A, which is at a higher elevation than point B, and because the Aligned option has been selected, we could just sample from point A and paste it all over the blemish at point B. Because the color is consistent vertically, the Clone Stamp would simply pull the gradient over the blemish and hey presto, it would disappear. The color at point A and B is exactly the same, even though they are at different heights.

With our sphere example however, the color changes both vertically and horizontally. Oh no! To try and compensate for this we are going to select from a point very close in color to what we think the blemish should be (once it is removed).

10. Now we need to sample an unblemished area of the sphere, which will be our source of paint to use to cover up this damn spot. At this point, you'll find that it really helps to zoom in to the image, so do this now.

11. So, making sure that you don't overlap with any of the blemished area ALT/OPTION-click just above the dark spot. You'll notice the cursor changing to the precise cursor as you press ALT/OPTION.

12. Now click over the top of the blemished area to apply it.

13. Try taking a graft from just to the left of the blemish and pasting it on the left hand outer part of the blemish. Basically, we're going to take samples from all around the blemish and paste them over the top of the boundary of the damaged area, in this way reducing it. The image below shows where color was selected from, and where it was pasted to. So color was taken from **1** and pasted at **2**. Similarly, color was taken from point **a** and deposited at point **b**.

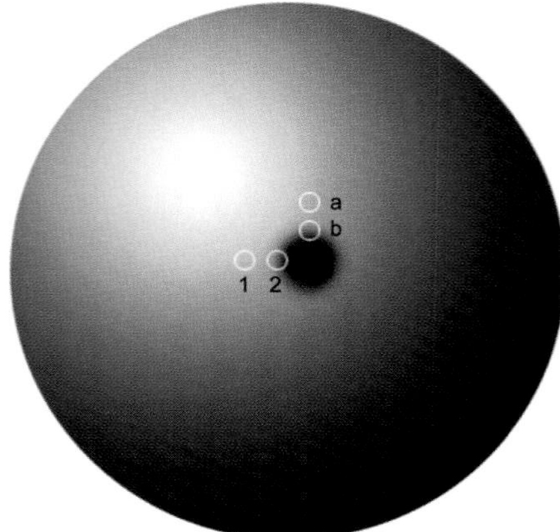

14. Because we're using a fairly low opacity brush, sometimes you might need to click more than once to deposit the freshly grafted color. How many times you click is up to you: the more you click, the more paint you deposit on that spot. Clicking too many times will obviously force the graft to totally dominate that area – which might not work too well.

The picture below shows the effects of effectively grafting from **a** to **b** and **1** to **2**.

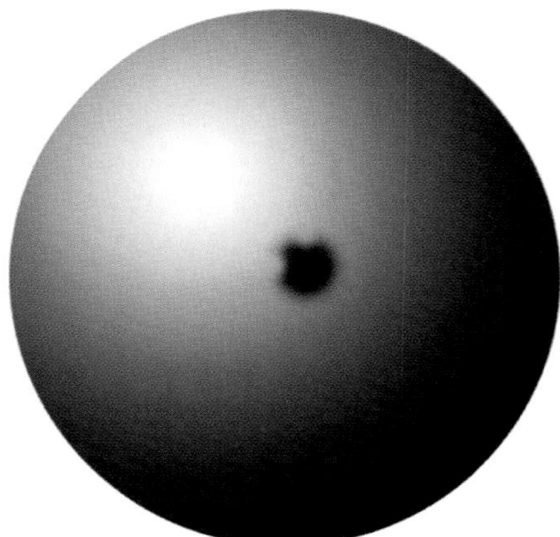

Notice how the blemish has been dented at those two points, and in fact has been visibly reduced. By applying this technique: Grafting from just outside the blemish and painting over the blemish boundaries next to the graft, in no time we can remove it completely.

15. You will probably notice however that the gradient is not as smooth in our retouched areas, as it is in the untouched areas. There's probably a slightly mottled look to the retouched area. In order to eliminate this

you can drop the opacity of the brush a little bit more – to around 10% – and then gently graft from areas very close to the mottle, slowly evening these kinks out.

16. I have actually chosen a fairly technically demanding example – fine changes in gradient combined with fine changes in color are often really hard to smooth out, as it's hard to find a good area to graft from. Using a low opacity brush helps a lot though.

Well, hopefully you've now got to grips with the Clone Stamp tool, so let's go back to our initial problem.

DIGITAL MAKEUP

1. If it's not already, open up the `highcontrast.jpg` image, and as before we'll start off by duplicating the background layer.

2. As mentioned earlier, there is more than one way to do duplicate a layer, this time click on the picture of the layer in the layers palette and drag it to the small icon at the bottom used to create new layers.

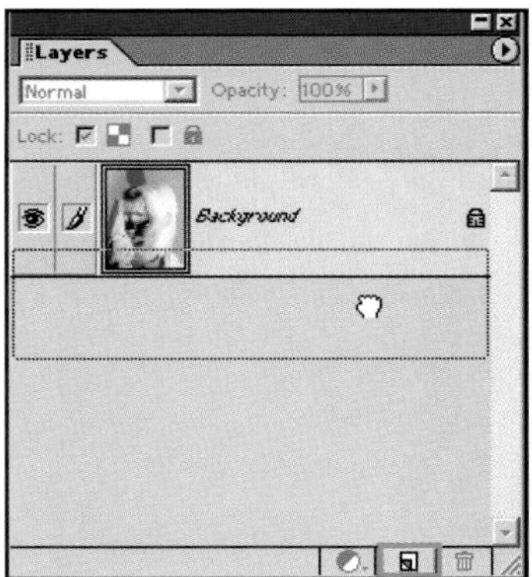

This creates an exact copy of the background layer and places it immediately above. Notice that this new layer is called *Background copy*.

3. The important thing to watch out for is the flow of the gradient. When grafting, we want to try and keep the hue and brightness of the color as consistent as possible. So before you even start to graft, try getting a sense of the flow of the gradient.

4. On the next page is an exaggerated illustration of the gradients at play in this image. Once you have spotted the general flow, try and graft from areas that fall within the gradient, and not across the gradient. In the straight gradient example above, things were simple – we just had to keep the grafting sample and pasting in a vertical line. Here we have no such luck, so keeping a close eye on the flow of the gradient is important.

5. To achieve this effect yourself, duplicate the layer of which you wish to expose the gradient. Then, perform a Hue/Saturation adjustment on this duplicated layer and drop the Saturation right down. To begin with, click an **Image > Adjustments > Posterize**, and use a level of 8. Now apply **Filter > Artistic > Paint Daubs** with a brush size of 19 and a sharpness of 0.

Remember that when using the Clone Stamp tool, it's better to use a low opacity brush and apply the paint over and over, than to just use a completely opaque brush and slap the paint down. You have far more control using the former. Also, it can be tempting to drag the mouse treating it like a paintbrush, but this can result in blurred areas. It is far better to apply the sampled areas using multiple clicks to achieve a nice clear image.

When we're finished, we should end up with something similar to the image below. Without prior knowledge, the flaw should be almost impossible to spot.

TAKING THE PERFECT SHOT EVERY TIME

Often you can find the perfect location, the perfect lighting but due to unforeseen circumstances something gets in the way of 'the perfect shot'.

On the other side of the coin: sometimes we miss the perfect shot because we think conditions aren't perfect – "if only that guy would just move out the way". This is where the beauty of Photoshop Elements, and specifically the Clone Stamp tool comes into play.

1. Open up the image entitled: `beach.jpg`.

Here we have your classic solitude beach walk type shot. But it's not quite perfect is it? Well minus the guy fishing and the odd bather, it's pretty close. The great thing about using a digital camera is that you can confidently shoot this kind of photograph, knowing what you'd like to get out of it, safe in the knowledge that you can remove the little imperfections at a later date. Well now is that date!

There are a number of problems with this image; apart from the other people on the beach, the hint of clouds tends to mess with the purity of the image – they'll just have to go! Similarly, the wave that's just broken on the left is undesirable.

2. Removing the wave residue and the clouds is fairly straightforward. Let's start by duplicating the original layer, and working off this layer. It's probably easier for the clouds and wave residue to use a brush size of around 45. Observe that there is a slight vertical gradient to the cloud area, so take care to select along similar gradient colors horizontally. Again, zoom in to get a clearer view of the area you're working on.

3. Right, with that done, let's get rid of our unwanted guests. We are going to start with the fisherman. This is a fairly tricky task as he's quite close to our model. We should therefore use a fairly small brush size: 13.

The first thing we need to do is analyze the flow of the image. Where will we find our grafting areas? It's quite clear that most of the flow we can see is horizontal. There is a white band of wave, which the fisherman is standing in. His head is touching a similar white band and his fishing rod is passing through a number of similarly horizontal striations.

A similar sense of flow can be found for all the other people on the beach, and getting rid of them is fairly straightforward. The only problem that we might come across in this task is the fact that the fisherman's legs and model's head are fairly close together. Using a diffuse brush might mess with the model, which we don't want to do.

4. We need to define the area that the Stamp tool will affect. First delineate the whole area with the Marquee tool, we want to leave the girl's head out of the selection, so we'll use the Lasso tool to draw around this hold down the ALT/OPTION key to subtract from the rectangular selection as shown in the image below.

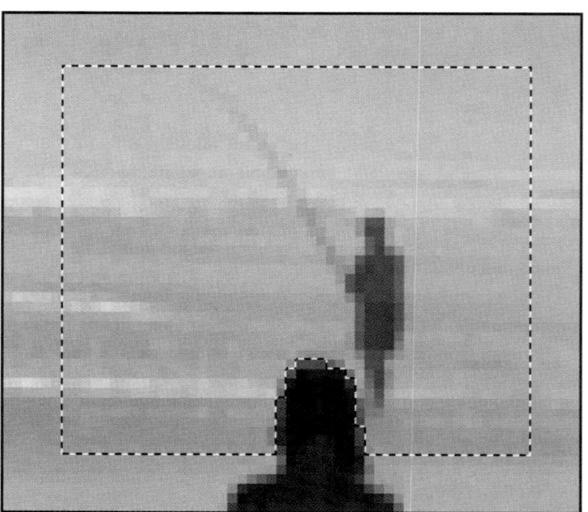

5. Using the methods we have learnt above, it is now a fairly straightforward task to remove the fisherman. Remember to use the Clone Stamp tool with a 13 pixel diffuse brush, set to a fairly low opacity, roughly 20%. A good method of painting for this task is to ALT/OPTION click on a good horizontally lined up grafting area, then click and drag over the fisherman in horizontal strokes a couple of times. In this way, you end up pasting strips of grafting area over the fisherman, and not just blobs – which will end up looking a bit dappled. One unwanted guest gone.

6. There's only one tiny problem with our great clone stamping spree: If you look carefully at the right hand side of the model's head you'll notice that I got a bit close with my marquee, and therefore the boundary between her hair and the sea is a bit sharp, and distinct from the hair which is almost on her shoulders.

7. In order to fix this, we're going to use the **Blur** tool (which looks like a teardrop). If you have the same problem with your image, simply select this tool, (using a brush size of 13 and a pressure of 50%) and paint over this area. This will soften up the hard artificial line and make it look more like the rest of the image.

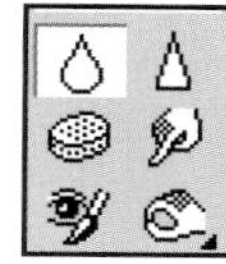

Similarly, the tool to the right of the Blur tool, the **Sharpen** tool, which is shaped like a triangle, is used to sharpen blurry images. We don't need to use this tool in this exercise, but the sharpen tool can be handy for tidying an image up.

8. Now, we can quickly remove the leftover people. Just one small point of observation: when removing the bather on the right, the shoreline that passes behind him does so diagonally from top left to bottom right, hence when we select our grafting area, it will be vertically higher than our pasting area (we have to paste along a diagonal line):

9. Don't be afraid to use a smaller brush size for this task – dropping down to a brush size of 5 is probably necessary to graft from and into the smaller areas. Similar to the horizontal strokes used to get rid of the fisherman, we will use diagonal strokes to paste over the bather.

10. With this task done, we end up with what we originally wanted: the classic beach solitude shot. You can have a look at this finished piece on the CD by opening `beach done.jpg`.

Analyzing the image a little bit closer, there is still something we can do to improve it. Have a look at the area just to the right of the model in beach done.jpg. This area is particularly hazy.

Even though this was part of the shot, it tends to detract somewhat from the effect of the image: the haze should just be coming from the sea. Let's see what we can do about this.

11. In order to make this area a little bit darker, we are going to use the **Burn** tool.

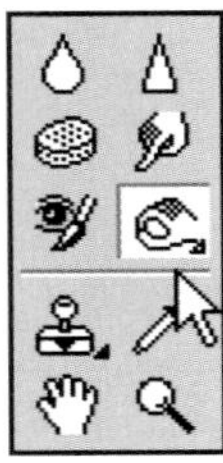

This tool acts like holding a flame under a piece of paper – a dark mark appears where the flame is – the longer you hold it there, the darker the mark gets. This tool is quite powerful, and seeing as how we only need a very slight change of brightness, we are going to set the power (exposure) of it way down. This is like holding the candle further away from the paper.

It's not a bad idea at this point to make a duplicate layer of your work so far. Using the burn tool can really adversely affect your image if it's not used carefully.

12. What we are now going to do is set the exposure to 10% and gently drag the tool across the light hazy area. You might have to gently dab the odd spot that burnt a little bit unevenly, but after this, we are done with creating our perfect shot:

If we, on the other hand wanted to make this area a little bit lighter, we would have used the **Dodge** tool (the icon of the pointing hand just above the burn tool) in much the same way as we have used the burn tool. Getting subtle and quick changes to lighting was never this easy!

Using the tools that we have learnt in this chapter can greatly improve the flexibility with which you can now take photographs. Creating the perfect picture is often an almost impossible task: Imagine the exasperation of the non-digital photographer trying to achieve what we have in this chapter...

By using the Clone Stamp, along with the Burn, Dodge, Blur and Sharpen tool that task is now quite a bit easier for us. In the next chapter we'll have a look at the filters and effects available in Photoshop Elements, and learn even more ways of manipulating our photos.

6 Filters and Effects

Up to now we have covered practical methods for correcting and adding elements to your digital photos. This chapter takes a well-deserved departure from the more routine applications of Photoshop Elements and gives you a chance to play around a little bit. We'll be taking a look at the various Filters and Effects available in Photoshop Elements this chapter, and how they can add life to your photos and create some pretty interesting images.

Before we start, let's first get this important distinction out of the way: the difference between a filter and an effect. A **filter** applies a specific change to the active layer in a document, such as an artistic remix, a blur, or a distortion. For example, you can use the Filter > Artistic > Watercolor filter to give your photo a quick painterly look in one command. An **effect**, however, is more complex – an effect is a pre-made series of actions that may include filters, Layer Styles, and/or other functions of Elements that are applied to the active layer. For example, if you apply the Bricks effect from the Effects palette, Photoshop Elements automatically goes through the steps necessary to create the Bricks effect – you actually get to watch them, one after the other, live as they happen.

Filters

Now that you understand the difference between the two, let's take a look at some of the features of the different filters available in Elements and how they can enhance your images. First of all, it's important to note that the same filters are available in both the menu bar under the **Filters** option, and the **Filters** palette. For this section I will use the Filters palette. The advantage of using the palette is that if you are unfamiliar with the behavior of filters it provides you with a thumbnail sample of what each filter does. Go ahead and drag the Filters palette out of the palette dock so it is fully open on your screen.

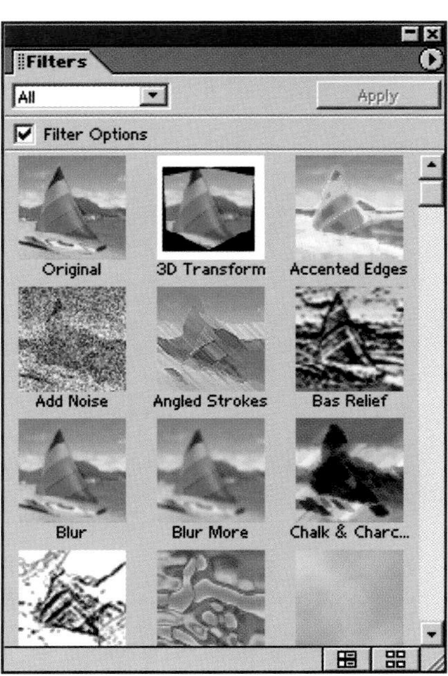

Before we start playing around with filters, let's make sure we have a grip on the way the palette works. First of all, take a look at the dropdown menu just under the Filters tab. This menu allows us to only display certain categories of filters, which is useful if we know the broad generic group we want to choose from.

Notice the **Filter Options** checkbox in the top left hand corner. By default this is checked, and this ensures that when you apply a filter through the Filters palette a dialog box appears that allows you to customize the settings of the chosen filter. If you unchecked this, the default settings would automatically be used. I suggest leaving it checked – you definitely want to be able to adjust filter settings.

There are three different ways to apply filters through the Filters palette. With a filter highlighted in the palette, you can click the **Apply** button. You can also double-click a filter thumbnail. Or if you like, you can drag a thumbnail on to the canvas. Do whatever is most comfortable for you – I prefer to double-click because it's the quickest.

You can view the Filters palette in two different ways. The default view for the Filter palette is **Thumbnail View**, but you can change it to **List View**. This allows you to see more filters at once, but you can only see the thumbnail of the one you have selected. You can toggle between the two views using the icons at the bottom right of the palette, or using the menu which is accessed via the small arrow in the top right hand corner of the palette.

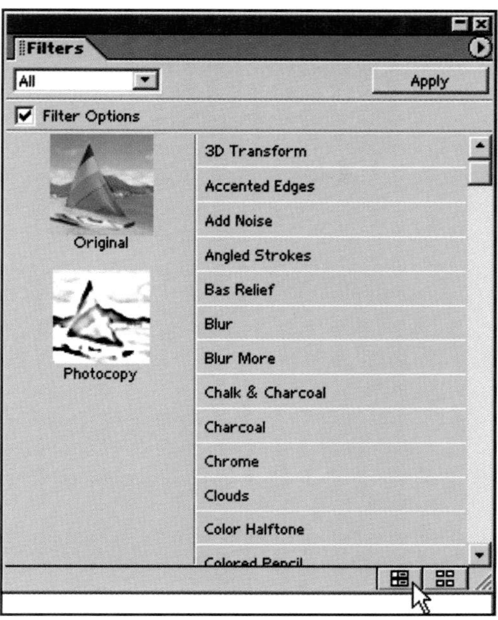

You're not always going to want to apply a filter to an entire layer – sometimes you'll want to only affect a certain area. Well, fortunately, with most filters you have the option to create a selection and have the filter only apply to that area.

There are almost 100 different filters; we won't cover each one individually, instead we'll look at the different groups of filters and what each one has to offer.

First, though, we need an image to work on.

1. Open up `Legodudes.jpg`, or your own image. If it's big (like Legodudes) then resize it to around 800x600 pixels (**Image > Resize > Image Size**) so the file size is smaller and we don't have to wait as long for each filter to process.

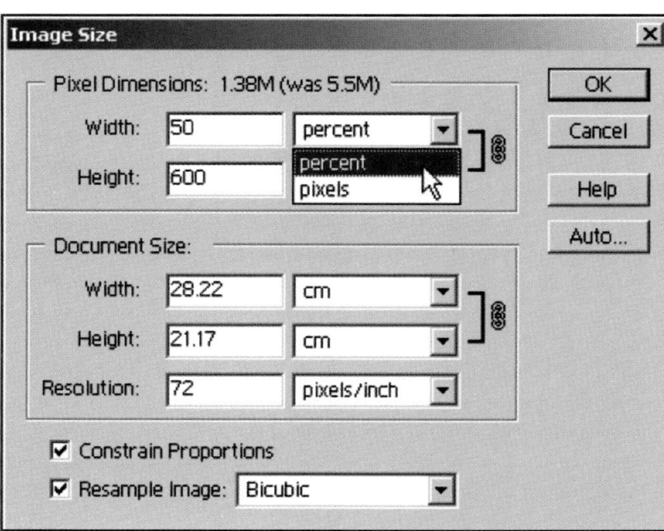

Artistic

2. We'll start by looking at the first group of filters in the popup menu, **Artistic**. These are useful for turning a photo into an instant work of art. Portraits, scenic shots, and still life shots work best here. You can achieve results with these filters that emulate paint, pencil, chalk, and more. Let's take a look at a few of them.

The **Dry Brush** filter is one of the filters that create a paintbrush-style effect. It does this by reducing the image to areas of similar color rather than the full range of photographic shades, which gives the appearance of an image painted with broad, flat colors.

3. Double-click on the Dry Brush thumbnail and let's look at the settings that come up.

Notice the interface of the filter's settings. This is typical of the settings window that most filters have. In the upper left corner there is a preview of how the filter will look; this updates as you adjust the settings. By clicking and dragging you can scroll around the preview window (as with the Hand tool) and zoom in and out using the plus/minus buttons under the preview. The preview changes as you change the **Brush Size**, **Brush Detail**, or **Texture**. For instance, you should be able to see the brush strokes widen and the image lose detail when you increase the Brush Size. Once you have settings that you are happy with, click OK and the filter will be applied. I'm using the settings pictured.

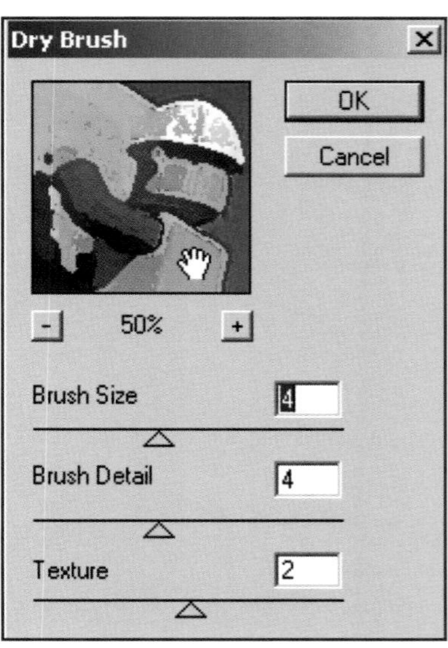

It's as simple as that. Double-click the filter thumbnail, adjust the settings, and the magic ensues. This simple process makes it easy to quickly test several different filters to decide which effect you want. Let's try another one from the Artistic group so we can see some different settings.

4. Undo the last filter (CTRL/CMD+Z) and double-click the **Rough Pastels** thumbnail.

5. Here, we're introduced to some different options, namely the **Texture** settings. Click on the Texture dropdown menu and you'll see that there are others besides **Canvas** to choose from. Try adjusting the **Scaling**, **Relief**, and **Light Direction** settings to achieve different texture effects. Relief refers to the extent to which a texture will appear raised from the canvas. Take note of the thumbnail preview to see what each setting does to the image.

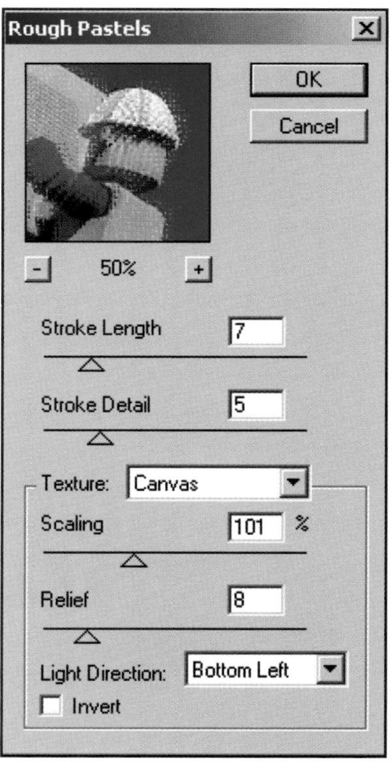

The Texture options are also available in some of the other filters – they can be useful for giving your photo the illusion of being on a different surface. Also, notice how in areas of bright color the texture doesn't show through as much, while in darker areas where there is less chalk the texture stands out more.

Try experimenting with the rest of the Artistic filters to get an idea of the various traditional media effects you can achieve. After all, you can undo after each try.

Blur

Let's move on to the Blur filters, the next group available in the Filters palette dropdown menu. The Blur filters are useful for simulating camera focus effects, camera motion, and can also be used to correct areas of an image that need smoother color gradations. These filters are best used on a selected area or specific layer – applying them to an entire image will blur everything out of focus. Let's try a couple of Blur filters out on our `Legodudes.jpg` image.

1. To set up the image, we'll draw a quick selection around the main figures using the Polygonal Lasso tool. Feather the selection by 1 pixel.

2. Create a new layer by copying the selection – **Layer > New > Layer Via Copy** (CTRL/CMD-J).

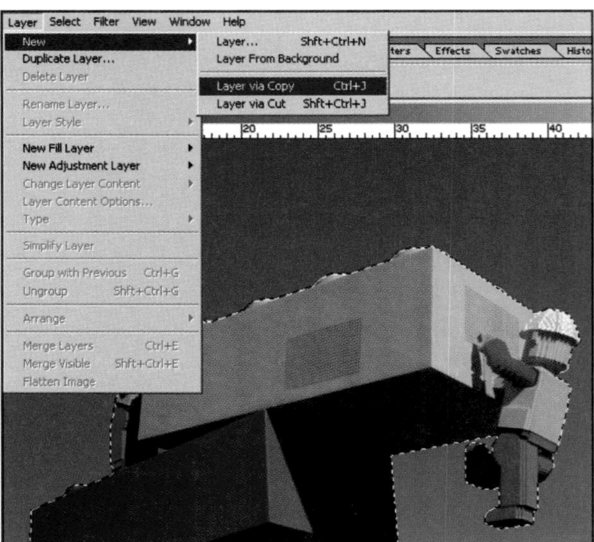

3. Select the background layer by clicking on it in the Layers palette. We'll apply some Blur filters to the background layer in order to bring more focus to the top layer.

4. Select the **Gaussian Blur** filter from the palette – this effect adds an evenly distributed hazy blur to an image or layer. Make sure you have the Preview box checked so you can see the effects as you adjust the settings.

5. Change the Radius setting to 10 pixels, and see how the background layer changes. By blurring the background we add depth to the image. Click Cancel and let's move on.

6. This time select the **Motion Blur** filter, set the Angle to 10, and the Distance to 70 pixels. See how we can create a dynamic feel to the image by simulating camera movement?

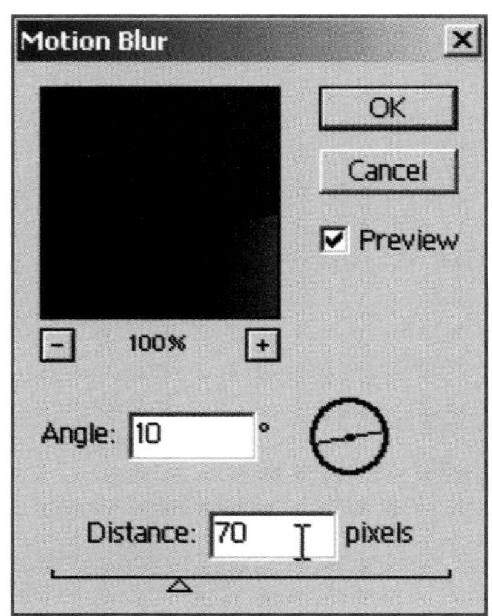

7. Hit Cancel and now select the **Radial Blur**. With the Radial Blur you can either create a **Spin** or **Zoom** effect but because this takes a while for the computer to calculate, there is no preview so you have to make do with a rough representation.

8. Let's first try the Spin effect, set the Amount to 25 and make sure Spin is selected as the **Blur Method**, and that Good is chosen for the **Quality** setting. Click OK. Notice how this effects simulates a rotating camera blur.

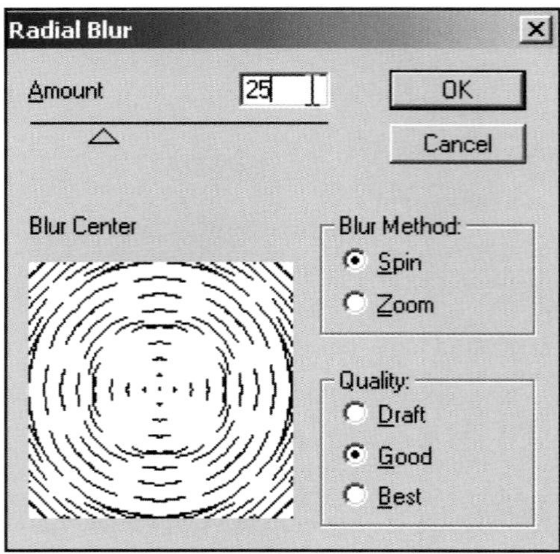

9. Undo this last step (CTRL/CMD+Z) and let's try the Radial Blur again but this time with the Zoom effect. Increase the Amount to 75 and set the Blur Method to Zoom.

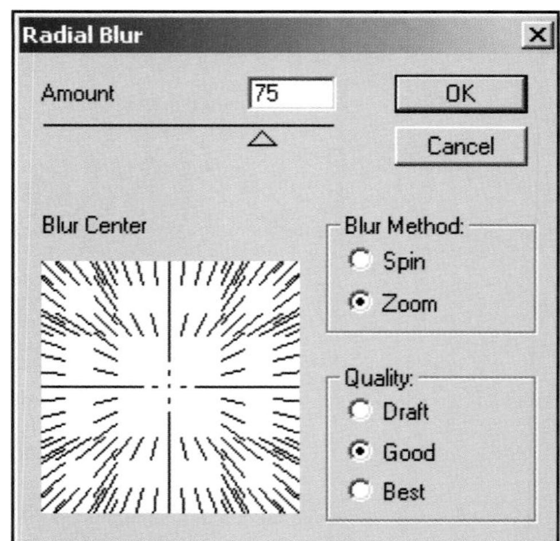

As you can see, the blur filters can generate a range of depth effects to give your images motion. When applying a blur to an entire layer make sure that in the Layers palette, you have deselected the **Lock Transparent Pixels** option. Otherwise it will not blur the edges of the layer.

Brush Strokes

The **Brush Strokes** filters are very similar to the Artistic filters group. They can add traditional brush and ink artistic effects to your images. Flatten the `Legodudes.jpg` image (**Layer > Flatten Image**) and try out some of these filters, experimenting with the different settings. Here you can see the Crosshatch filter.

Distort

The **Distort** filters are for the most part impractical, but fun nonetheless. This group of filters can tweak your image in several different ways – we'll take a look at a few of them here. Undo any previous effects and select the **Glass** filter. Play around with the sliders and watch the Preview box to see how the image is being affected. Choose the Canvas texture with a Distortion value of 10 and Smoothness of 5.

This reminds me of a reflection on water, the **Ocean Ripple** and **Ripple** filters create a similar effect. Try experimenting with those too if you want to achieve a really watery feel.

Let's briefly take a look at the **Liquify** filter, which we'll be coming back to later in the chapter. Undo any previous effects (or if you've applied several effects and don't want to apply Undo a million times, use the Revert command under **File > Menu** to go back to the last saved version of our image, which should be when you opened it) and select the Liquify filter.

The Liquify filter is unique in that it combines the power of several filters in one tool. You have eight separate tools to choose from: **Warp**; **Twirl Clockwise**; **Twirl Counterclockwise**; **Pucker**; **Bloat**; **Shift**; **Pixels**; **Reflection**; and **Reconstruct**. You can control the size and pressure of the brush that you use for each one. We'll modify an image using this filter later in the chapter, but go ahead and experiment with it a little now if you like.

I suggest experimenting on your own with the rest of the Distort filters. You really learn them best by experimentation, since there are no standards set for their use. Try at least a couple different settings for each one – you'll find that each one can produce several variations by making slight shifts in the settings.

Noise

The **Noise** filters not only add noise to your images, but they are also useful for removing noise as well. Undo all effects done to `Legodudes.jpg` and select the **Add Noise** filter. Take a look at the preview and see how this gives your image a grainy look similar to old film. Take note of the two modes of distribution: **Uniform** adds a more subtle grainy effect while **Gaussian** creates more of a speckled look, and **Monochromatic** strictly preserves the original color tones of the image.

The Add Noise filter can be really helpful when working with scanned photos. Sometimes, retouching scanned photos can look unnatural because the digital effects are too clean compared to the natural noise that appears in a developed photograph. Using the Add Noise filter to the retouched areas can help it blend in better with the original photograph. This is a good time to mention that filters often work well when combined. For example, applying a noise effect then adding a motion blur can provide interesting results.

The other three Noise filters are for removing noise – they basically detect small discrepancies in an image and change them to match the surrounding pixels. These filters are useful not only for cleaning up old photographs with dust and scratches, but also for using on newer scanned photos with visible film grain.

Pixelate

The **Pixelate** filters can be used to create some interesting graphic effects. They work by grouping similar pixels together to create uniform patterns. Let's take a look at a few of these. One of my favorites is the **Halftone Color** filter. This filter simulates halftone screening (like if you looked at a newspaper photo with a magnifying glass), but at a much larger scale. Try this filter out on our Legodudes image, and leave the default settings.

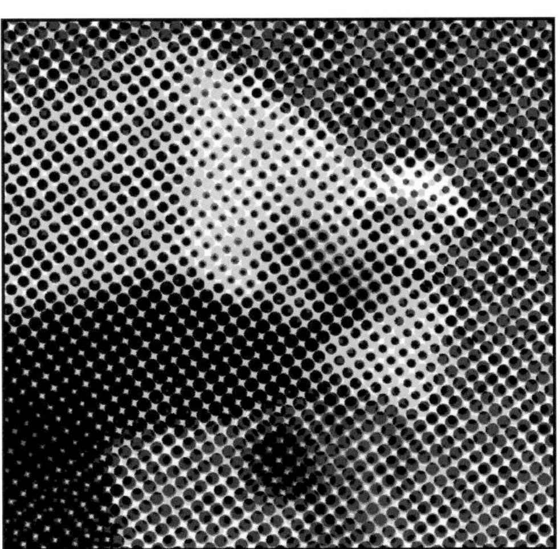

I've zoomed in slightly in order to emphasize the effect, but as you can see we can achieve instant Pop Art with this effect.

Render

The **Render** filters are a collection of 3D shaping tools, natural cloud patterns, and various lighting effects.

Here's a brief overview of what each one has to offer:

- **3D Transform**: This filter takes your image and "fits" it to a cube, sphere, or cylinder shape. You can manually draw a wire frame then rotate it with the image mapped to it. There are several options for setting the perspective of the shapes, combining shapes, editing the shape anchor points, and including the background in the render.

1. Select the 3D Transform filter, and choose the **Cube** tool to make a cube shaped wire frame.

2. Use the **Trackball** tool to rotate the cube slightly to the left, and then click on the **Options** button to bring up further choices, in this dialog uncheck the **Display Background** box.

   Your image should look something like this:

- **Clouds**: This creates a random cloud pattern using the foreground and background colors as the tones. It's best to create a new layer or work on a blank canvas before using this filter.

- **Difference Clouds**: Creates the same random cloud patterns with the foreground and background colors, but uses information from the current layer to create varying color.

- **Lens Flare**: The Lens Flare simulates the effect of a camera pointed at a strong light source. You can choose from three different types and also specify the location and brightness of the flare.

- **Lighting Effects**: This complex filter allows you to choose from and fully customize several types of light sources, apply more than one at a time, and load textures as maps for lighting.

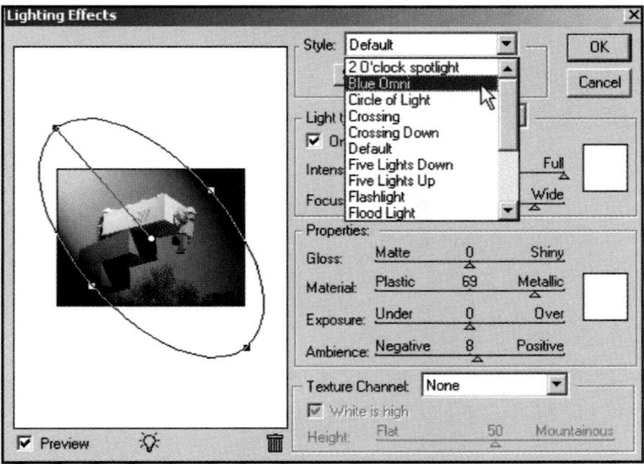

Sharpen

The **Sharpen** tools provide fairly simple methods for making slightly blurred images seem crisper. They can't repair images that are severely unfocused, however, so still make sure you focus your shots as best you can when shooting. The **Sharpen** and **Sharpen More** filters have no settings – they are simply one-click solutions for image sharpening, and, as you can probably guess, the Sharpen More filter applies a stronger amount of focusing than the regular Sharpen tool. The **Sharpen Edges** filter sharpens only areas of high contrast, so as a result the edges of your photos subjects are focused while more uniform areas of color remain unchanged.

For more precise control over sharpening, the **Unsharp Mask** filter allows you to adjust the sharpening percentage, the pixel Radius to be affected, and the Threshold level. Unsharp Mask is useful for sharpening scanned photos, or removing the half toning from scanned printed materials.

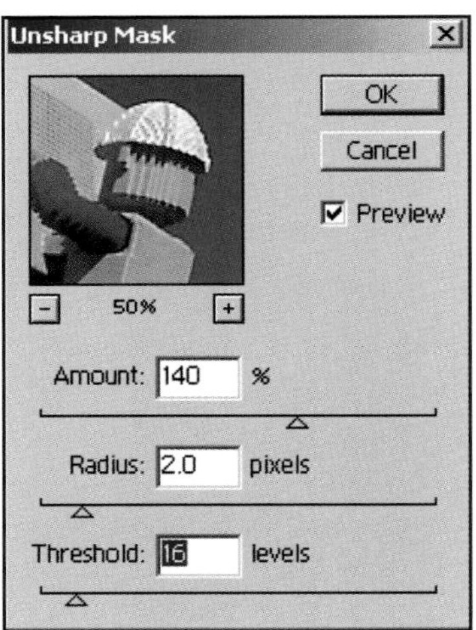

Sketch

The **Sketch** filters, similar to the Artistic and Brush Stroke filters, simulate not only traditional art effects but also include some filters that create stunning three-dimensional effects such as chromed objects. We'll take a moment here to cover these features.

- **Bas Relief**: Simulates a low-relief sculpture (one that is slightly raised from the surface); be sure to choose a foreground and background color as they will be used for the highlights and shadows.
- **Chalk & Charcoal**: Uses the foreground and background color as the dark and light charcoal tones, respectively, and creates a sketch of your image on a gray background.
- **Charcoal**: Similar to the Chalk & Charcoal filter, but uses the foreground color as the chalk and the background color as the paper.
- **Chrome**: One of the more fun filters – makes your image appear as if has been covered in chrome, with settings to adjust the smoothness and detail. This filter works best on images with less detail.

- **Conte Crayon**: This simulates drawing with a Conte Crayon on textured paper – uses the foreground and background colors in a similar way to the Chalk & Charcoal filter.
- **Graphic Pen**: One of my favorite filters, it simulates the effect of an ink drawing done with parallel lines in any direction you choose. The foreground color is used as the ink color and the background color for the paper.

- **Halftone Pattern**: Turns the image into a halftone pattern of your choice – Circle, Dot, or Line, and you can set the size and contrast of the pattern.

- **Note Paper**: Simulates a low-relief papier-mâché construction of your image.
- **Photocopy**: Another one of my favorites, this filter simulates the high contrast and graininess that often results when photocopying an image.

- **Plaster**: Displays your image as if it were molded in plaster, using the foreground and background colors for the highlights and shadows.
- **Reticulation**: Simulates traditional film grain, using the foreground and background colors. You can adjust the density of the grain as well as the dark and white points of the grain.
- **Stamp**: This filter takes an image and reduces it to two colors – the foreground and background colors. This is more effective on black and white images.
- **Torn Edges**: Works a lot like the Stamp filter, but makes the edges of the foreground color areas appear torn and ragged.
- **Water Paper**: Makes your image appear as if it is bleeding into wet paper, with settings to control the paper's Fiber Length, Brightness, and Contrast.

Stylize

These are an interesting group of filters that include 3D, object edge, and blur effects.

- **Diffuse**: Takes the edges of the subjects of your image and jumbles up the pixels to make it appear out of focus.
- **Emboss**: Finds the edges of the subjects of your image and raises them – the background is turned gray and the edges are based on the original colors of the image.
- **Extrude**: Creates a neat 3D effect by making your image appear as if it's projecting off of the canvas in columns of blocks or pyramids. You can customize the depth and size of the blocks among other settings.

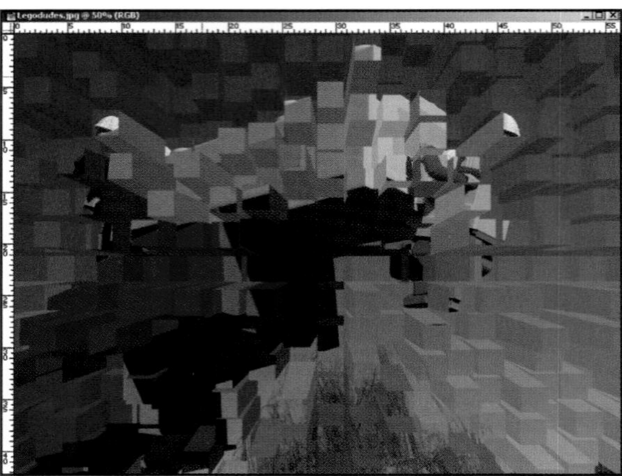

- **Find Edges**, **Glowing Edges**, and **Trace Contour**: All three filters create various effects by finding the edges of the objects in your photo and applying different effects to them. Find Edges will create dark lines on a white background, Glowing Edges will create glowing lines on a dark background, and Trace Contour will create very thin outlines on a white background.
- **Solarize**: Simulates the effect of a photo being exposed to sunlight in the development process, with warped colors and gradations.
- **Tiles**: Similar to the Extrude filter, but only on a two-dimensional level. Separates your image into tiles, letting you set the spacing and options for how to display the background.
- **Wind**: Makes your image appear as if it is being blown by wind, with settings for the strength and direction of the wind. Look at our poor little Lego dude being buffeted!

Texture

The Texture filters are fairly self-explanatory: they allow you to give your images the appearance of being on different materials or media. One of the most effective is the **Texturizer**, which has a dialog box which allows you to choose from **Brick**, **Burlap**, **Canvas**, or **Sandstone** and adjust the depth, scale and light direction. You can even load a texture of your own from another file – to do this select **Load Texture** from the Texture dropdown menu and choose a file with an image of a well-defined texture.

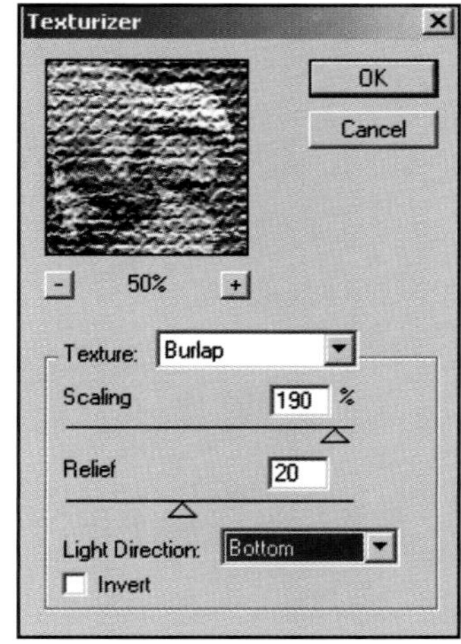

Video

The two filters in this group are used when working with images that are either captured from video or being prepared for use in video. The **De-Interlace** filter removes the "interlaced" lines (think of these as the scan lines that you can see on a television screen) that appear in images captured from a video source. The **NTSC Colors** filter prepares your image for television by restricting the range of colors used.

Other

The **Other** group of filters allows you to make more advanced effects with very specific uses, such as creating your own custom filters. The chances are you won't have to use these in day-to-day image editing, but let's very briefly look at each one.

- **Custom**: As the name suggests, this option allows you to customize your own filters by changing the brightness value of each individual pixel. Each pixel is given a new value based on the values of the surrounding pixels.
- **Dither**: This option allows you to create a custom dither pattern for a selected RGB color.
- **Maximum and Minimum**: Are used to modify masks. The minimum filter shrinks white areas, and spreads out black areas. The maximum filter does the opposite.
- **High Pass**: This retains the edge details where sharp contrast appear, but suppresses the rest of the image.
- **Offset**: This will offset a selection of an image, either horizontally to the right, or vertically downwards.

Effects

As we've already noted, effects differ from filters in that they tend to perform a series of combined 'actions' to produce their effect. Now let's take a moment to cover some of the various effects available in Elements and how they can contribute to your photos. The effects are organized in groups via the Effects palette much like the Filters palette.

Frames

The **Frames** effects, as you might suspect, create various frames around your images. These effects are best used on final images, because once you apply a frame it's difficult to do more editing to the image without affecting the frame too. The image below has the **Spatter** frame attached to it.

Textures

Not to be confused with the Textures filters, the **Textures** effects create more sophisticated textures by combining several filters into a series of steps, which are executed when you select one of them. Once the texture is complete and on a separate layer, experiment with the Layer blending modes to modify the textures with interesting results.

Below I have used the **Cold Lava** effect, and then adjusted the layer blending mode to Hard Light, in order to let the background layer show through the effect.

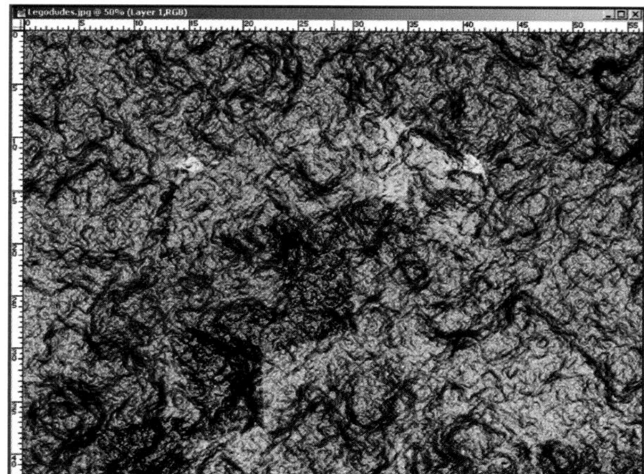

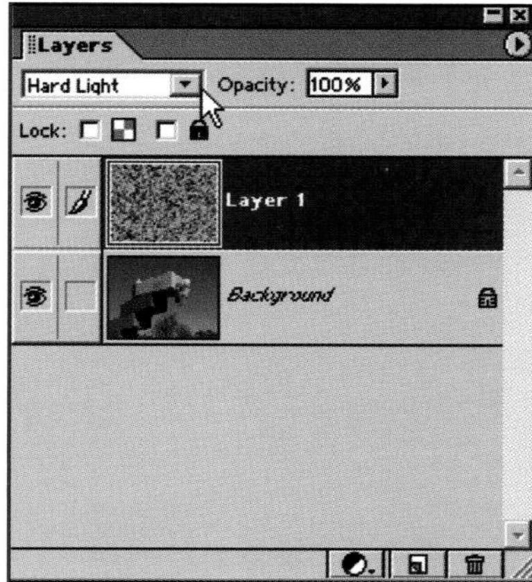

Text Effects

These effects can be used to quickly create jazzy text graphics. Use the Type tool to write a slogan on your canvas, and try applying these effects to it and see the range of effects that you can obtain. Below I've added a **Clear Emboss** to the text, to give a subtle look.

Image Effects

Image Effects make creative use of combining different filters to create effects that could not be achieved through the use of one filter alone. Try some of these out and take note of the processes – you might get ideas of your own for filter combinations. Below I've used the **Blizzard** which uses the Pointillize filter combined with blending options and a motion blur to achieve the final result.

Recipes

Stepping away from Filters and Effects, let's briefly discuss the **Recipes** palette. You might be curious by now about what it can be used for and how it can benefit you. In simple terms the Recipes palette is a kind of built-in tutorial machine for common tasks in image-editing. You can learn how to achieve certain result by watching it walk though a process.

Try selecting a recipe from one of the categories and notice how you can follow the steps on your own or have Photoshop Elements perform certain steps for you that are marked with a Play button.

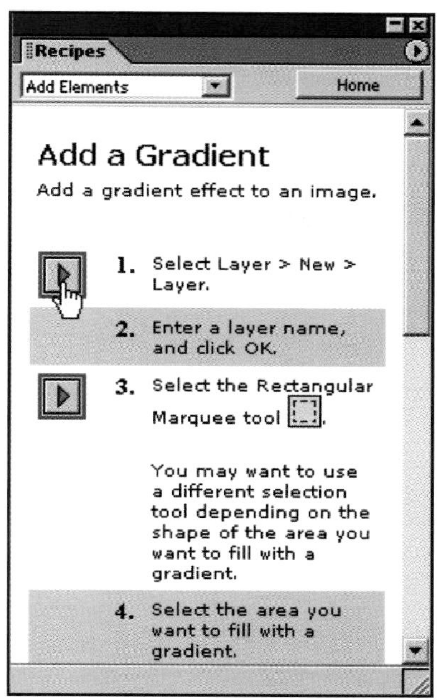

Try out some of the recipes, they are a great resource for when you need help solving a particular problem or when you simply wish to do some basic image-editing tutorials.

TUTORIAL: USING THE LIQUIFY TOOL

Let's go back to the Liquify tool and create a little havoc with it.

1. Open up `Einstein.psd`.
2. Select Liquify from the Filters palette or select **Filter > Liquify**. We're going to tweak this monument to Einstein with the Liquify tool to make it more of a caricature.
3. Choose the **Bloat** tool (fifth icon down on the left) and set the brush size to 100 and the pressure to 25. Let's enlarge Einstein's left eye a little to make it more dramatic for our caricature.

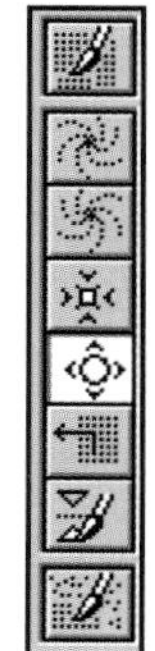

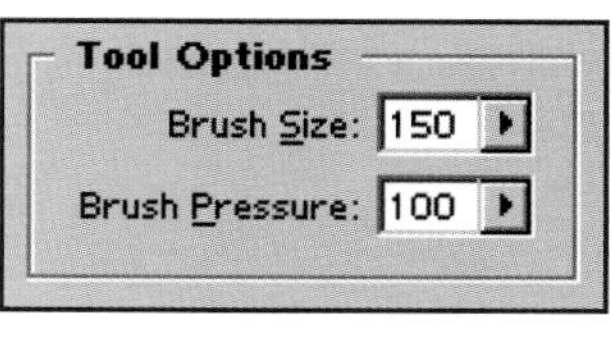

4. Click on the eye and hold the mouse down until the eye bulges out a little bit.

5. Now use the **Pucker** tool to shrink the other eye a bit. Select the icon just above the **Bloat** tool, use the same settings as before, and this time click and hold on Einstein's right eye till it shrinks a bit. As you can see the Bloat and Pucker tools expand or contract areas of your image.

6. Let's see what else we can do to Einstein using the Liquify tools. Select the **Warp** tool and let's give Einstein a pointy ear. The warp tool basically "pushes" pixels as you drag, so with the Brush Size at 50 and the Brush Pressure still at 25, click on the top of the ear and drag it upwards to pull it to a point. You might have to apply the tool a couple of times to get the desired effect.

7. Use the same tool with the same settings to stretch the points of his moustache. Click and drag on each end until you get the moustache's shape to your liking.

8. We now have a problem, though – in tweaking the right side of Einstein's moustache, we've also distorted the red column of the building behind him. Fortunately, the **Reconstruct** tool allows us the freedom to restore our image in areas that we accidentally distort. Select this tool and click and drag over the edge of the red column until it is restored to its original, straight form. It's an imprecise method, as it doesn't restore the original image exactly, but rather an approximation, which is sometimes inaccurate.

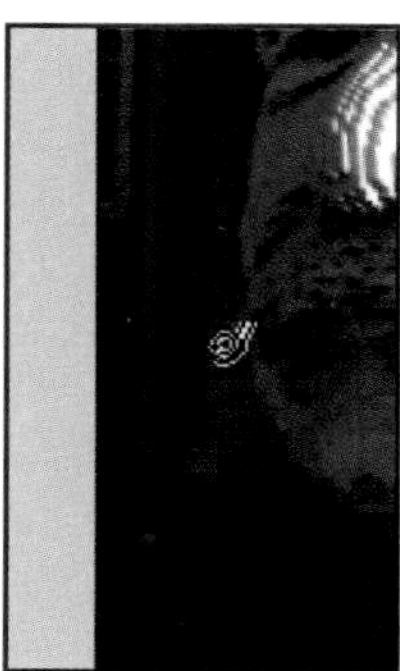

9. To put some final touches on the image, let's use the two **Twirl** tools to rotate the eyes a little. Select the **Twirl Counterclockwise** tool and set the Brush Size to 125. Click on Einstein's left eye until it rotates enough to add a little more character to his expression.

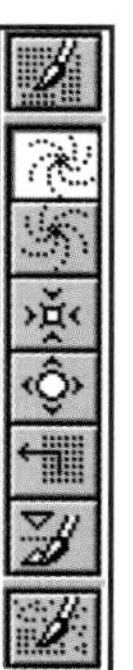

10. Switch over to the **Twirl Clockwise** tool and apply a similar effect to the other eye, but choose a smaller brush size since the eye is smaller. I used a setting of 75. Remember, you can always use Undo to take one step backward, or use the Reconstruct tool to restore accidents. If you really mess up an image, use the **Revert** button to restore the image to its original state.

Here is our final image:

Now we've run through the main filters and effects available in Photoshop Elements you'll be well equipped to use them to add some character to your images.

If you enjoyed the caricature exercise that we've just completed, why not try the same trick on your friends and family? If you dare!

7 Layer techniques

We've been touching on layers in a couple of the previous chapters. This chapter will take a closer look at them. Using layers is an important part of Adobe Photoshop Elements. Reworking practically any image will require the use of layers.

Layers are often likened to the sheets of acetate that are used in traditional animation. These save animators a great deal of time as they can draw one background and re-use it many times by altering foreground layers. That's why, if you buy an animation cel, you might get half a character's arm and nothing else.

In Photoshop Elements though, you can do a bit more than just put layers on top of each other. It doesn't just see layers as on or off; you can adjust their level of visibility and even apply effects to them. Let's have a quick look at this in Elements.

QUICK TASK: MAKING THREE LAYERS

Open up Adobe Photoshop Elements and click on the layers tab in the Palette well to bring up the Layers palette. We are going to detach this from the Palette well by simply clicking on it and dragging it onto the main work area. I always position my palettes to the right of the image I'm working on, but you can place them anywhere you feel comfortable with. Before we get into exactly how all the aspects of layers work, let's look at how to use them.

First layer

1. Create a new image by either clicking on the icon (the first one along on the shortcuts bar) or selecting **File > New**. Let's make this new image 600 by 400 pixels in size, 72dpi with a white background.

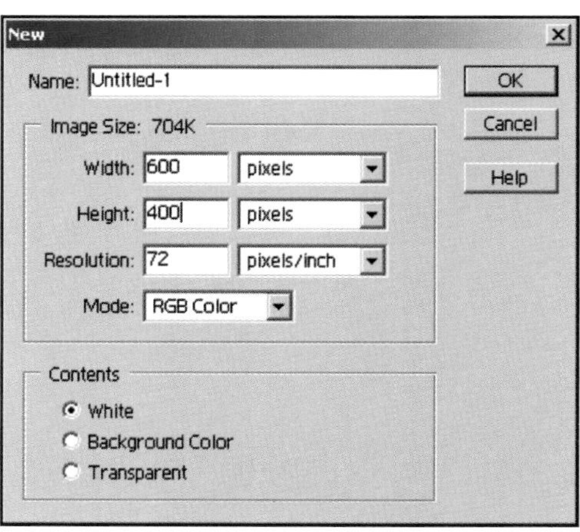

As you can see, we only have one layer, 'Background', so let's make another, by clicking on the Create new layer button (bottom of the palette).

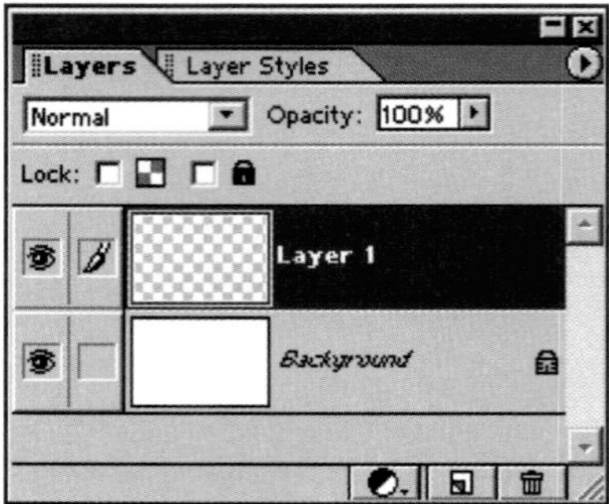

2. Let's draw a big red square on this layer. Using the Marquee tool, click and drag to make a square shape of roughly the size shown in the picture below. If you hold down the shift key while making your marquee, Elements will constrain the proportions of the shape produced to create a square. If you'd like to be precise about the size of a marquee that you're drawing, click on the info palette and watch the width and height reading in the bottom right hand corner.

3. Select your foreground color and pick a nice bright red.

4. Now we are going to fill the marquee with the red we have chosen. To do this, simply click **Edit > Fill**. This will bring up a dialog box. Make sure that you wish to use Foreground Color as the contents of your fill. Leave everything else and click OK.

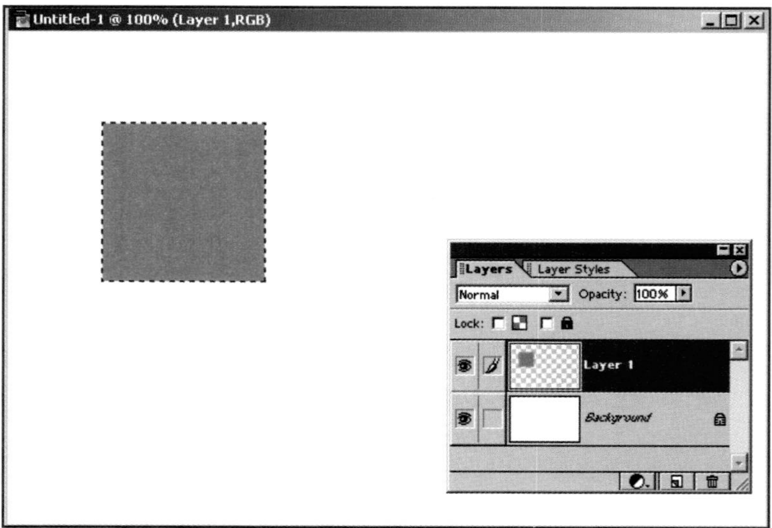

5. Click anywhere else on the canvas to deselect your red square (or you could always go to the Select menu and choose Deselect or press Ctrl/Cmd-D).

6. Now select the Move tool and drag your square around the canvas. Let's drag it into the top left hand corner. As it gets close to the corner it should snap neatly into place. If it doesn't, or if you would like to turn this feature off, go to **View > Snap** and either check or uncheck this option.

Another layer

For the purpose of this exercise, we are going to make two more layers, one with a green square, the other with a blue square. We could do this by going through the steps outlined above once again, but there is a quicker way – we are simply going to duplicate the layer and change the color of the red square.

1. Go back to your layers palette. RIGHT-CLICK/CTRL-CLICK the layer. Select Duplicate Layer. When the name box pops up, call the layer green.

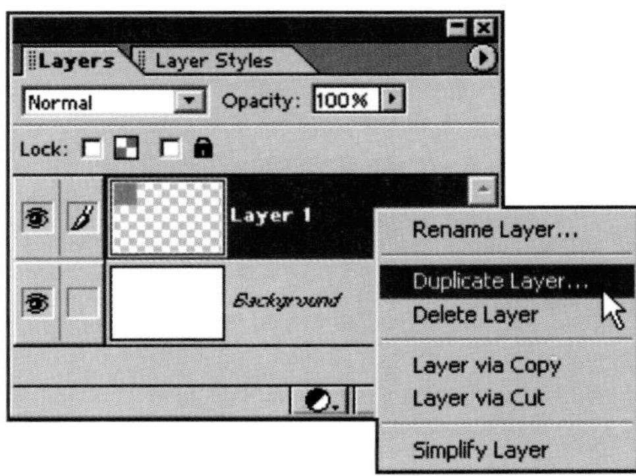

2. We've now created an exact duplicate of Layer 1. Let's rename the original layer; RIGHT-CLICK/CTRL-CLICK and choose the Rename Layer option. Call the layer *Red*.

3. Because the two layers that we now have hovering above the background layer are identical in every way except name, all we can see is one red square in the top left. Using the Move tool, click on the green layer and drag the square to the bottom right hand corner, allowing it to snap into place. What we now have should resemble the picture below. Not terribly exciting stuff yet!

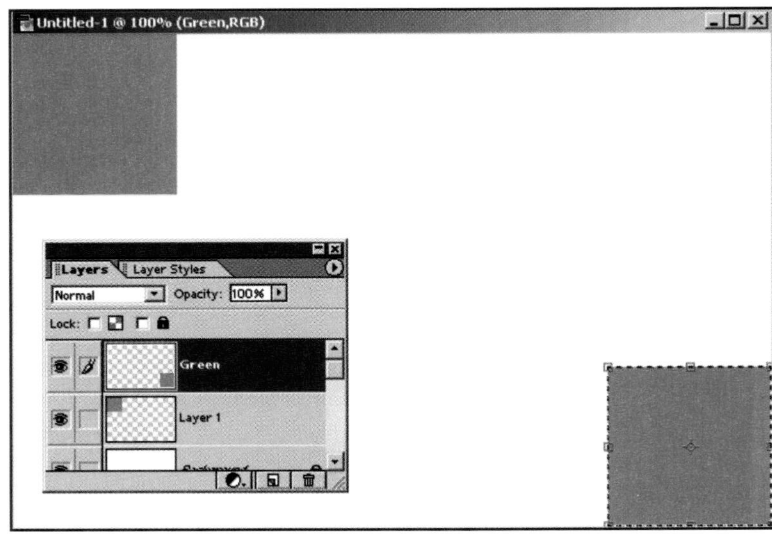

4. Time to change the red square on the green layer into green! First take a look at the small checkerboard icon in the top left hand corner of the Layers palette.

5. This option allows you to **Lock transparent pixels** on this layer. This means that when the box is checked, we will only be able to edit areas that are already drawn on – we cannot add anything new to the layer. If we now fill it with color, the only area that will be affected is the non-transparent part, the red square. Let's select a nice green as our foreground color and fill it as before.

Another thing to notice is that Elements puts a little padlock sign on the right hand side of the layer to indicate that the transparency has been locked. We could also prevent the layer from being edited in any way by clicking on the padlock checkbox (the second of the two checkboxes at the top of the palette) but we won't do that right now.

You'll see a similar padlock sign on the background layer. This lets you know that its contents cannot be moved around. The background layer acts more like the light table that you're putting your acetate sheets into than an actual layer itself. And clearly it's easier to move the acetate layers than drag your table around the studio!

6. Using the same technique as above, create another layer by duplicating the green layer, lock the transparency and fill it with blue. Let's put the blue square right in the middle of the screen.

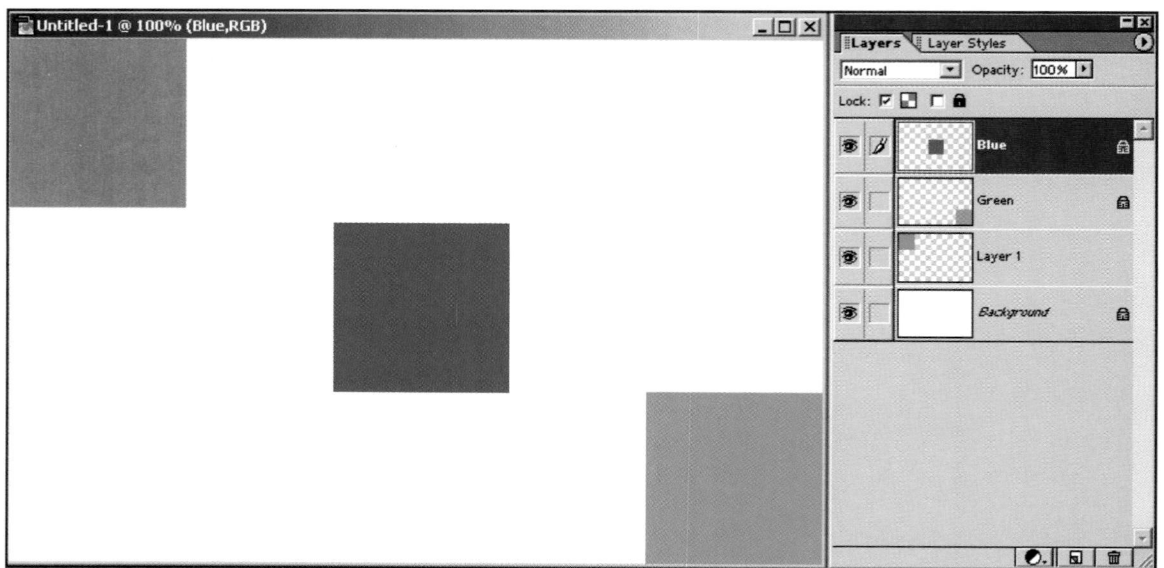

And more...

Let's create a new layer above all the others. Click on the blue layer so that it's selected as our current layer.

1. Click on the **Create a new layer** button at the bottom of the palette to create a new layer above the currently selected layer.

2. Let's make a selection using the Rectangular Marquee tool from the middle point of the red square, in the top left corner, to the middle of the green square in the bottom right corner.

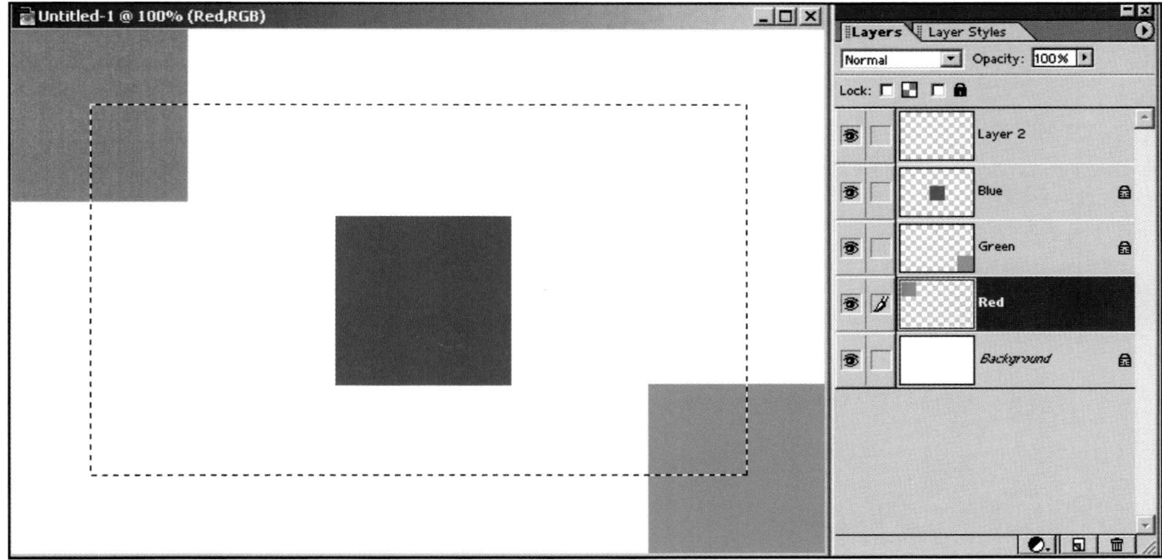

3. Select a fairly bright yellow as the Foreground Color and fill the marquee with it (**Edit > Fill**).

4. Because the yellow rectangle is on the uppermost layer, it totally blocks out our view of the blue square, and partially obscures the other two. Using the Opacity slider in the top right hand corner of the layers palette, drop the opacity of the yellow layer (which we can rename to Yellow at this point) to 50%.

Now we can see the blue square showing through. It's not looking very blue though! Notice that when you drop the opacity of the top layer, you blend the two colors together. It's like taking two candy wrappers, one yellow and one blue, and holding them up to the light together – you get a greenish blend.

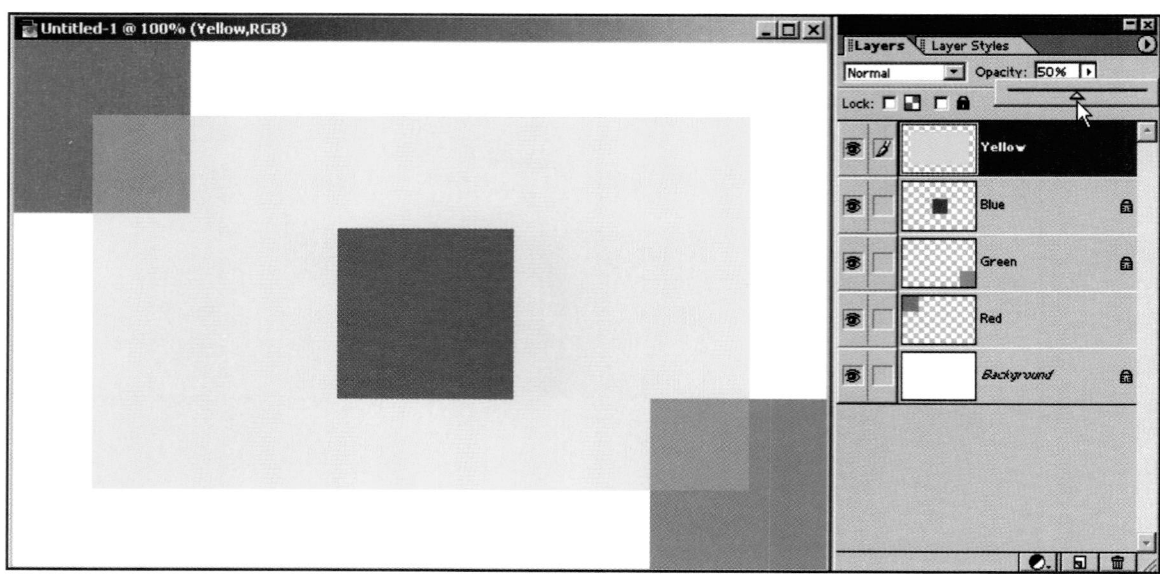

It is important to note that whatever you do to the layer applies to the whole layer. So if you drop the opacity of a layer, everything on the layer will now be partially transparent. This includes things that you draw on the layer afterwards.

Blending modes

There are many different ways to combine layers in Elements other than simply dropping the opacity of one. We call these different methods **blending modes**. To the right of the Opacity slider at the top of the Layers palette is a drop down box of the different blending modes available in Elements. Change the opacity of the yellow layer back to 100%. Have a look at the different blending modes by dropping down the selection box. So what are they and what are they used for?

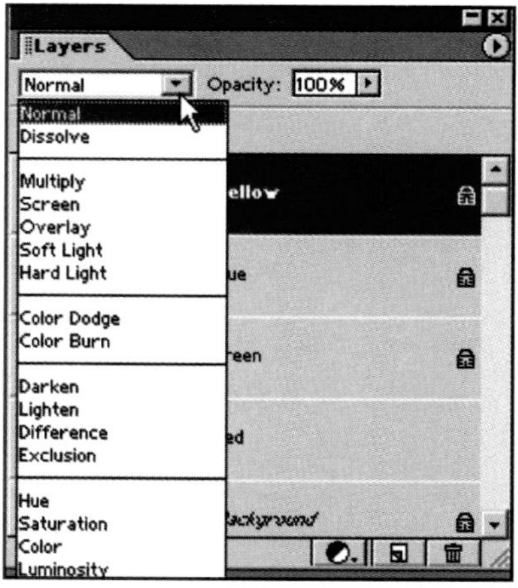

Using blending modes to dictate the way layers interact is one of the most powerful features of Photoshop Elements. Let's have a look at what some of the more commonly used ones do. Instead of taking a technical approach on how modes actually blend the colors, we're going to look at the impression created and possible uses for some of them.

Open up `exercise-generic.psd`, which will allow you to examine different blend effects compared to the original image.

- **Normal** This is the default mode. Up to now we've been using the layers in Normal mode. Unless we drop the opacity of the layer, this layer will not affect any other layers below it: where the layer is opaque, nothing of the layers below it will be visible.

- **Multiply** This mode takes the layer and combines the color in it with the layers below. The brighter/whiter the color, the more transparent the light area of the top layer becomes, and the darker colors are combined with the layers below to become even darker.

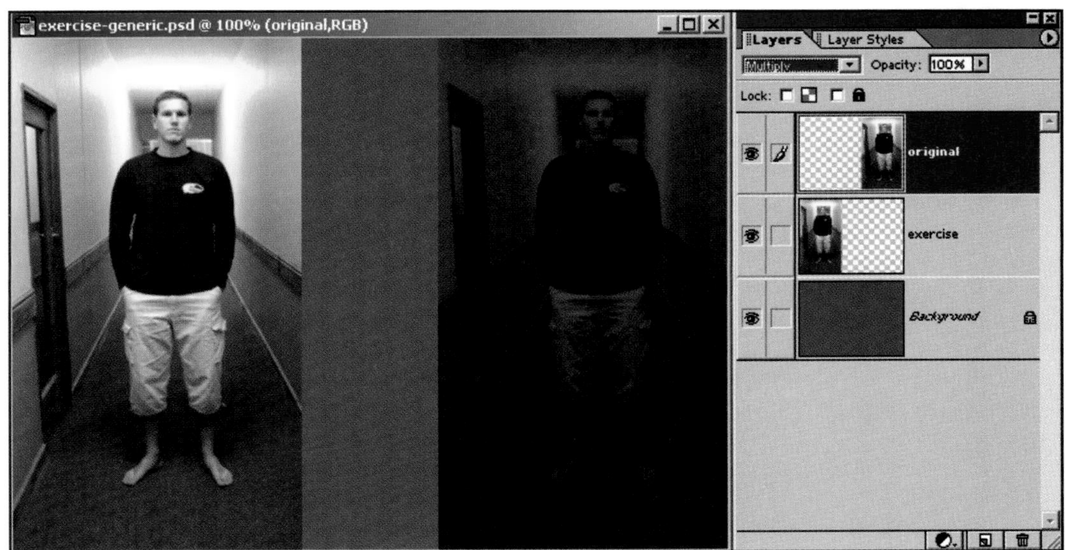

For instance, if you wanted to use your own handwriting on top of a photograph you would either take a digital picture of your handwriting or scan in a page you'd written on. Either way you'd have a lot of black text on a white page. So how do you remove the white page that the black text is on? Well you could try selecting it all and deleting it, but this will not only take a lot of time, but will also not be very effective. Enter the multiply mode... Using this mode on the layer will drop out all the white and leave the text on a seemingly transparent background.

- **Screen** Screen works in pretty much the opposite way to Multiply: combining the layers to make a lighter result. All the darker colors become transparent with the darker colors becoming lighter as they are combined. Another similar mode to this is Lighten which, when used with darker underlying layers, gives more contrast than Screen but has no effect on lighter ones.

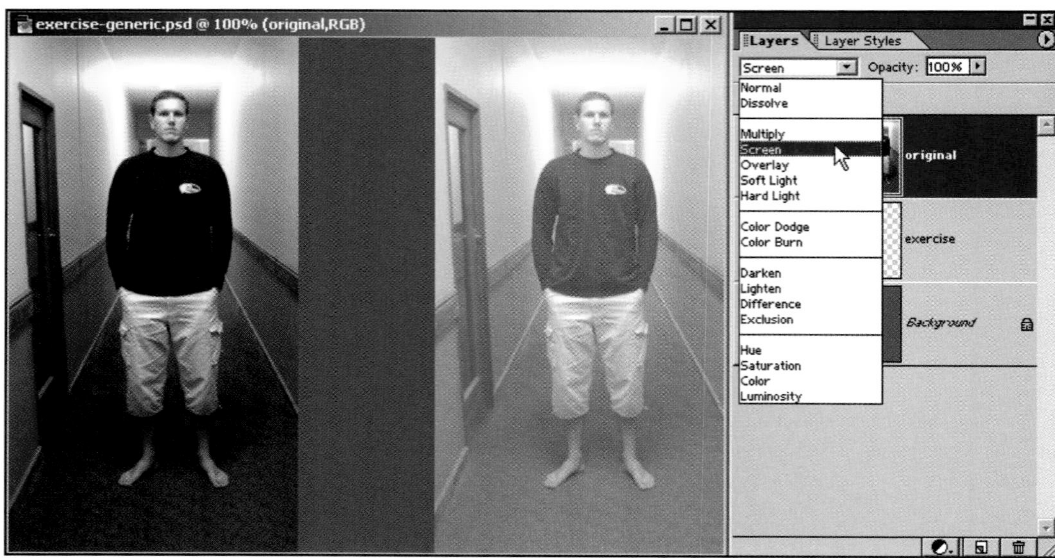

- **Overlay** One of the most frequently used blending modes, Overlay is a combination of Multiply and Screen. With Overlay, the colors are not made darker or lighter, but mixed together, so that the resultant blend takes on the coloring of the underlying layers. Very similar to this mode is Soft Light, which performs a similar operation, only with a softer result. Another variation on this theme is Hard Light, which works in much the same way but with a more severe effect.

- **Luminosity** This is also a commonly used blending mode. Basically it takes the color of the underlying layers and coats the layer with it. So if we have a predominantly gray hue coming through from the underlying layer(s), we get a grayscale image. In the screenshot below I've drawn a gradient on the background layer, so you can see how other colors are affected.

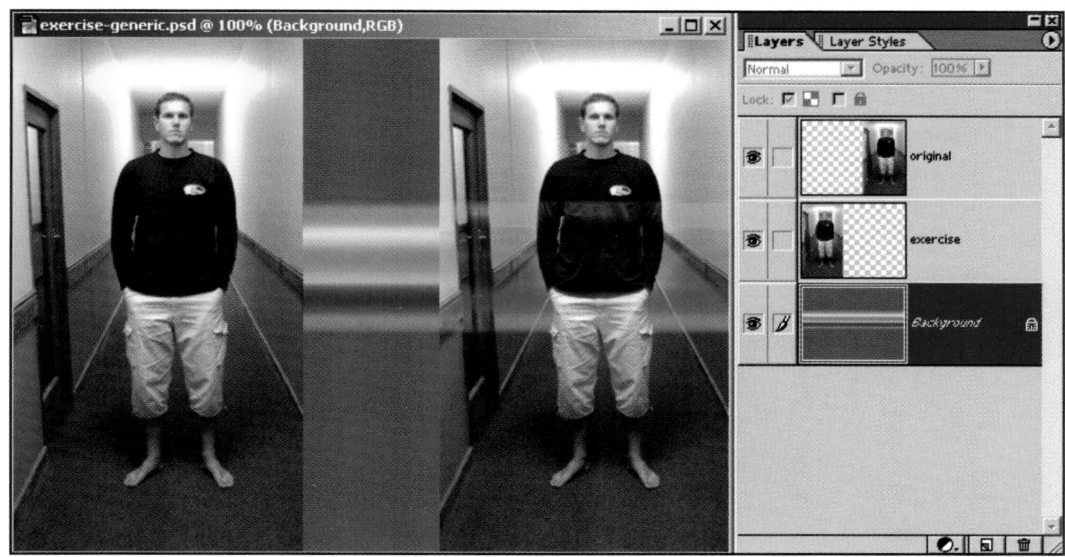

While the other blending modes each have their purpose, they are perhaps more specific to particular tasks and therefore not as widely used as the ones mentioned above. We will, however, be looking at all of them in the next set of exercises.

QUICK TASK: MOVING LAYERS

Open up `exercise1.psd`. Notice that there are three layers: a colored background layer, an exercise layer (which you are going to work with) and an original layer, which has already been tampered with.

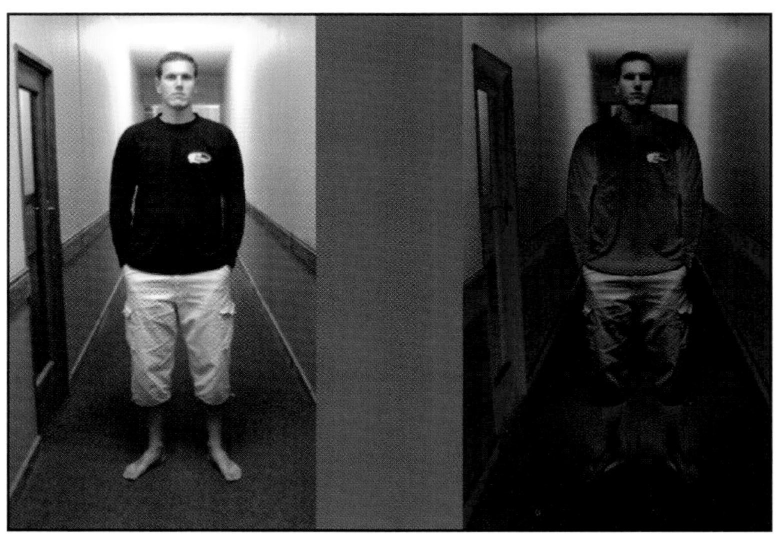

Your task, should you choose to accept it, is to go through the layer blending modes for the exercise layer till it matches up with the original layer. Repeat this procedure with exercise 2 and 3.

Another useful thing about layers, like their acetate counterparts, is that they can be shuffled into a different order at any time. Open up `exercise4.psd`. Notice how the Multiply and Luminosity layers combine to give the image on the right a rather dingy appearance. Now let's put the Luminosity layer above the Multiply one.

Click and drag the Luminosity layer to above the Multiply one, you'll see a black highlight line appears above it, that's when you then drop. As you can see, when the layers change order, the effect of the blending modes also changes. A Luminosity blend applied to a Multiply blend is not the same as a Multiply blend applied to a Luminosity blend.

Often we will use blending modes in this way: to enhance other blending modes. The range of ways we can alter the image becomes endless. In the following tutorial, we will put this process to the test.

RETOUCHING WITH BLENDING MODES

We are going to use the same picture that we worked with in Chapter 5, complete with the retouching that we performed. If we look at the image critically, we can see that the lighting is rather stark, which also gives the color a fairly lifeless look. Wouldn't it be nice if we could soften the harshness and warm the light touching the model's face? The effect we're going for here is a healthy glow, and a softer overall effect.

1. Open up `tutorial1.psd`.

2. The first thing we need to do is duplicate the background layer. Let's call this layer 'working'.

Now we'll look at the different ways we can blend the 'working' layer onto the background layer. Because they are the same image, we should get some good mileage out of blending modes that add light or dark colors together. Just doing this will give us some good contrast as a result. We're going to use Color Burn as the blending mode on the working layer – it has plenty of contrast!

One point to remember is that what we are now seeing on the screen is a **resultant** image. If we look at the above image of the layers palette we can see that both the thumbnails of the layers are the same, it is only the blending mode – the way the two layers are combining – that is making the image look so contrasted.

The minute I change the blending mode on that layer, the entire resultant image will change. We don't want this to happen however. We want to record this particular state of the image on it's own layer. Why? The way the image looks now shows stark contrasts between light and dark areas. We are going to use these contrasts to our advantage.

3. Select the entire canvas using **Select > All**.

4. Now use **Edit > Copy Merged**. This will treat all the layers as one, and copy the image as it appears, regardless of layers. Now paste this to a new layer (**Edit > Paste**).

5. As you can see, we have created a new layer, which in Normal blending mode looks like our two other blended layers. If we turn the visibility of this layer on and off it won't affect the way the image looks. Let's name this layer: *merged blend*.

6. Because the merged blend layer looks the same as the layers beneath, we'll now turn off our working layer, as it is no longer needed.

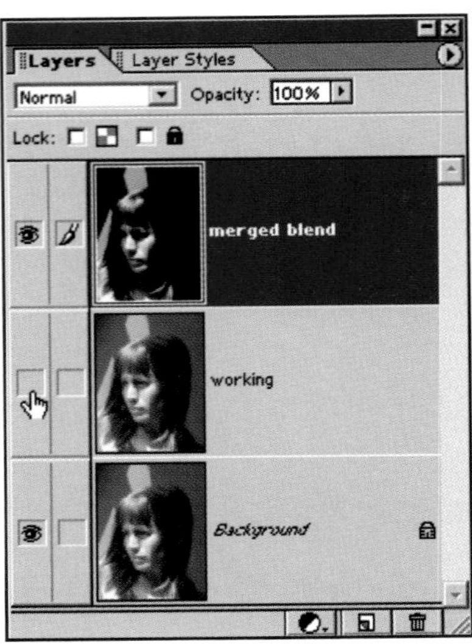

We are going to use this merged blend layer to highlight areas of the background layer, by changing its own blending mode. We'll use the strongly contrasted image (which we got from making a blend) to bring out and highlight areas of our image. This should bring the image to life. But what about softening?

7. Let's apply a Gaussian Blur to our merged blend layer. In this way, when we blend it, it will create more of a soft glow than a harsh light, which is more suited to our purposes. Using **Filter > Blur > Gaussian Blur** and a setting of 5.2 we can apply a fairly strong blur to the layer.

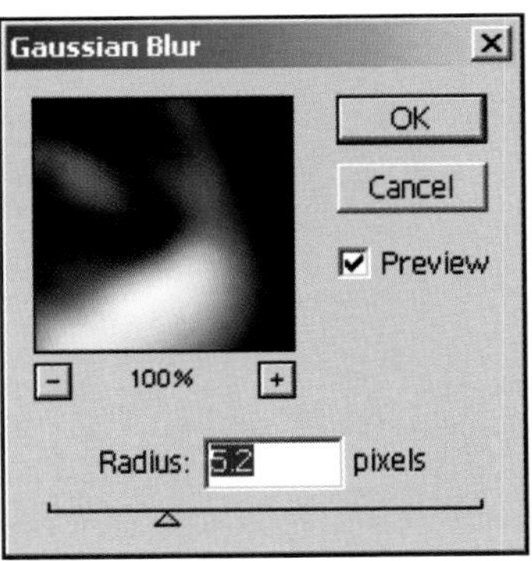

8. All that we need to do now is find the right way of blending our layer to the background. Change the blend mode from Normal to Screen.

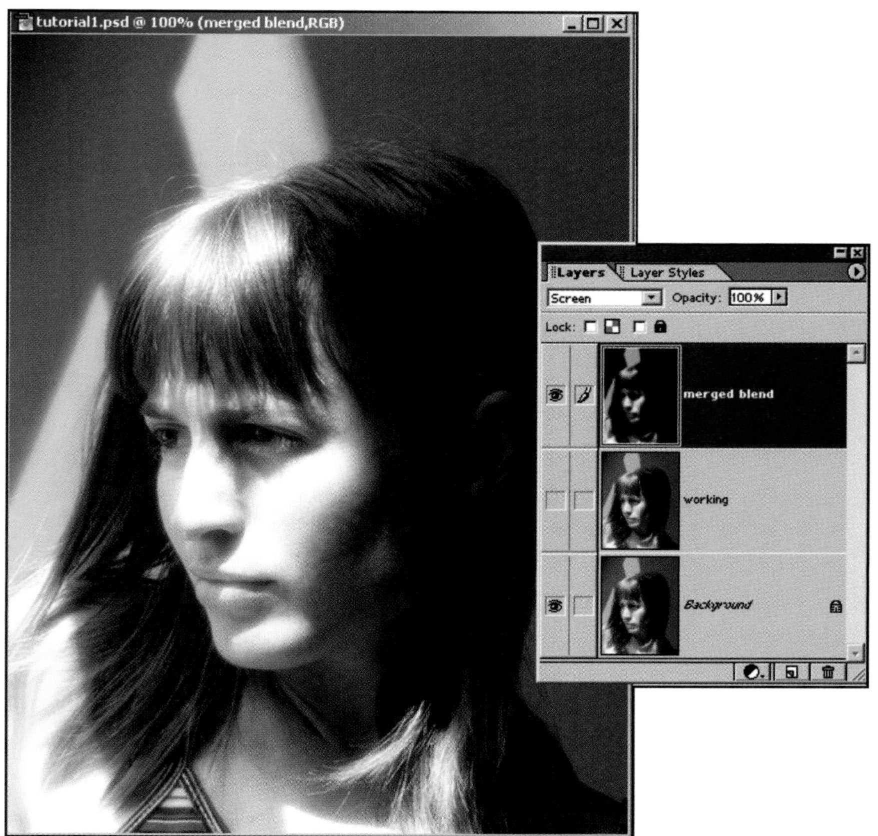

Notice how the color is much richer and softer because of the combination of blurring and screening. Click the visibility of this layer on and off a few times to see the difference between the original and our modifications. You can also experiment with modifying the opacity of the layer to limit its effect.

Adjustment layers

Often, if we want to change an image's tonal range or color, getting the desired effect is a process of trial and error. This can be frustrating if we are three steps down the line and we suddenly decide that we would rather not have turned the picture blue, we no longer have the original image to work with. If we want to go back and change the color, we will lose all the work we have done since then. Once we have modified a layer by blurring it or darkening it, there is no way to change this modification back.

Adjustment layers allow us to play around with changes, without committing to them. An adjustment layer lets you experiment with color or tonal adjustments to an image without permanently modifying the pixels in the image. If you decide you don't like the effect, or want to change it after doing more work on it, you can amend it later.

QUICK TASK: COLOR ADJUSTMENTS

1. Open up `exercise5.psd`. Have a good look at the picture.

If we wanted to use it in a photo-montage that was predominantly blue, no problem. We'd simply use **Enhance > Color > Hue/Saturation** and adjust the color slider to the left to give the image a blue tinge. But what happens if, after further time-consuming changes, we wanted to change the color to something else? Would we have to start all over again? A rather dismal outlook indeed!

2. Instead, let's create an adjustment layer: **Layer > New Adjustment Layer > Hue/Saturation**.

3. A Hue/Saturation dialog will appear and we can simply move the slider into the blue band of color and click OK.

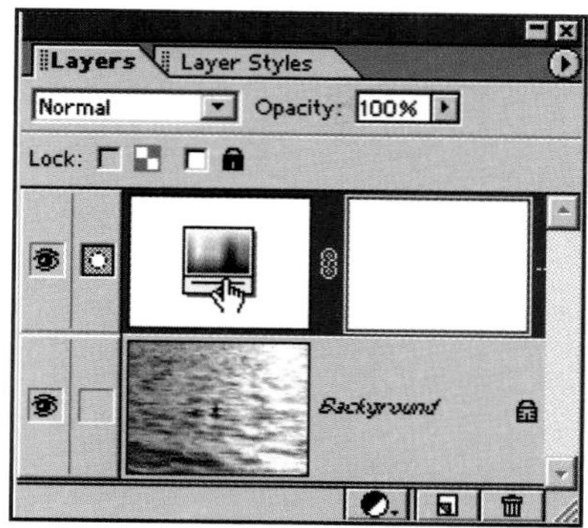

4. Should we want to change it later, we simply double click on the left hand **Layer Thumbnail** icon in the adjustment layer and adjust the Color slider until we have the tint we want, or delete the adjustment altogether.

So the color or tonal changes reside within the adjustment layer, which acts as a veil through which the underlying image layers appear, instead of us actually permanently altering the image layer(s).

Adjustment layers and blending modes

With a blending mode changed to a layer we observed that the blending mode affects the entire layer. This is not necessarily true of an adjustment layer. This is really useful because it means that not only can we come back later and change the way the layer is modified, but also we can decide how much of the underlying image is affected by the adjustment layer.

The adjustment layer is a rather strange looking layer isn't it? If we look at the Layers palette we see that there are two thumbnails on the layer. Notice that the little paintbrush icon that normally precedes each layer, to tell us we can draw on it, has been replaced with a small white circle. This tells us that anything we draw on this layer will act as a mask.

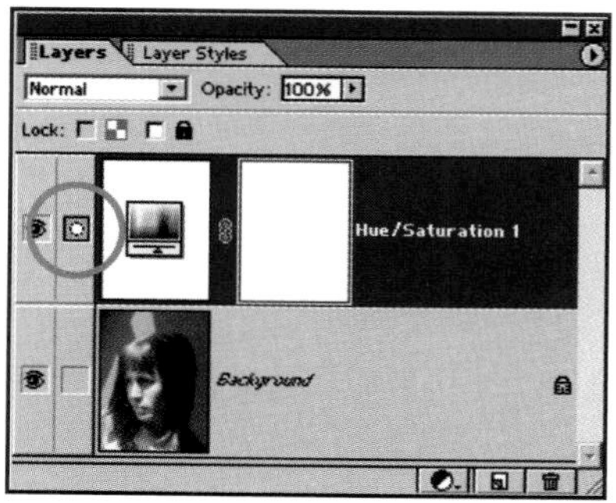

As you can see, the entire right-hand thumbnail is white. This means that the adjustment layer is being applied to the entire layer. Now if we draw on this layer using black, we are basically erasing the effect of the adjustment layer at that point. Also, if we paint with a shade of gray, the adjustment layer will be applied at that point as a percentage of its normal strength: the lighter the gray, the stronger effect the adjustment layer will have at that point.

1. Let's create a large circular marquee in the middle of the image, on the adjustment layer. Select the Elliptical Marquee tool.

2. Now fill this area with black. What happened? Notice the big black circle that has appeared on our thumbnail. Remember this is telling us that wherever there is black, the adjustment layer is not being applied. Looking at our image confirms this: the blue tinge is not affecting the area defined by the circle on the adjustment layer. We have effectively masked out a part of the adjustment layer.

3. Let's make this look a little more artistic: apply a Gaussian blur of around 50 to the adjustment layer. Notice how the thumbnail changes.

Now let's see what happens if we want to change the adjustment layer:

4. Double click on the left thumbnail in the adjustment layer and adjust the slider so that the sea is tinged with red. Notice how the central area under the black dot is not affected by this change.

So adjustment layers allow us to isolate an area of an image, and change the tones and brightness, while leaving the rest of the image unaffected. Throughout this chapter we've seen how we can create new layers, move layers, and use layer blending modes to adjust the appearance of an image. Isolating and adjusting different areas of an image in this way can open the door to a whole new and powerful range of artistic expression, some of which we'll get to grips with in the next chapter.

Advanced layers

In Chapter 7 we saw how layering can be used to enhance an image. In this chapter we will fully explore layers and how they can be used to the maximum potential. Before we dive in, let's take a step back and look at the different kinds of layers. There are basically four different types of layers that we will use in Elements, with very different purposes – drawing layers, fill layers, mask layers and layer styles.

Drawing layers

The most frequently used type of layer in Elements is the drawing layer, which we have already used many times (for example blurring the background but not the foreground of the `legodudes.jpg` image). Apart from placing our photographs and artwork on these kind of layers, we can affect them in two different ways: firstly by changing their opacity, and secondly by changing their blending modes. We can also lock the transparency and movement of these layers. With drawing layers, whichever layer is on top will obscure all subsequent layers beneath it, unless there are some areas of transparency.

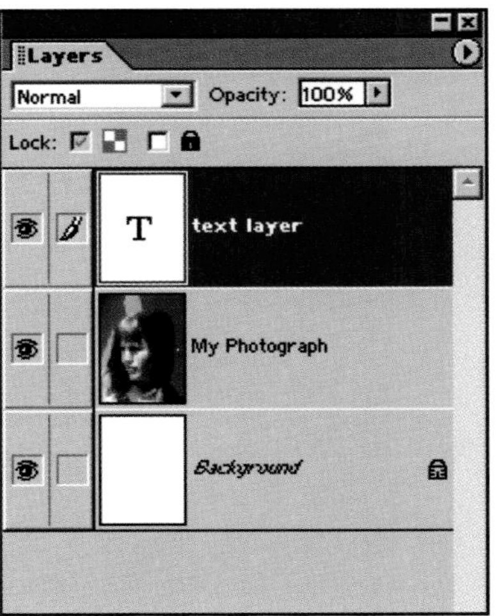

Fill layers

Fill layers are very similar to standard drawing layers, with two exceptions. Firstly the effects used are editable at a later stage; so if you don't like the way they are, you can come back and change them. Secondly, fill layers have a mask attached to them, which means you can decide to only apply the fill layer to certain parts of your image – by editing your mask. To create a fill layer click **Layer > New Fill Layer**, you then need to choose which type of fill layer you need, there are three different types of fill layer, we'll have a so let's look at their properties now.

- **Solid Color:** This kind of fill layer is just an entire layer of solid color – the same as if you'd created a new layer then filled it with a particular color of your choice. So why use a fill layer instead? Fill layers come with a handy mask attached, which means you can delete parts of them (by drawing with black on the mask) and then still be able to change this mask at a later date.

- **Gradient**: This is a similar kind of adjustment layer to Solid Color except, as it's name suggests, it relies on gradients.

- **Pattern**: You would use this adjustment layer to achieve a patterned effect. By selecting a rectangular area of your work and then using: **Edit > Define Pattern** you can then use this pattern across your entire fill layer.

Adjustment layers

Adjustment layers work in a very different way to standard drawing and fill layers. As we saw in the previous chapter, adjustment layers work on existing drawing layers; their sole purpose is to modify the layers below them, they don't achieve anything by themselves. These layers automatically come with a mask attached; this mask is created by Elements each time we create a new adjustment layer. A linked thumbnail allows you to determine which part of the normal layer the adjustment layer will affect. Adjustment layers do not cause permanent changes to your project, but allow you to come back at a later stage and alter the adjustment. In this way, they are comparable to a filter for a light: while the light is still actually white, a red filter, for as long as it is used, makes the light appear red.

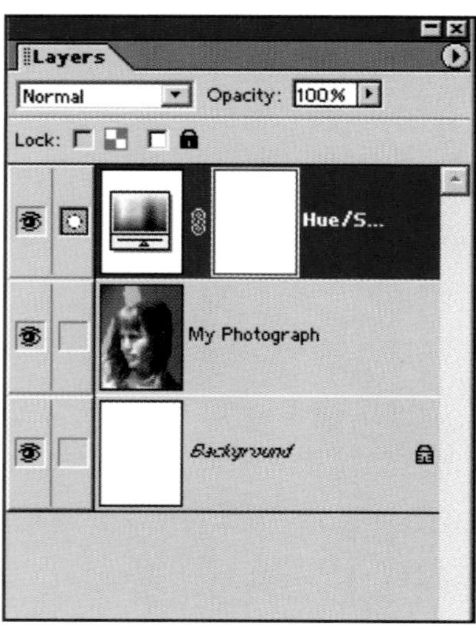

As we can see from the image on the left, the Hue/Saturation adjustment layer is being applied to the entire image. If we wanted to only apply this adjustment layer to the model, and not the background behind her, we would use black paint on the mask thumbnail. As we discovered in the last chapter, this right hand thumbnail indicates where the adjustment layer is applied to the image. We can paint in black on this layer, by clicking on this right hand thumbnail, and using a black brush on our canvas, wherever we paint, the adjustment layer will not be applied to the image.

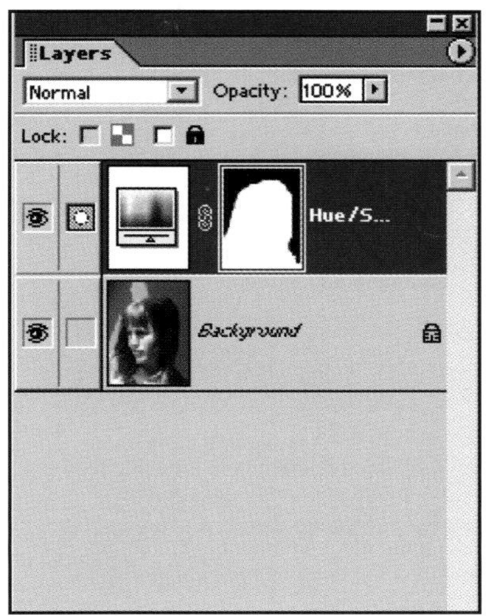

Adjustment layers affect all the layers below that point. This can be extremely useful; corrections can be made to multiple layers by making a single adjustment, rather than having to make each adjustment separately. There are seven different types of adjustment layer; we looked at the most common ones in the previous chapter, now we'll look at the full list in detail.

Brightness/Contrast

As its name reveals, this adjustment layer modifies the overall brightness and level of contrast in the image. Open up `tutorial.psd`, which we used in the last chapter. If you have saved the changes that we made to this PSD, remove these until you are only left with the layer containing the model. (To delete layers, click on the layer that you wish to delete and then click on the tiny icon of a trash bin in the bottom right hand corner of the Layers palette).

There are two ways to make an adjustment layer. The first is to click on catchily titled **Create new fill or adjustment layer** icon. This is the little black and white circle icon in the bottom right hand corner of the layers palette.

Then, simply select the Brightness/Contrast option from the drop down menu. In the following dialog you can adjust the sliders to change the brightness and contrast of the image.

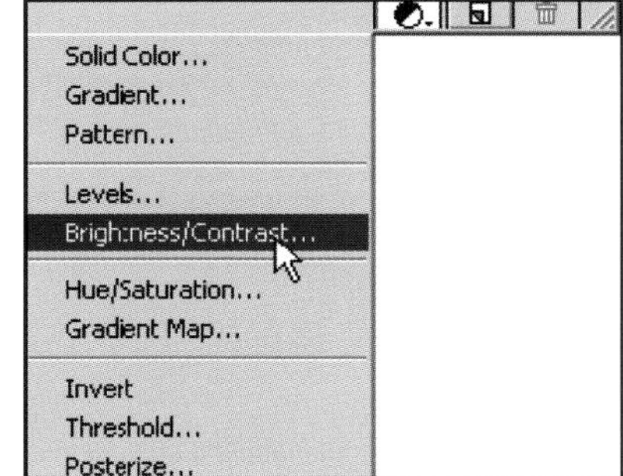

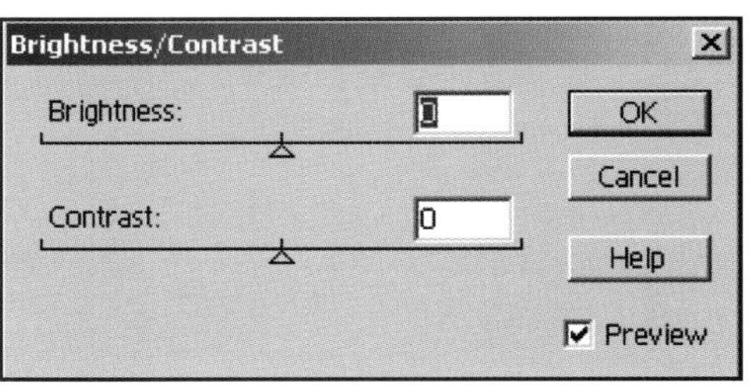

Alternatively you can click on **Layer > New Adjustment Layer > Brightness/Contrast**, and you'll be greeted with an initial dialog box.

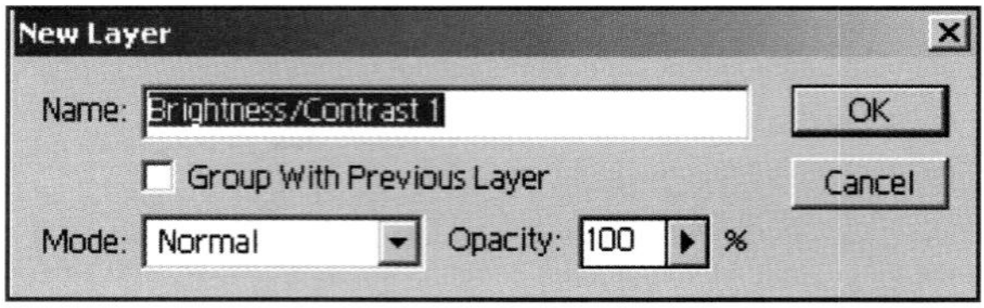

Notice that we can rename the adjustment layer to whatever we want. Why would we want to do this? Sometimes we will use more than one adjustment layer to change an image in some desirable way. We touched on this briefly in the previous chapter. Notice also that there is the option to group this layer with the previous one. Effectively what this means is that the adjustment will affect only the layer(s) to which it is grouped, leaving the rest untouched.

We will come back to grouping and other layer manipulation techniques later in this chapter, however an important point to observe at this stage is that when we create an adjustment layer using the Layers palette icon, Elements assumes that we want to apply the adjustment to the entire set of layers below that point and also automatically names the layer for us.

If we want to rename the layer we simply need to right-click/CTRL-click the layer and choose the rename option. Grouping layers is a little bit more complicated and we will deal with it when we discuss layer manipulation.

Levels

The Levels command is similar to using Brightness/Contrast except quite a bit more powerful. In the same way that we applied the Brightness/Contrast adjustment layer we are going to apply a levels one. Before doing this however, let's delete the brightness/contrast layer so that it won't interfere with what we're doing.

Right, let's apply a Levels adjustment layer to this image. Click **Layer > New Adjustment Layer > Levels**.

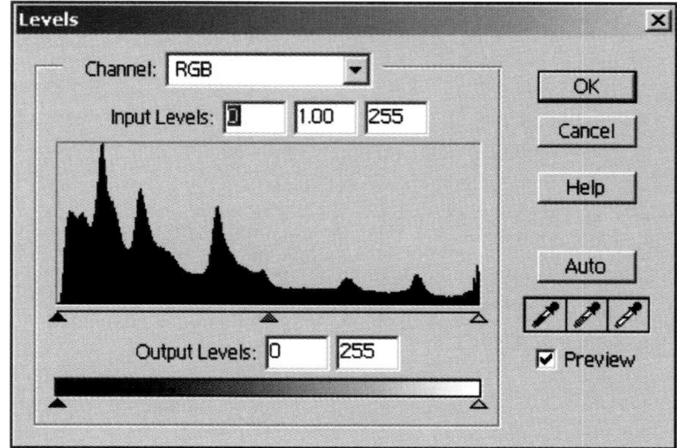

The Brightness/Contrast command adjusted the entire image, but with the Levels command we are able to adjust the brightness and contrast of the highlighted, midtone or shadow areas of the image separately. These are represented by the three tiny arrows underneath the dark mountain of the histogram.

The histogram is a basic graphical depiction of the tonality (the range of tones from light to dark) of the image. For instance, here we can see that there are basically two areas of shadows, represented by the two spikes in the left of the histogram. These probably represent the large dark area of the model's hair and the darker parts of the green background. At a glance we can also see that on the whole there are a lot more dark areas than light in this image – there is a lot more volume on the left hand side of the histogram than the right. By dragging one or all of these tiny arrows we can affect different areas of the image.

Try dragging the middle gray arrow left and right to see the effect it has on the image. Notice that if you drag the highlights triangle to the left (the tiny white triangle on the right) the shadow/dark areas of the image are left pretty much untouched. The Output Levels slider at the bottom determines the percentage of light or dark in the image. Notice also that by dragging the black triangle on the left towards the right, the entire image becomes lighter.

Hue/Saturation

This adjustment layer is particularly useful when tweaking your digital photograph's color. The dialog box is fairly straightforward:

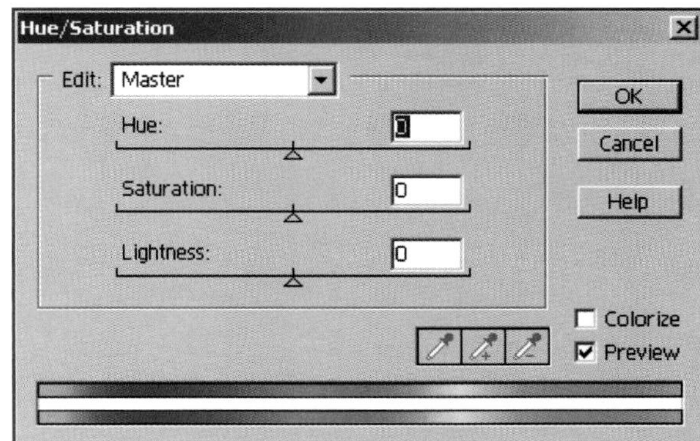

The top slider adjusts the general hue of the image. Dragging this slider slightly either to the left or right can give the image a totally different coloration. Similarly, the saturation slider either saturates (dragging to the right) or desaturates all the color in the image. Sometimes it's essential to adjust the tonality of the image while making color adjustments, so a Lightness slider allows for this.

In addition to this we can color the entire image with one color – like a sepia tone – by checking the Colorize tab. Another useful feature of the Hue/Saturation adjustment layer is that we can, if we choose, adjust only a particular range of hue and not the entire spectrum.

1. Let's have a look at this in action: Open up `exercise1-huesat greenremove.jpg`. You'll find this on the CD.

There are many ways in which we could desaturate the amount of green in this image. We could apply a Hue/Saturation adjustment layer, set the saturation way down, then mask out the bug by painting on the adjustment layer's mask (and hence returning the bug to full saturation). But, look at the image; it would be a fairly rough task to draw a mask around the bug. Let's try another method.

2. Create a new Hue/Saturation adjustment layer . At the top of the dialog box is a dropdown box that currently says Master. We only want to edit out the green, so from this drop down box choose: Greens. Notice that all sorts of little goodies start appearing on the bottom color slider:

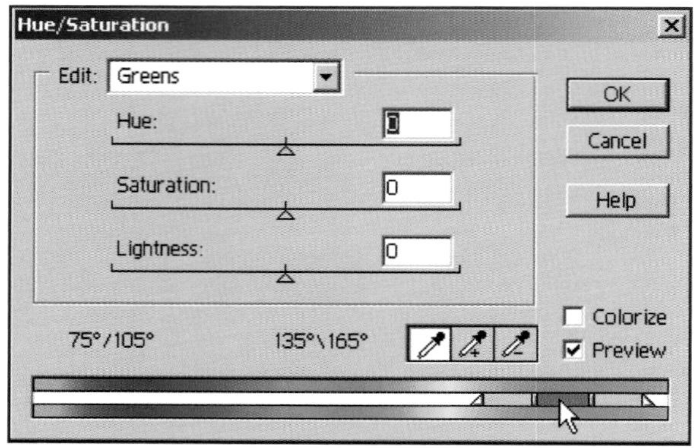

What we can see in the dialog box is a dark gray rectangle flanked by two light gray rectangles supported on both ends by two small triangles. This allows us to select the range of color that we'll be affecting.

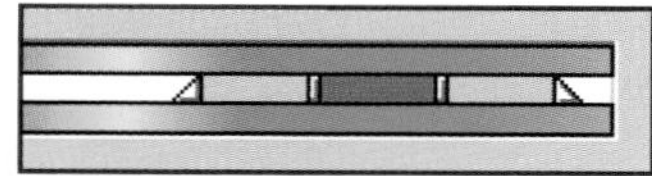

By moving the dark gray rectangle around, we can determine which colors come under fire. By moving the light gray rectangles away or towards each other we can determine the range of hue – in this case the range of green being affected. We can also change the size of the light gray rectangles by moving the tiny triangles, or the upright struts that separate the light gray and dark gray areas.

What does this do? The light gray areas look at how much fall off we want: Our Hue/Saturation effect will not just abruptly end; it will fade out, becoming weaker as it goes. This light gray area determines how fast it fades out. If we want to be strict and make this fadeout abrupt, then we will make this fall off area very small – by dragging the left hand triangle right up close to the strut that separates it from the middle dark gray block for example. Keep in mind that if you do limit the fall off too much like this, there's a good chance that you will create artificial boundaries between adjusted and non adjusted areas – in other words you will see where the effect starts and ends too easily, which will make your changes look artificial.

3. We've already observed the large range of green in this image; hence we are going to have to drag the light gray rectangles wide apart from each other – which will increase the size of the dark gray rectangle significantly, thus affecting more tones/shades of green.

4. The aim of our task is to reduce the amount of green in our image, so drop the saturation way down.

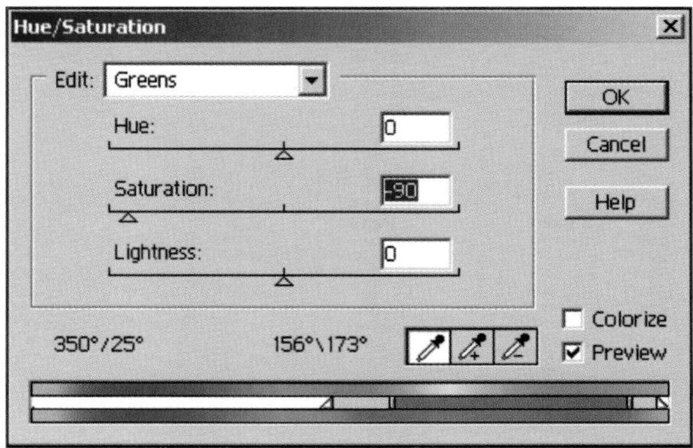

Hey presto, the green background falls into gray, and the only thing left in glorious color is the big blue bug.

What if the color is not contiguous? What if there are two separate areas of the same color and we only want to desaturate the one? Enter our trusty mask that's connected to the adjustment layer: We simply remove the effect of the adjustment layer at the point we want to remain in the original color, by painting on it using black, as we have done previously. Let's demonstrate this now, by returning the green color to the leaf that our bug is sitting on.

Make sure that the Hue/Saturation adjustment layer is selected in the Layers palette. Using a black Paintbrush at about 35 pixels, paint over just the foremost leaf. We'll see the color return to this section of the image, while the rest remains desaturated. If you look in the layers palette you'll see where your layer mask has been painted over.

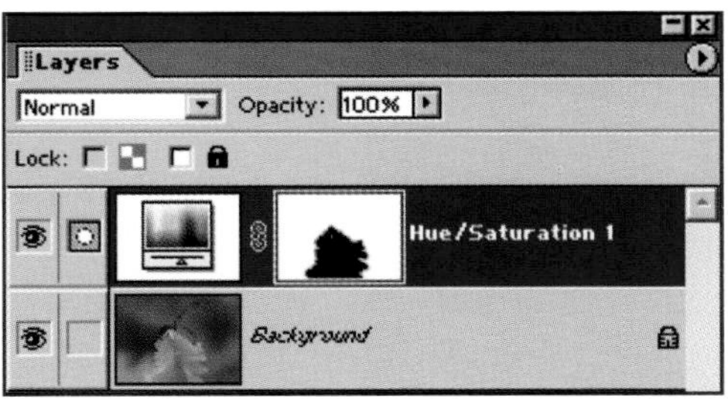

And do you know the best part? We can come back at any point and put the green back: double-clicking on the adjustment layer thumbnail will reopen the dialog box. Select 'Greens' again from the top and you will see that your settings are exactly how you left them. We can even re-saturate the image slightly giving it a little bit of green – whatever takes our fancy.

Gradient Map

This adjustment layer works a little bit like the Colorize option in the Hue/Saturation feature: Instead of using just one color to colorize the image with, a gradient of color is used. While Colorize basically takes a particular hue and applies it to the entire image, darkening and lightening it, in keeping with the image itself, Gradient Map changes the color used as the tonality of the image varies, darker colors in the image are replaced by the color on one side of the gradient, and lighter colors from the other.

Let's use the same image from the last example, deleting the adjustment layer so that we have only the unaffected image to work with. When deleting an adjustment layer, be careful to drag the left hand thumbnail, rather than the right hand one, as this will only delete the layer mask, and you'd then need to repeat the process to delete the rest of the layer.

1. Go to **Layer > New Adjustment Layer > Gradient Map**, and click on the small arrow on the right hand side of the gradient to open the Gradient picker. Select the fifth gradient along, violet to orange. Check the Preview box; so you can see how this affects our image.

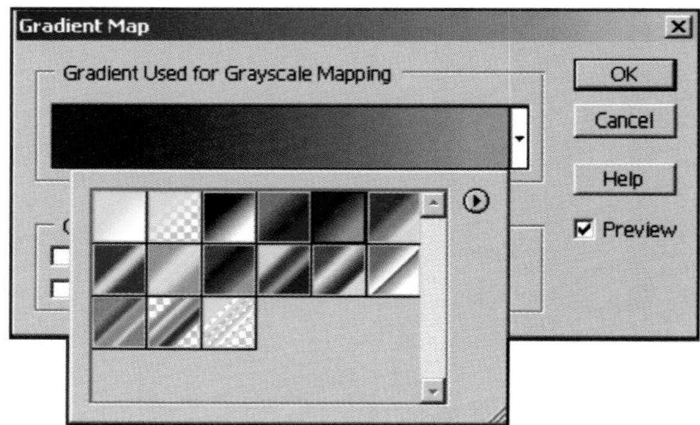

2. Notice how all the darker colors are replaced with violet, and all the lighter ones with orange. We could reverse this by checking Reverse in the bottom left hand corner of the dialog box. Continue to resist the urge to click OK; we're not sticking with this vision in orange.

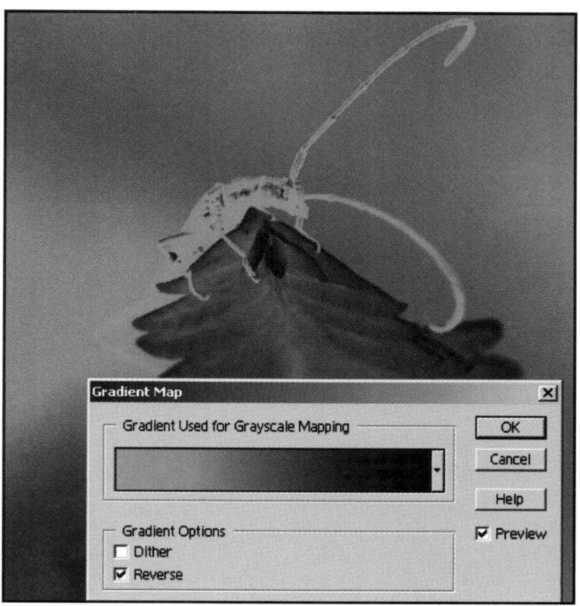

3. If you have already applied a Gradient Map adjustment layer to your image, then double-click the layer thumbnail in the Layers palette to reopen the dialog box. Now select the red green gradient, the fourth one along, and check the Reverse box so that it's used as green to red.

4. Hmm, lovely...! Let's change the blending mode of the adjustment layer to Soft Light, (remember we do this in the top left hand corner of the layers palette). Now, as if by magic, our picture is transformed into something far more pleasing to the eye.

What we've done is tinted the colors with red and green. The leaf that the bug is climbing on we've given a red tinge which, when blended as a soft light, gives it a slightly more yellow appearance than the rest of the background – so it stands out more. We've also brought out the color of the stem of the leaf more. The only problem is that it's gone a bit dark.

5. Time to add another adjustment layer: Levels. Click on the **Create new adjustment layer** icon at the bottom of the Layers palette, and select Levels from the menu.

6. Let's make the midtones a tad brighter by dragging the middle gray triangle to the left a bit. Remember, this histogram represents all the colors in the image: how light or dark they are. By moving the middle triangle we are affecting the midtones: all the colors that are of medium brightness.

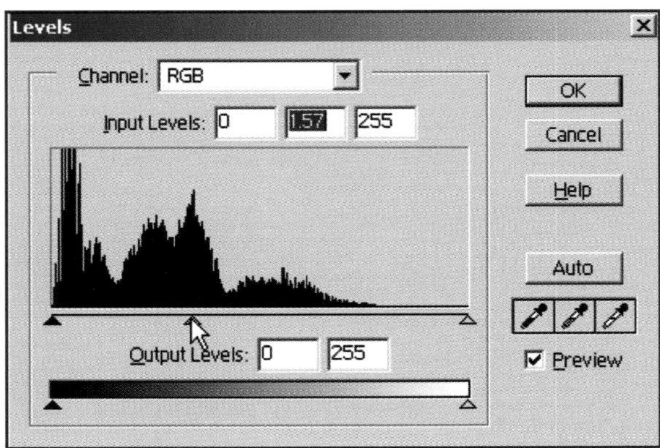

We've radically changed the appearance of the image, but most importantly, because we are not working on the image directly, our original is left intact. At any point we can turn off or delete the adjustment layers and our original image will still be there.

Invert

This adjustment layer takes the image and inverts the color of an image to produce a negative effect. This is mainly useful if you're doing really artistically altered work.

Threshold

When you bring up the Threshold dialog you see a little histogram, which represents the tonal range of our image, going from shadow to highlight. The bottom slider allows you to select a particular tone; Elements will then compare this tone to the others in the image, and fill every pixel darker in tone with black and every lighter pixel with white. Basically, this command converts grayscale or color images to high contrast black and white images. It is useful in determining the lightest and darkest areas of an image.

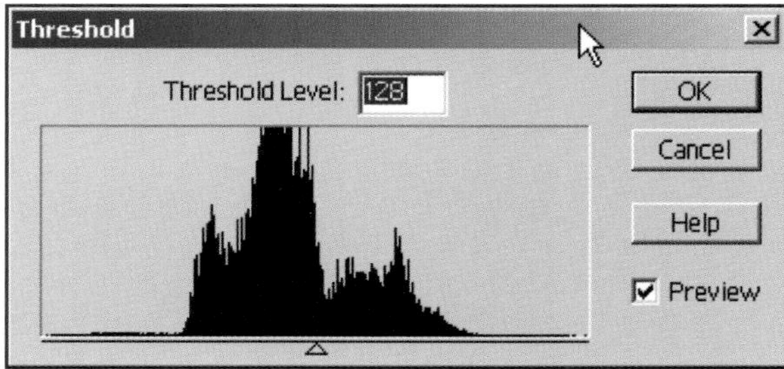

1. Although this adjustment layer is normally used to uniquely style an image, we can apply it to our current bug image to darken the bug.

2. Create a Threshold adjustment layer above our original background image. Set the Threshold Level to 55, and see how we are left with a strangely isolated black bug on a white background – except for a few black dots.

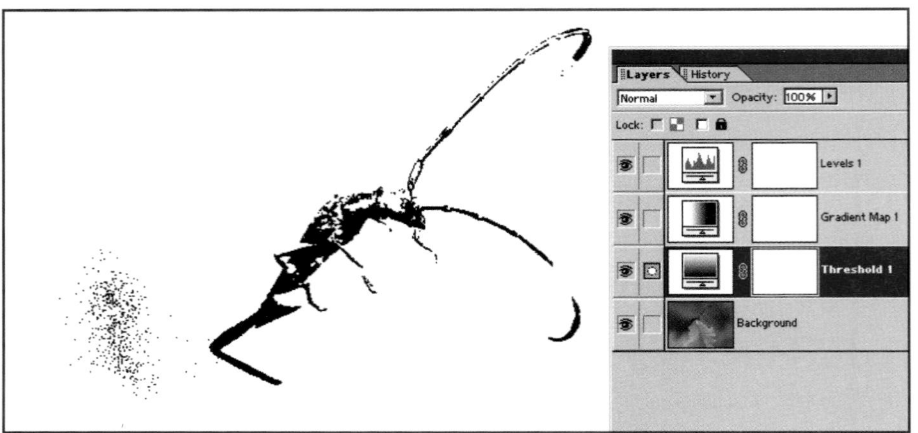

3. We need to get rid of those black dots though. Let's use a 100% opacity brush of size 27 and draw on the mask (we select it by clicking on it's thumbnail which is the thumbnail on the right, if we're looking at this adjustment layer in the layers palette). By drawing on the dots with this black paintbrush (while on the adjustment layer) we can easily remove them.

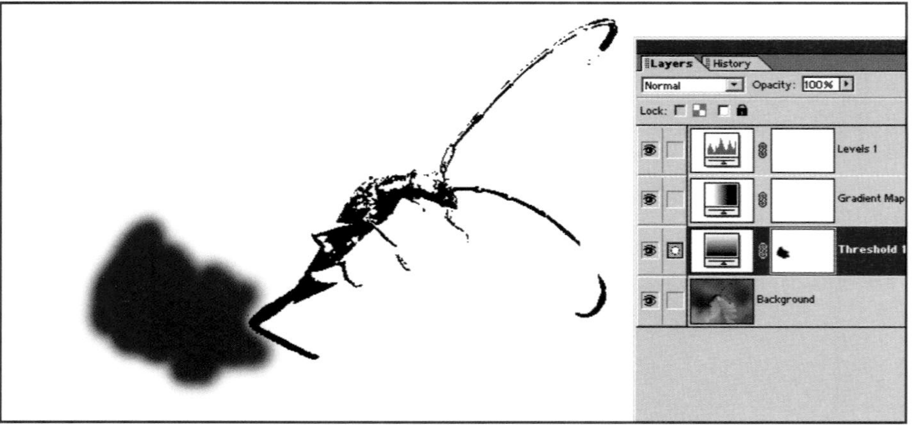

4. Now let's color burn this adjustment layer and set the layer Opacity to 55%, and the result is that we've managed to darken the bug without interfering with its surroundings and leaving the original intact.

Posterize

This type of adjustment layer is similar in artistic goals to Threshold. Posterize lets you specify the number of tonal levels (brightness levels) for each color range (red, green and blue). It has more value as a way of stylizing a photograph than enhancing it in any way. Posterize can also be used to highlight where the dark and light areas are in an image – and in which directions the gradients flow – as we saw in Chapter 5.

Mask layers

By now, I'm sure you are aware just how useful masks are in Elements. But how do we attach a mask to an ordinary layer instead of an adjustment one?

Adjustment layers always have a mask attached to them so that we can specify which parts of our image our affected by the adjustment. Remember, that where we paint on the mask (which we select by clicking on its thumbnail) with black paint, the mask is rendered useless at that point – it is not applied. What would be really useful is if we could do something similar with ordinary layers, so that where the mask was black the image wouldn't be seen, and where it was white, it would.

Well, we can achieve this kind of partially masking by grouping layers together. We've already seen how to link layers together by toggling the link chain icon on or off. We can take this one step further by grouping the layers. Grouping a layer means that the bottom layer is used as a mask for the top one. We can then use the opacity of a layer as the mask for another, so the areas that are transparent on the layer we are using as the mask, make the same areas on the grouped layer transparent.

This is a different and more primitive kind of mask than the ones we've used: We actually need to delete parts of this layer as opposed to drawing on the layer with black or white to indicate transparency, so we're going to find a work around for that.

1. Open up Exercise2 – `bug masking.psd`. Here we have the bug on a different layer to the background. Select the background layer, then create a Fill Layer, **Layer > New Fill Layer > Solid Color**, and fill with white. We are creating this new layer at this position so that it is directly below our bug layer – the layer being used as a mask should always be directly below the one we wish to partially mask. Now, with the big layer selected, use **Layer > Group with Previous**.

Notice how Elements indents the bug layer and puts a downward pointing arrow on the layer. This is telling us that the bug layer is now grouped and therefore dependent on the Color Fill adjustment layer. Effectively, whatever happens to the one layer happens to the others in the group. Applying filters, deleting areas applying adjustment layers... all these modifications happen to all members of the group.

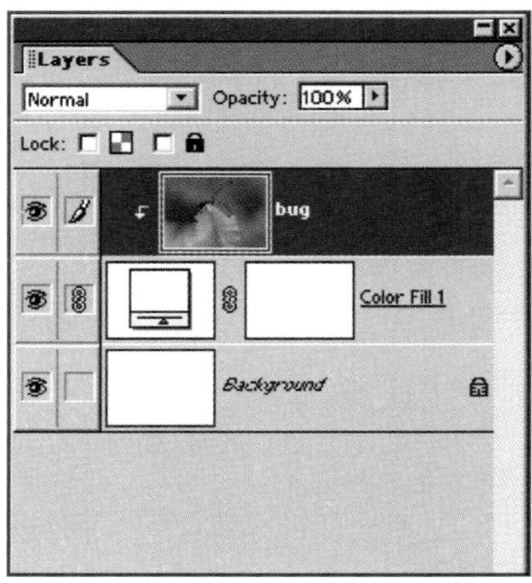

2. Now we can draw on the Fill Layer's mask with black and because the bug layer is grouped, it will also be affected. Let's fill the background layer with a red, just to differentiate it from the Color Fill adjustment layer.

So we want to remove everything from the picture except the bug. But how? Well we could simply use the eraser tool – but then the parts of the image that we erase would be lost forever. How would we accomplish this task and still keep the image intact?

What we need to do is draw a marquee around just the bug, then invert the selection (select everything except the bug) and finally fill this selection with black while on the mask of the Color Fill Layer.

We know that because the bug and Color Fill layers are grouped, drawing with black on the Color Fill layer's mask will act as a way of erasing the bug layer. It's as if the mask on the Color Fill layer were really a mask on the bug layer. But how do we cleanly select the bug?

3. Let's duplicate the bug layer. Notice that the duplicated layer is still grouped to the mask. With this new layer selected, **Layer > Ungroup** fixes this. Now we are going to remove all the green and replace it with a solid color – which will therefore be easy to select using the Magic Wand tool.

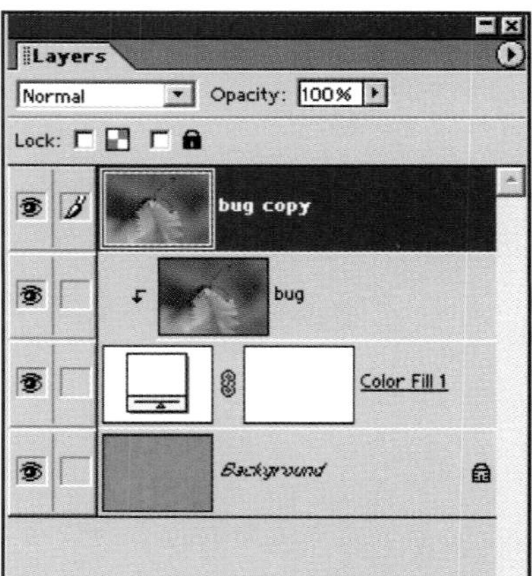

4. So, we'll click **Enhance > Color > Replace Color**. This will give us the following dialog box:

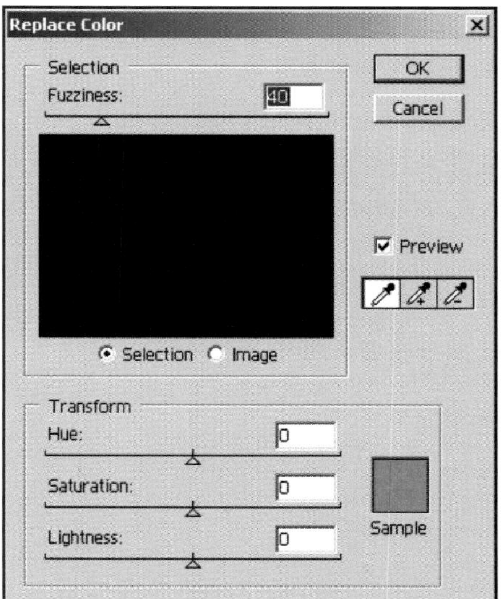

5. The top fuzziness slider sets the accuracy of the colors we are about to select, let's use the default value of 40. Notice that the preview window is totally black – this means we currently have no colors selected.

6. Just to the right of the preview pane are three little eyedroppers. We'll use the middle one – which allows us to select more than one color at a time. Let's also preview the image instead of what is currently selected. We do this by clicking on the **Image** radio button. We now see a miniature version of our layer. In order to select colors for replacement we are going to click and drag around the green area, keeping the mouse button down, staying away from the bug. Do this all around the bug being careful not to click on the bug itself. Now switch back to Selection mode by clicking on the **Selection** radio button. You should see something like this:

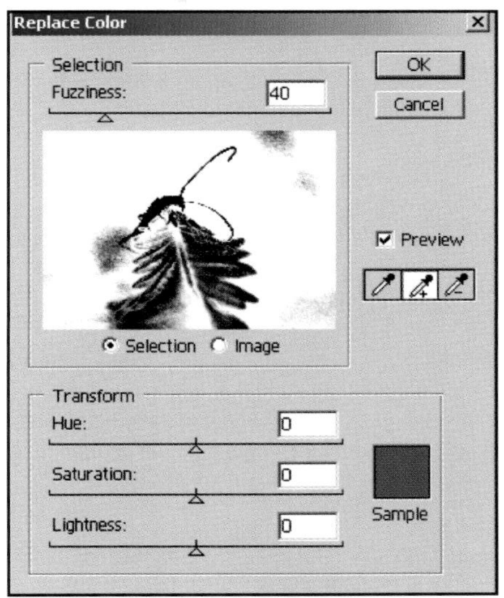

The white areas indicate all the color that we are going to replace (and fill with a flat color). We need to get rid of more black. By using the same technique of clicking and dragging around, drag the cursor over as many of the remaining black areas as you can, still being careful not to draw on the bug. You can also use this color picker on the main drawing, and not just its miniature replica, which can make things easier as it is a lot bigger.

If you do accidentally draw on the bug, you can always start over by holding down the ALT key, which changes the Cancel button into a Reset button.

Finally you should have a black bug in the middle of a white background:

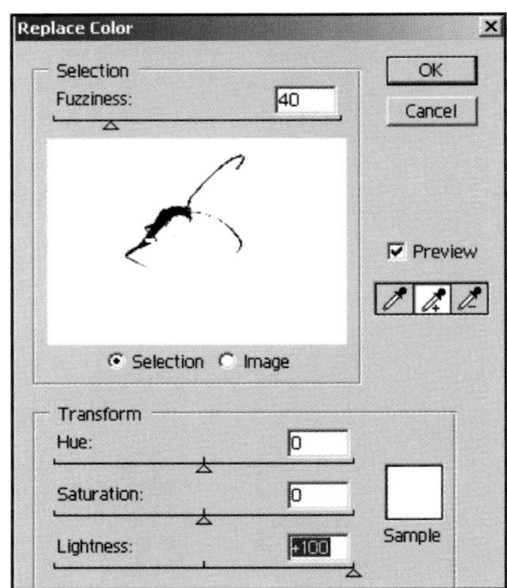

7. Now let's slide the Lightness slider all the way to the right. Click ok and see the background-less bug!

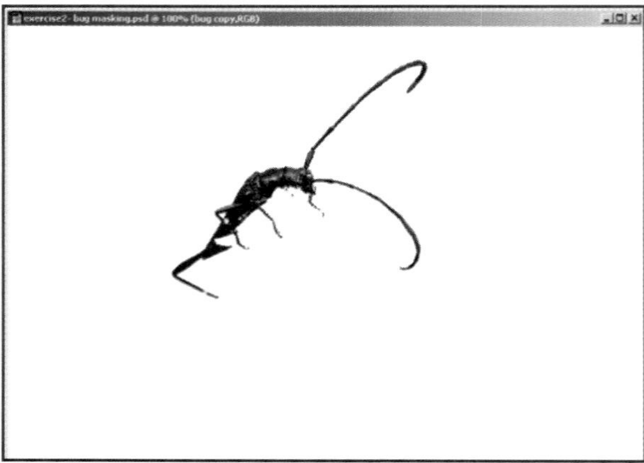

8. Now what we need to do is select the background of the bug, which we just made white. In order to do this we need to use the Magic Wand tool. Select this tool then click on the background – anywhere on the white area. We need to add a small piece to this selection: the tiny triangle of white encompassed by the bug's hind leg. Still using the Magic Wand tool, SHIFT-click in this area. This adds the triangle to the selection.

9. Now click on the right hand thumbnail while on the Color Fill layer. **Edit > Fill** (using Foreground Color) now fills the mask with black using our selection as a guideline. Deselect everything (CTRL/CMD+D). All that remains to be done is to delete our top copied bug layer: select it and click on the Trash Can on the layers palette. And there we go. Our bug is now floating in a sea of red.

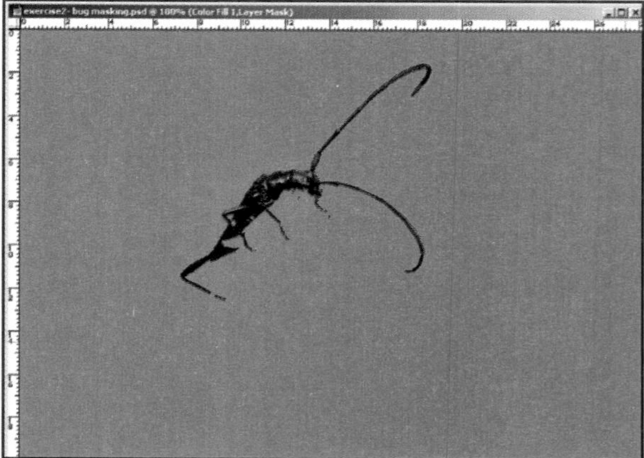

A quick glance across at the layers palette will show us that our original image is still intact: we are just hiding part of it.

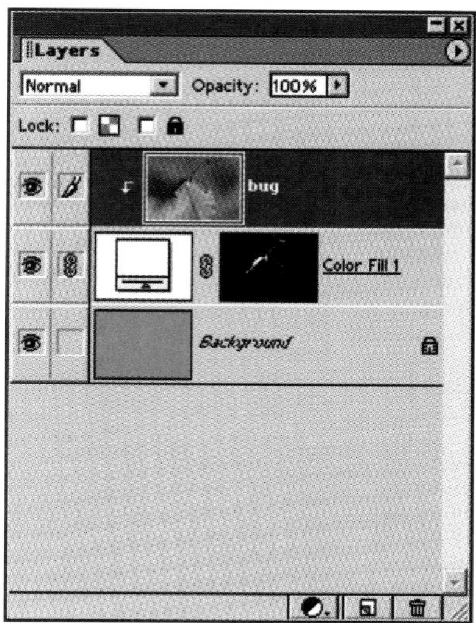

So now we have learnt how to hide parts of the image without actually tampering directly with the image itself. If needs be we can also merge layers together (kind of like using glue). This works best with normal layers, as merging layers changes the blending mode of all the layers involved in the merge back to normal. If you need to do this with adjustment layers, you will need to do it one layer at a time: link two, merge down, link the next two, merge down etc.

In order to merge layers we simply link the layers we wish to merge together and then use **Layer > Merged Linked** or Merge Down. Try and only merge layers that are adjacent to each other: If you are trying to merge two layers with another layer in between and that middle layer uses an Overlay blending mode, this effect will be lost after the merge, as the contents of the new merged layer will be different from the original. To achieve this kind of merge you will have to use a Merge down on the top two layers, then another merge down on the single merged layer (that you just created) and the remainder of the three directly below it.

Layer Styles

Layer styles work much in the same way as adjustment layers: While the visible image changes, the original remains untampered with. Most of these styles are more suited to adding effects to text layers, which we will see the use of in later chapters. These include: adding drop shadows, adding outer and inner glows and all sorts of bevels.

Note that adding a drop shadow to our bug would not work: Layer styles, similar to adjustment layers work on entire layers. Even though our bug appears to be floating by itself on a red sea, we just need to look at the layers palette to remind ourselves that the bug is still part of the original picture; we have just hidden those parts. Layer styles, therefore do not use masks as a reference, and tend to totally ignore them. If we wanted to put a drop shadow on our bug, we would have to cut him out of the background and apply the style to this layer.

MAKING FAIRIES REAL

In this tutorial we will look at creating a flower fairy using a few digital photographs as raw material. While it is easy to cut the images up using the Eraser tool and patch them together, we will see during the progress of this tutorial the value of using mask layers.

1. Open up `fairy.jpg`. We are going to use this person as the basis for our fairy.

2. Let's duplicate the background layer and call it simply 'fairy'. We're doing this in order to place a layer below the background layer – this will be our mask. We're now going to work a little bit strangely - instead of using a color fill layer, we are going to create the shape of the mask first, then make it into one. Why? With our bug example there was clear definition between colors – we don't have that luxury in this example.

3. Now we need to create a layer above our fairy layer. We'll call this new layer 'fairy mask'.

4. On this layer select a bright red color and draw neatly over the fairy using a 100% opaque brush of around size 9, to ensure precision. To make this easier set the layer opacity of this layer to around 60%, and zoom in on the figure, so that we can see what we're doing. Remember, we are not drawing on the fairy; we are drawing on the layer above her.

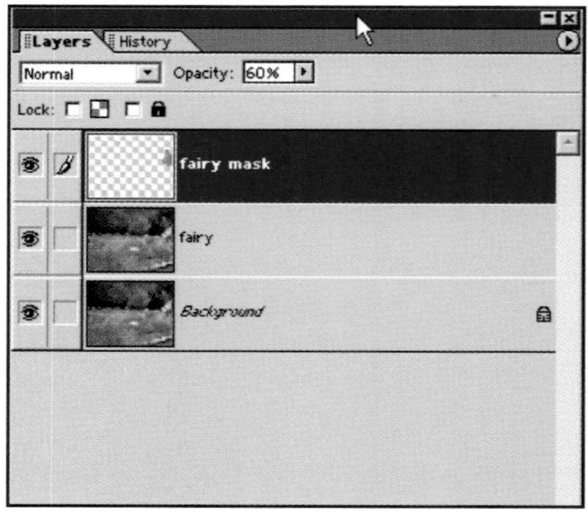

5. Drag the fairy mask layer to just below the fairy layer. We are finished drawing on this layer, so set its opacity back up to 100%. Now link these top two layers together to keep the mask with the fairy, remember that we do this by clicking on the chain link icon, and then group them by going to **Layers > Group Linked** (CTRL/CMD + G).

6. Let's fill our background layer with white, so we're able to see just our fairy by herself. Go to **Edit > Fill**, and in the Contents section select white. The reason we're doing this is because I like a solid color to work off, and there's nothing better to see exactly how well your masking is going than to have a layer of solid color behind it.

7. Because the layers are linked we can use the Move tool to drag our fairy (and its mask) into the middle of the canvas. Now we need to insert the background image that we are going to use.

8. Open up `fairyflower.jpg`. We are going to insert this image just above our background layer and just below the fairy, so click on the background layer then, going back to the other image, drag the fairy flower image across to our project and drop it anywhere on the canvas.

9. Drag this image around till it snaps into place: it's the same size as our background. You'll be able to see in the layers palette when it's centered properly. We can call this layer 'flower'.

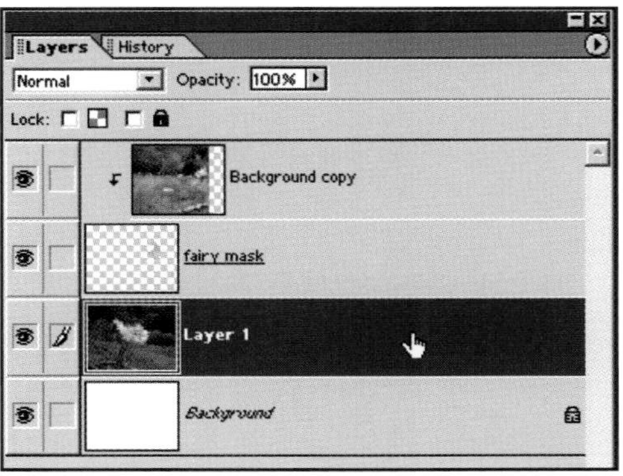

10. Now click on the fairy mask layer. Let's drag the fairy to the top of the flower so that she is just sitting in it. We are going to hide her boots behind some of the petals in a minute, but first let's get her into the right position.

This would be a good time to hide part of her behind the flower. The obvious way to do this is set the opacity of the fairy mask layer back down to 60% so that we can see the flower behind her, and then delete parts of the fairy flower layer. As these deleted parts will no longer be a part of the mask, it will be like erasing part of the fairy. But what if we want to move the fairy at a later stage? Well, as you'll see we can work around this by making full use of the flexibility of our mask layers.

11. CTRL/CMD and click on the fairy mask thumbnail to load the fairy as a selection. We are now going to make a Solid Color fill layer, which will appear just above our fairy mask layer. Use a bright red as the fill color. Notice that most of the mask for this fill layer is black: we only filled the selection, which in this case was our fairy.

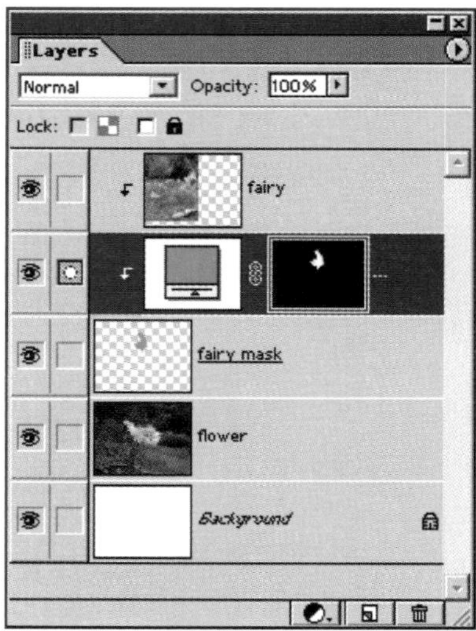

12. We are no longer going to use our fairy mask layer (but keep the technique in mind) so it should be deleted at this point.

Whoops. Because we deleted this layer, our fairy layer no longer has anything to use as a mask, so we suddenly see the entire image reappear. Was all our hard work for nothing? Not quite! We are going to use our newly created Fill layer as the mask.

13. Group the fill layer and fairy layer together by selecting the fairy layer and then using **Layer > Group with Previous**. Ah there we go! Now we have our masking back for our fairy. So what has changed? Well for one thing, it is going to be a lot easier to mask out the fairy's boots.

14. Time to hide the fairy's boots – fairies don't have boots do they! Drop the solid color fill layer's opacity down to 60%, and using a 100% opaque paintbrush of size 9 and black paint, we are going to draw on the fill layer's mask (remember to select it by clicking on its thumbnail to the right of the fill color thumbnail in the layers palette).

15. Although the fill layer is a 100% opaque layer, because we have dropped its opacity, we can see through to the layer below, which is our flower layer. Now we are going to draw on the fill layer's mask, using what we can see of the layer below as a guideline. Draw on the parts of the flower that overlap with the fairy's boots. These are the parts of the flower that would not be visible if the fairy was fully opaque. Remember we are not actually drawing on the flower, we are drawing on the mask layer, so we are in effect erasing her boots using the shape of the flower as a guide.

Don't worry if you draw on some other area that is not the flower, you can simply switch to using white paint and draw over your mistake; this is one of the pleasures of using masks.

16. But fairies have wings! Open up `butterfly.jpg`. We are going to use just the right hand wing of the butterfly, as if to suggest that the fairy's wings are closed. Click on the flower layer in our project, and then drag the butterfly image onto the canvas. Let's name this layer 'wings'. By clicking on the flower layer, we are ensuring that this new layer appears just above it.

17. Drag the butterfly around so that it's body is hidden behind the fairy. And the right wing protrudes from her back. Let's rotate the contents of this layer a little to make it more realistic. Using: **Image > Rotate > Free rotate**, let's enter a value of –20 in the options bar:

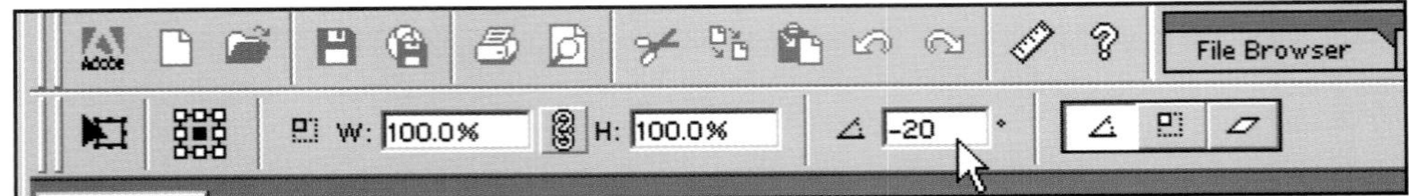

At this point, we should have something looking like this:

All that now remains for us to do is mask out the unwanted portion of the wings:

18. Let's create another Solid Color fill layer just above our wings layer. We are going to use a bright green as the fill color this time. Wow, the green just goes everywhere. Let's fill the Solid Color mask with black. This means that the fill is not being currently applied anywhere: Remember white paint on a mask means reveal the fill/adjustment at that point, and black paint basically hides the fill/adjustment layer.

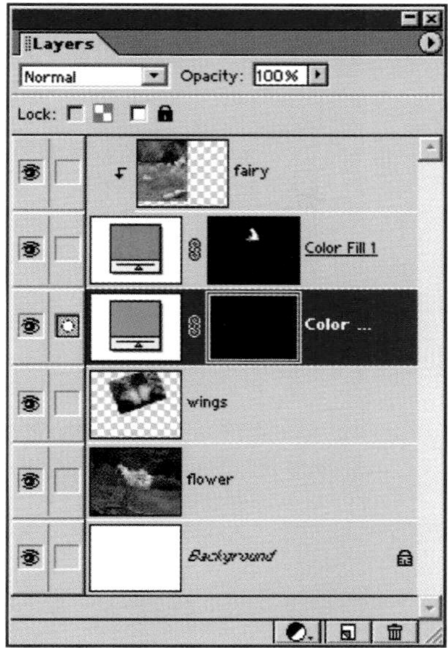

Remember how we created the mask for the fairy? We're going to repeat that process now!

19. Using a 100% opacity white paintbrush of size 13, paint over the part of the wing that we want to use. Your paint should come out using green. This makes sense, as we are now using white brush strokes to reveal our fill layer.

20. Now we have very little left to do. Swap the order of these two layers (the fill and wings layers). Link the two layers together then group them. Now we can see our wing take shape.

21. Once again we will want the foreground flower to be in front of the wing, so we need to drop the opacity of our green color fill layer to 60% and then using a 100% opacity black brush size 9, paint on the parts that overlap with the wing and the flower. Remember we are painting on the solid color fill layer mask, and not on the image itself.

This means that at those points the wing will not be visible – which is what we want, seeing as how the flower should be in front of the fairy's wings.

22. Set the opacity of the layer back up to 100%.

We have finally brought our fairy to life. You can compare notes by opening up `fairy.psd`, which contains all the layers discussed in this tutorial. Our final product should look something like this:

We have looked at many different ways to use layers in this chapter. In the next chapter we will combine much of what we have learnt to maximize digital retouching.

Even though we could have completed the above tutorial without using masks, we now have the flexibility to change our work at any time, without having to redo lots of it. This is particularly important should you be using Photoshop Elements in a business environment. Even if you're not, clever use of layers and masking can save you a lot of time and give the final result a much more polished and believable look.

9 Photo retouching

Over the past few chapters we have looked at different techniques to remove blemishes and change the lighting of our digital photographs. In this chapter we will not only see how to combine these various techniques, but also learn ways to actually improve upon our shots.

In this chapter we are going to look at a particular scenario: Your Resident's Association has a district improvement scheme on the cards. As a member of the Association, you realize that by using Elements you could create a digital makeover of the area, and thereby provide some incentive to getting the real-world development approved. So, you offer to take some photos of the area and improve them digitally, to create a 'Before' and 'After' view of the neighborhood.

CLEANING UP THE NEIGHBORHOOD

In this tutorial we are going to make use of more than one photograph, and combine them to create an improved rendition of the scene that you have captured.

Open up `street_scene.jp`

Wow. Some of these houses are in bad need of repair.

Before we start, let's outline the general areas we think should be improved:

To describe the tasks ahead:

- Firstly, there is an initiative to place the unsightly power cables underneath the roads. These will need to be removed. As you can see, these power lines not only bisect the hill in the background, but also cut across a few of the chimneys and roofs.
- And look at those roofs! Many of the roofs and walls are in desperate need of repair.
- Finally, we are going to make a few cosmetic changes, such as removing drain covers, telephone poles and the odd electricity box.

Subtle landscape improvement

Let's start by getting rid of the power lines. As a warm up, we'll use the Clone Stamp tool to remove them where they interfere with the hill.

1. The arrows indicate where we are going to get our Clone Stamp raw material from, and where we are going to paste it. Using a 40% opacity brush of size 17, let's go about this task.

2. ALT-click at the base of an arrow and paste the cloned area at the point – over the power line. If you're a bit lost, take another look at Chapter 5, which discusses the ins and outs of using the Clone Stamp tool. In this way, we can fairly easily remove the unsightly power lines.

The Clone Stamp tool works best with a "softly, softly" approach. We are going to be pasting cloned imagery into an area that is a slightly different color to the source. If we were using a 100% opacity brush this would pose a severe problem: the result would be all patchy, and therefore easy to spot. It is better to use a lower opacity brush and keep selecting raw material from different areas (above and below the area being replaced).

Also remember that if you select from an area immediately adjacent to the area that you are adjusting, this can often be spotted by the way the pasted area will be identical to the piece you stole it from – and will form a kind of pattern, which looks unnatural and obvious.

With this in mind, carefully go about removing the power lines until this area of your image looks something like this:

Fortunately this hill lacks any clear definition, so telltale patterns can easily be kept at bay. As we'll see later on, when working on areas with significant texture, selecting from multiple and varied sources is problematic as the result will be all blurry and confused. In the meantime however, we can enjoy this flexibility.

3. While we're in this area, let's get rid of that telephone pole on the left and the aerial on the chimney on the right. For the telephone pole, we are going to have to be precise about where we choose our raw material from: we'll need to make sure we select carefully along any given horizontal so that everything matches up.

When you choose an area to clone from, make sure that you paste the raw material directly horizontally from where it came. Notice where the telephone pole crosses a white horizontal line: the top of a roof. You will need to reconstruct this area that the pole obscures from either the direct horizontal left or right of this spot.

The cables are still intersecting with the roofs. Let's finish getting rid of all the power lines. We're going to go across all the roofs being careful now to watch our alignment of source and target. Let's do the tin roof in the foreground. There are vertical grooves on the roof, which we will need to observe. As opposed to selecting multiple sources, select one correctly aligned source (preferably from just above the problem area) and paste it over the blemish:

4. With this in mind, we are going to tackle the tin roof, and then moving to the right, we are going to go across all the houses' roofs, including the chimneys, until no more power cables can be seen. Points to observe for each roof:

   - Watch the flow of the gradients. If you have zoomed in to get finer adjustments, always zoom out to see if you're on the right track, in this way you might spot slight color changes that you've built into the cloned area without noticing it.

   - If this is the case, drop the opacity of the brush down to about 15% and then resample a nice dark area (we're assuming the discolored patch is lighter here) and, observing the groove patterns where possible, gently apply this darker clone over the lighter area to even out the color difference.

   - You may also experiment with the Lighten and Darken blend modes to achieve the same effect.

   - Choosing an area to clone from and then pasting this diagonally takes some getting used to. Take your time with this task. Try to be as much of a perfectionist as possible. You've always got the Undo option, (CTRL/CMD+ Z).

The one nice thing about working on a fairly textured background is that slight variations in color and grain won't be noticed so we can clone whole chunks of areas at a time.

As you can see, all the cables have been removed but there are still a lot of things wrong with this area. The unsightly rusted leak area on the left hand chimney has also been removed. There are two major tasks to achieve for this area:

1. Firstly, the tin roof to the bottom left of the dark middle roof doesn't match at all. Let's clone a piece from the main roof over this area, so that it matches. In order to help matters, let's make a marquee around the tin area, so that we won't accidentally mess up the surrounding walls. Don't worry about the chimney in the middle of the tin roof; we're going to get rid of it anyway:

2. Now let's select as a clone source somewhere in the middle of the black roof, preferably the middle of a chunk about the same size as the selection we've made.

3. We want to match the pattern with the roof above, which is what we're cloning from. This means we don't want to use a massive piece of it, and we want to select carefully, so use a brush sized approximately 21 pixels, at 100% opacity.

This guy really needs to fix his roof. Let's do some repairs for him. Both above and below this area the gutters are falling apart. Let's make a uniform gutter:

4. Select a small area of the roof, as shown below, then use: **Image > Resize > Scale** and drag the right hand side of the selection to the right, thus smearing it across the damaged area – giving the impression of a uniform look:

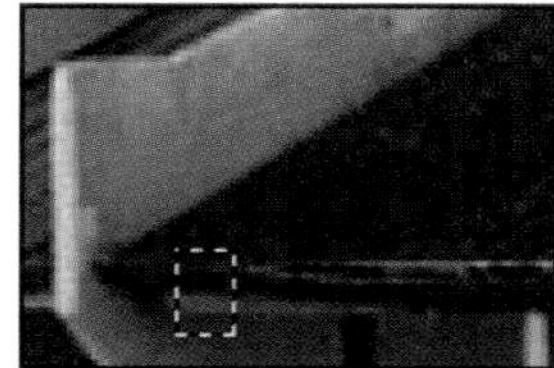

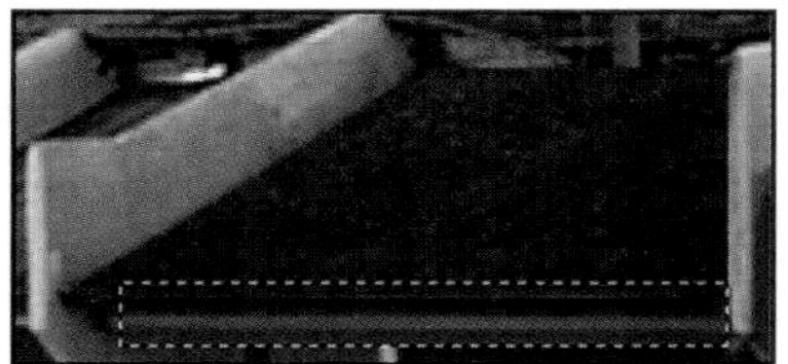

5. Let's repeat the process with the damaged area just above this piece of roof, which would pretty much completely get rid of the pipe. Wow, the walls here really need repainting. Luckily we have just the right kind of paint!

Let's start on the motley purple wall on the right.

Notice that it will be very difficult to use the Clone Stamp tool here – there are hardly any useful areas of flat color to clone from.

6. Instead we'll use the standard paintbrush at 50% opacity, with a brush size of 9. Remember, by using the ALT/OPTION key and clicking, we can select the paint color as we go, so we don't have to be too unyielding to the various contrast changes in this area.

Here's a bit of a poser: there's purple and green paint on the same wall. Looks like the guy couldn't make up his mind either, so just didn't bother to paint this area.

7. Use the same size brush as before at about 20% opacity and just blend the two colors together by going over the area with both.

8. We can apply the same techniques to all the unpainted areas using both the Clone Stamp tool (for realistic continuation of the wall grain) and the paintbrush (to smooth out rough areas and create a continuity of color). See which works best for you, and which gives you a result that is more believable. We really should charge for these home improvements...!

After attending to the roofs, let's concentrate on some of the walls. As they're in the foreground, they are certainly going to be noticed.

9. Using dabs of flat color on the red wall should even out any mildew problems, and cloning color from the middle of the white wall and using it along the bottom of the wall should neaten up the area considerably.

10. One more important thing to attend to is the sill of the white wall, which is tarnished. Using the Polygonal Lasso tool again, make a selection and use the Paintbrush to repaint this area. Select an existing color from this area by using the Eyedropper tool (ALT/OPTION-click). Use a fairly low opacity brush (20%) so that the grain of the wall isn't totally destroyed: We don't want it to look too smooth.

Leave the left and right hand parts a little unpainted, or the new paint will look a little bit unrealistic. We can use this technique on the red ground by the gate on the right too.

11. Let's start on the wall immediately below this area. Create a new layer immediately above the background layer and call it 'gray wall'.

12. Using a 40% opacity paint brush of size 17 use ALT/OPTION-click to pick one of the colors off the wall – preferably a fairly light one – remember to be on the background layer when you select this color.

13. Going back to our 'gray wall' layer and using this color, gently cover the wall with a coat of this paint. In order to pay attention to the finer areas, you might try zooming in to 200%. Once you've completed this task, use the Luminosity blending mode.

Why use Luminosity, as opposed to, say, the Color blending mode? Luminosity will take our opaque paint and give it the color of the layer below. Using the Color blending mode will take the layer below, and apply the color of the gray wall layer to it, but it will lose its opacity and substance (and become just a color). We are plastering here, more than painting: basically smoothing out the wall, while preserving its original base color for authenticity.

14. Drop the opacity of the layer down to 80%, or whatever seems appropriate, to let some of the original wall texture show through.

15. Use the same technique to fix the red wall to the left – create a new layer called 'red wall' for this purpose. You could also take the chip out of the bottom of this wall using the Clone Stamp tool.

Tree surgery

What's missing? Well the street isn't very green is it? In fact, our neighborhood has a tree planting drive going, to make the area a bit greener. To give residents an idea of what will be achieved by this, let's add in a tree on the right. Just one street down, things are really going well: there are trees everywhere. Let's take one of their trees and put it in our picture.

Open up `one_street_down.jpg`. Notice that this shot is a lot bigger than the `street_scene.jpg`. That's ok. For cutting something out it's nice to work on a larger image – because we can create a more precise marquee and we can always scale it down afterwards.

1. Duplicate the background layer and place a new layer between these two, filled with white. This will allow us to see what we are erasing from the image. We need this additional white layer so that we can see the areas that we erase, otherwise we'd just see the duplicated picture on the background layer. This is an easy way to keep track of where we are.

We could use a mask to hide the parts of the image that we don't need, but in this case we're going to use the Eraser tool. Once we are done, we're going to drag this layer across to our street scene. Go back to the duplicated layer and let's start by removing everything around the trunk of the tree.

2. Zoom in around the target tree to ensure accuracy.

3. Using a 60% opacity brush of size 19, start erasing from around the trunk.

We've set the opacity to 60% as opposed to 100% in order to avoid making the edge of the trunk look too sharp and unreal. When we move this layer onto our street scene project, we will want it to blend in – as if it was always there. We are using a hard-edged brush of size 19 as opposed to a softer one because we also don't want the tree to be too fuzzy. Using a hard-edged brush at a slightly lower opacity will mean we can cut the tree out without the lines being too severe, but at the same time we won't lose any resolution on the outline of the trunk.

Try erasing right up to the trunk, without removing any of it. If we were using a softer brush we wouldn't be able to get this close to the trunk, and would have to leave some of the background in – which is obviously undesirable.

Because the tree is positioned on the extreme right hand side of the image, you might need to drop your brush size: If you go off the side into the scrollbar, instead of erasing you will suddenly start scrolling!

Erasing in between the central branches is quite difficult: with your round brush it's hard to get into those pointy areas without erasing some of the trunk. Let's use the Lasso tool. We'll start with the biggest central area.

4. Your Lasso selection tool is probably still set to the Polygonal mode, so hold down this icon and reselect the normal lasso from the pop up menu.

5. You don't have to draw the marquee all in one go, remember by holding down the SHIFT and ALT keys while clicking you can alternatively add or subtract from your marquee.

6. Using **Select > Feather** and a setting of 0.5 we can smooth out our selection a bit so that when we erase it isn't a harsh aliased line. Repeating this process with the other inner areas, and taking the Eraser tool as far up as where the leaves start, we now have the trunk isolated from the background.

7. Cutting out the leaves is going to be far more difficult. Let's make a marquee to more or less define where the leaves for this tree end.

8. This doesn't have to be completely accurate, make your marquee as you'd like the shape of the tree to be – just use a rather jagged line – as you go around some leaves and not others.

Using a 40% opacity brush of size 19, let's drag the Eraser around this border:

9. Now deselect everything and repeat this process, but this time do not follow exactly the same path: select the same route, but go around slightly different leaves. We could have simply deleted the first marquee and feathered the edges, but this would not give the desired effect. The entire tree does not fade into another tree – quite a few areas of it overlap houses and other objects, so it would be easy to spot where our tampering had taken place. Trees do not just fade away into a blur – especially in the foreground of a picture, instead they end in definite leaf-edges.

10. Now let's use the same settings on the Eraser brush and trace around this area in a similar fashion. Switching to a 70% opacity size 35 soft edged brush, start erasing the center of the marquee and pass briefly over the edge of it.

11. Now let's select the entire left hand part of the image that we don't wish to bring across to our street scene project and delete it. Leave a little portion of the pavement in tact, so that we have a reference point:

We'll make some finer adjustments to the tree once we've dragged it across to our street scene.

12. Go back to the street_scene project and click on the top layer – which is should be 'red wall'. Now drag the top tree layer from `one_street_down.jpg` onto the street_scene canvas – it will automatically put it on a layer above whichever layer is selected – so in this case we should now have our tree on the top layer.

13. Resize the tree using **Image > Resize > Scale** and move it till it fits perfectly on the right. You should have to scale the tree to roughly 74% of its original size.

If you lock the aspect ratio (as shown in the picture opposite) you can scale the horizontal and vertical size of the image together:

14. Using a size 21 40% opacity Eraser, dab at the edges of the leaves that are a bit hard. As you can see, the parts of the tree that are over the houses blend fairly well; the illusion is only really broken where the leaves meet the sky.

The problem with this, of course, is that the leaves do not actually meet the sky at this point – we have simply cut them out to look like they do. What we need to do is find a piece of tree that actually does end with the sky and stick it on top – that way the leaves on the edges will look authentic. We only need to do this where our newly planted tree actually meets the sky – the rest of the tree that's in front of the houses is fine.

Let's go back to `one_street_down.jpg`. There is a fairly large part of tree that interacts with the sky in this picture. Let's borrow some of it:

15. Using the Move tool, drag this selection onto the street_scene canvas. Position this new layer so that it's just above our tree layer. Call it 'new piece'.

16. It's not quite the right way around. Using **Image > Rotate > 90° Left** followed by the Move tool we can position the piece of tree over the area we wish to cover.

We'll probably need to move this piece around a bit until it's perfectly positioned, let's use a mask instead of the Eraser tool to remove unwanted pieces.

17. Create a new layer just below the piece we wish to mask. CTRL/CMD-click on the thumbnail of our new piece layer in order to select it, then click on the new layer and fill this selection with black.

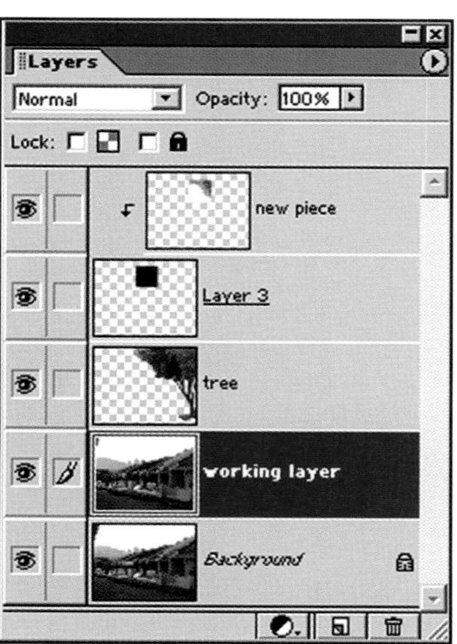

18. Now we can safely use the Eraser tool on our new layer and the layer above ('new piece') won't be damaged should we wish to make changes at a later date. Have a look at Chapters 7 and 8 for a more in-depth discussion of how layers work.

Right, let's get rid of all the sky that we inherited with our new layer.

19. Using a 40% opacity size 19 brush, get as close to the leaves as possible without actually erasing any of them.

20. To see if you've erased everything you need to, CTRL/CMD click on this new layer – whatever is surrounded by a marquee is still visible – you might have missed the odd spot – now would be the time to erase those. We are going to set the blending mode of this layer to Overlay – which effectively means our 'new piece' layer, which is grouped to it, will also be overlaid. The reason we have chosen Overlay is that it will allow us to blend nicely with the tree beneath. The texture of this layer will be transferred to the lower layer, but in general its color and tonality will be inherited from the layer beneath.

21. All that remains to be done is to soften the edges on the right and the top where our new piece mixes with the existing tree. We're going to use a larger brush of size 35 with an opacity of 25% to accomplish this task. Select the Eraser with the same settings as before, and gently erase from the new layer (Layer 3 in the picture above) until the new piece layer and the existing tree blend together nicely.

You might find that you delete quite a bit of this layer, but that's fine: we were only basically using it for the sections which show leaves meeting the sky.

22. You also might notice that some of the original tree layer sticks out into the sky to the left of the new piece. This is because we have deleted too much of the new piece layer, and part of it has been replaced by the old tree underneath, poking through. Carefully erase these dark areas; if there are any, making sure you're on the tree layer when you do so.

Finishing touches

So far so good, but because we have effectively overlaid the new piece, the color is far richer than it is over the existing tree. We used the Overlay blending mode on the 'new piece', which brought through the texture, yet dampened most of this layer's color, so there is a color discrepancy. We are going to have to tweak the color in on our 'new piece' layer to bring it in line with the rest of the picture.

1. Let's add an adjustment layer directly above the tree layer, so select the tree then **Layer > New Adjustment Layer > Hue/Saturation**.

2. For the time being we're going to leave the settings as is, so check **Group With Previous Layer**, then click OK. We don't want to apply the adjustment layer to the entire image, just to the area directly above our new piece.

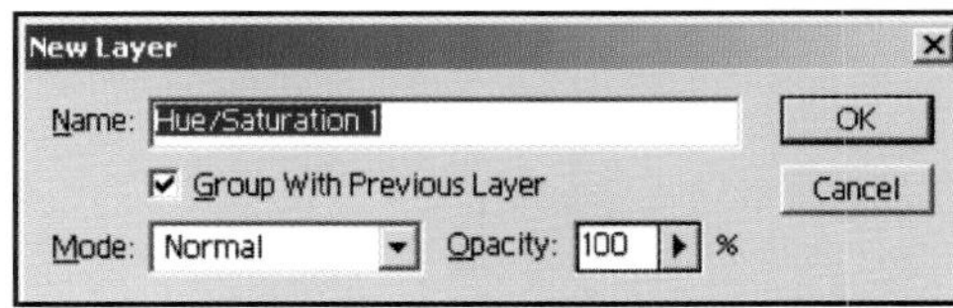

3. What we need to do now is click on the mask thumbnail (the one to the right of the adjustment picture) and fill it with black. This basically means that the adjustment layer will not be applied to any part of the image. We are then going to use 100% opacity white paint with a diffuse brush of size 35 and paint on the area just above our new piece.

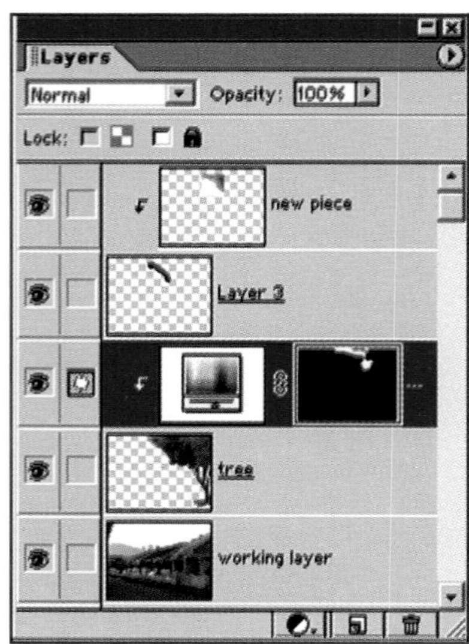

Notice that in the picture above I've painted quite a bit of white onto the mask – these are all the areas that are going to be affected by the adjustment layer.

4. Now we need to fiddle with the adjustment layer properties (**Layer > Layer Content Options...**) to bring the colors to life.

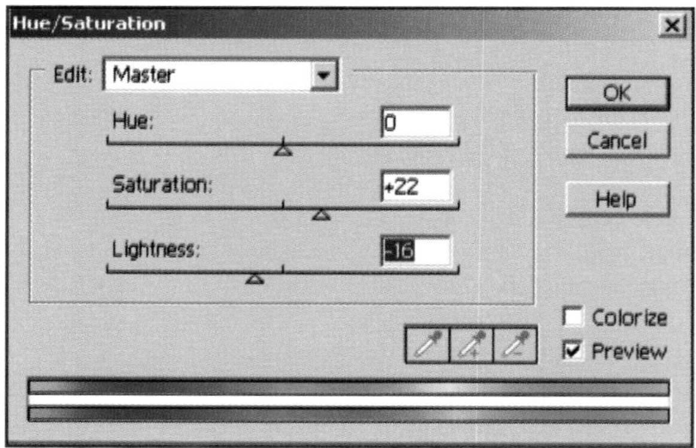

5. Use the above settings to bring out the color. Because this 'new piece' layer was much brighter than the layer we overlaid it onto, we are going to drop its lightness by a good deal. Doing this will affect its saturation, however: changing the lightness of the layer effectively means darkening, and so unfortunately, de-saturating the color. We need to compensate for this by putting the color back by increasing the saturation.

The final addition to our scene should be a different skyscape: the one we have now is so boring and lifeless.

6. Open up `knysna_sunset.jpg`. Select most of the sky area, and drag it onto our street scene. If it's not the top layer, drag it to the top.

7. Let's use the Darken blending mode and, using the Eraser tool with a soft edged brush setting with a size of 35 or greater and 80% opacity, erase the parts of the sunset layer that contain any land.

8. The only thing left to do is blend the sunset and the hill effectively. Using a large paint brush, roughly 65 pixels, with an opacity of 20%, run it evenly over the top of the hills once or twice, while on the sunset layer – this will lighten the area.

9. One last finishing touch: use the Eraser tool on the bottom of the tree trunk to remove the parts of the pavement that we brought across from the original picture.

Obviously there are other fine tweaks that you can still make to the image (for example, if this picture had been taken in less diffuse light, we would have needed to add a shadow for the tree). But I'll leave that up to you. The trick is to keep enough of the original image intact so that it's still believable. The changes should be subtle – we want to enhance the original image, and not change it altogether. Maybe as a final change to the image, you can look at placing a levels adjustment layer right at the top, to brighten up the image a little bit.

As you will have seen from this chapter, a fair amount of work goes into manipulating digital images, and with that, a fair amount of time. Sometimes it's not necessary to go into quite this depth to change an image, other times it requires even more work. Making something believable takes far more work than manipulating an image just to provide an effect: We could have just plonked the tree down to demonstrate what the street might look like with some added foliage, without going to such lengths to make it look like part of the original image. You need to decide this before you start any image manipulation: how much time and what depths you should go to on any image is determined by what you want the outcome to be.

A last note to consider: changing images digitally involves certain ethical considerations. We are able to make something look completely real, and yet it is not so. This power should not be abused.

10 A panoramic project

We're now going to look at how to create panoramas from sets of photographs. To ensure we create a perfect panorama we'll use of some of the tools that we have already covered, and hopefully this will serve to reinforce your understanding of them.

Before the advent of digital manipulation of photographs you could only create satisfactory panoramas through the use of a wide-angle lens. With digital cameras and digital photo manipulation this task is made so much easier: We can even create 360° degree panoramas. Try that with a normal camera – wide angled lenses don't stretch quite that far!

Back to basics

Let's go over some of the practical considerations you need to remember when shooting your pictures for a panorama. Firstly, if you can, use a tripod. If you don't have access to a tripod, try swiveling around on the same spot without dropping your hands – in a perfect horizontal arc.

As you take each picture, remember that you're going to have to connect all these photographs together – so allow for a bit of overlap between pictures – in other words, photograph some of the same ground from the last picture.

The most difficult thing about taking panoramic shots is maintaining consistent lighting. Most cameras, when facing towards the sun, will adjust the exposure to correct for the increase in light. What this translates to, is that the photographs in your panorama taken facing away from the sun will be of a different brightness (and most probably contrast) to those taken facing towards it.

Another interesting problem we find in panoramic projects is that of perspective. Because we are photographing 3-dimensional surroundings, moving our camera around in an arc, the perspective of the objects we photograph will change.

When taking the photographs, avoid making the overlapping areas anywhere near well-defined features. For instance, if we are shooting a panoramic street scene, we should avoid putting a car in the overlapping area between two of the photographs. A car has a specific, recognizable shape, and people will notice if we mess with it. Try to put the overlap on a wall, or something where a slight change of perspective will not be obvious.

Even if we take these precautions into account, we will most probably still have to adjust the perspective of our images manually in order to stitch them together.

As a general rule with panoramas, take more shots than you think necessary. This achieves two things: firstly, it means that our change in perspective between each shot is less, and secondly, it gives us more raw material to work with, should we need to "borrow" certain areas to stitch with using our clone stamp tool.

Introducing the Photomerge tool

One of the most remarkable and useful tools that you will learn to use in Photoshop Elements is the **Photomerge** tool. This tool left me with my mouth hanging open when I first saw it in action! Make no bones about it, stitching photographs together into a seamless and believable panorama can be a difficult and time-consuming process. This tool removes 90% of the labor involved in creating panoramas.

Although the tool has its limitations, it is most definitely an indispensable part of any panoramic project. We start off the practical section of this chapter by looking at its strengths. Let's see how it works.

SOUTH AFRICAN PANORAMA

1. From the File Menu, click on the Photomerge command, **File > Photomerge**. This brings up the following dialogue box:

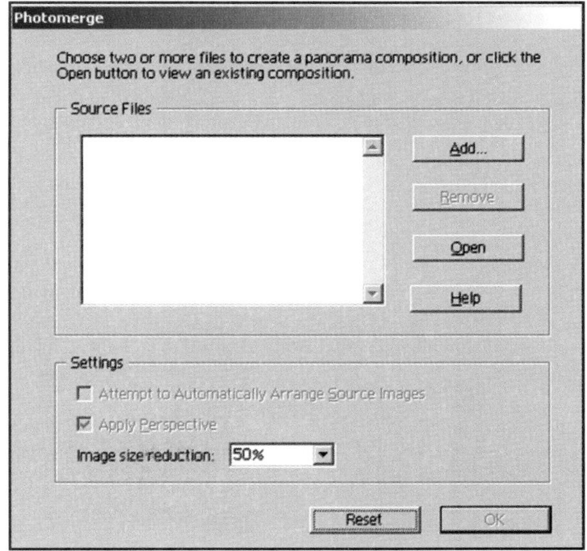

2. Using the **Add** button, select the images entitled `knysna_forest1.jpg`, `knysna_forest2.jpg`, and `knysna_forest3.jpg`.

I took these images while on holiday in Knysna, a small town 300 miles up the east coast of the Cape. This incredible view can only be accessed by a staggeringly bumpy dirt road, which proved both arduous and painful (as the driver of the 4x4 was slightly over-enthusiastic). It proved worth it when the clouds parted to reveal a most majestic view, which could only be captured properly as a panorama.

3. Once you have added all three images into the center box, check the boxes for **Attempt to Automatically Arrange Source Images**, and **Apply Perspective**. Then set **Image Size Reduction** to 50%. What does all this mean?

Checking the first box will allow Elements to arrange the photographs into (hopefully) the correct rotational sequence. Normally this works fine but beware; there is a pitfall. The Photomerge tool arranges pictures sequentially from left to right. The algorithm for connecting the images only seems to work properly in this order. If you have taken your images from right to left instead, then uncheck the Automatically Arrange box, and save yourself the headache of your pictures being out of sequence.

The second box, Apply Perspective, instructs Elements to adjust the perspective of each shot to create the best fit. Even though it doesn't always get this right, it is an incredibly powerful and useful feature.

Finally, we have decided that our output panoramic image will be much smaller than our originals. Remember that panoramas, once put together, are incredibly long images, so it's often a good idea to scale them down or we'll create a monster!

4. With all of this ready, click OK. Notice how Photomerge shuffles the images around and then presents you with a hybrid image. Not a particularly impressive one, however. The reason for this is that the seams are not yet lined up properly.

Notice how Photomerge has huddled all the images together. Let's separate them a bit. Using the **Select Image Tool**, drag the right hand image further over to the right. Observe the **Navigator** on the right keeping track of your images on the entire canvas.

Photomerge pitfalls

One of the shortfalls of this tool is that it falls outside the scope of the Elements History, which means that there is no Undo option if you make a mistake. Of course you are free to drag the images around without altering or damaging them in any way, so the use of the Undo states is not essential. But it does get a bit irritating when you line everything up perfectly and then accidentally drag it off the mark again!

Another point to add is that unlike linking layers together, the Photomerge canvas is totally freeform. This means that you will have to manually make allowances for the horizontal span of each image. As we saw when we were first presented with Photomerge's attempt at stitching the images together, they were all crowded together. So pretty much the first task here is to try and space the images out.

We need to do this at the beginning, as you cannot drag two images at the same time. Imagine if you'd lined up the outer four images of a 5-picture sequence, but had not made proper allowance for the middle image, you would then have to reposition at least three of your photo's all over again; what a waste of time!

5. Back to our Knysna project, drag the three images apart and arrange them so that they are just touching. In accordance with Photomerge's wishes, let's work from left to right.

When you drag an image in Photomerge, you can choose either **Blend** or **Ghost** mode.

- **Ghost** mode automatically adjusts the transparency of the image so that you can see both images at the same time. This allows you to line up the overlap much more easily.

- **Blend** mode blends the images together on the fly. This mode is more useful when you know that the images are not going to line up but you still want to force a panorama. This mode allows you to decide what's going to be the best blend. If you know the images will line up, however, stick to Ghost mode, because this will allow you to achieve a more accurate blend.

As you can see, when the images are not overlapping Photomerge leaves them alone:

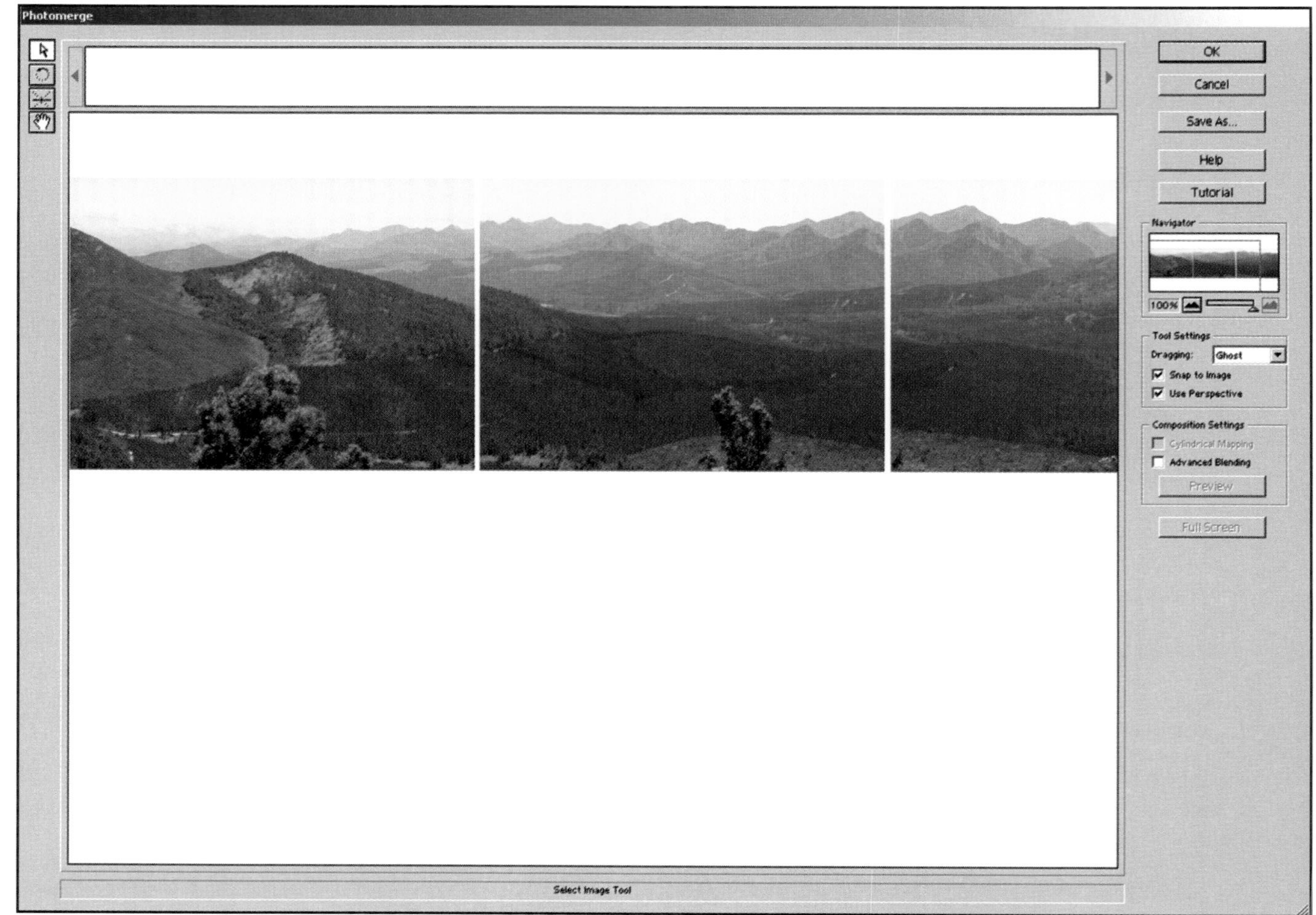

6. Let's start by dragging the middle image towards the left hand side one.

7. Because our subject matter is mostly background and very little foreground, let's turn off **Use Perspective** for the time being. Also, we are going to want to manually align the images, so turn off **Snap to Image** too. Photomerge will still snap the two images together but will no longer try and align the image with the entire canvas.

8. So once you have dragged the middle image over the left hand one and you think that they are more or less lined up, drop it there. Photomerge immediately blends the two together.

9. Repeat this procedure, dragging the right hand image over the middle one. Once again, turn off Perspective and Snap to Image. Photomerge should now have seamlessly merged the three images together:

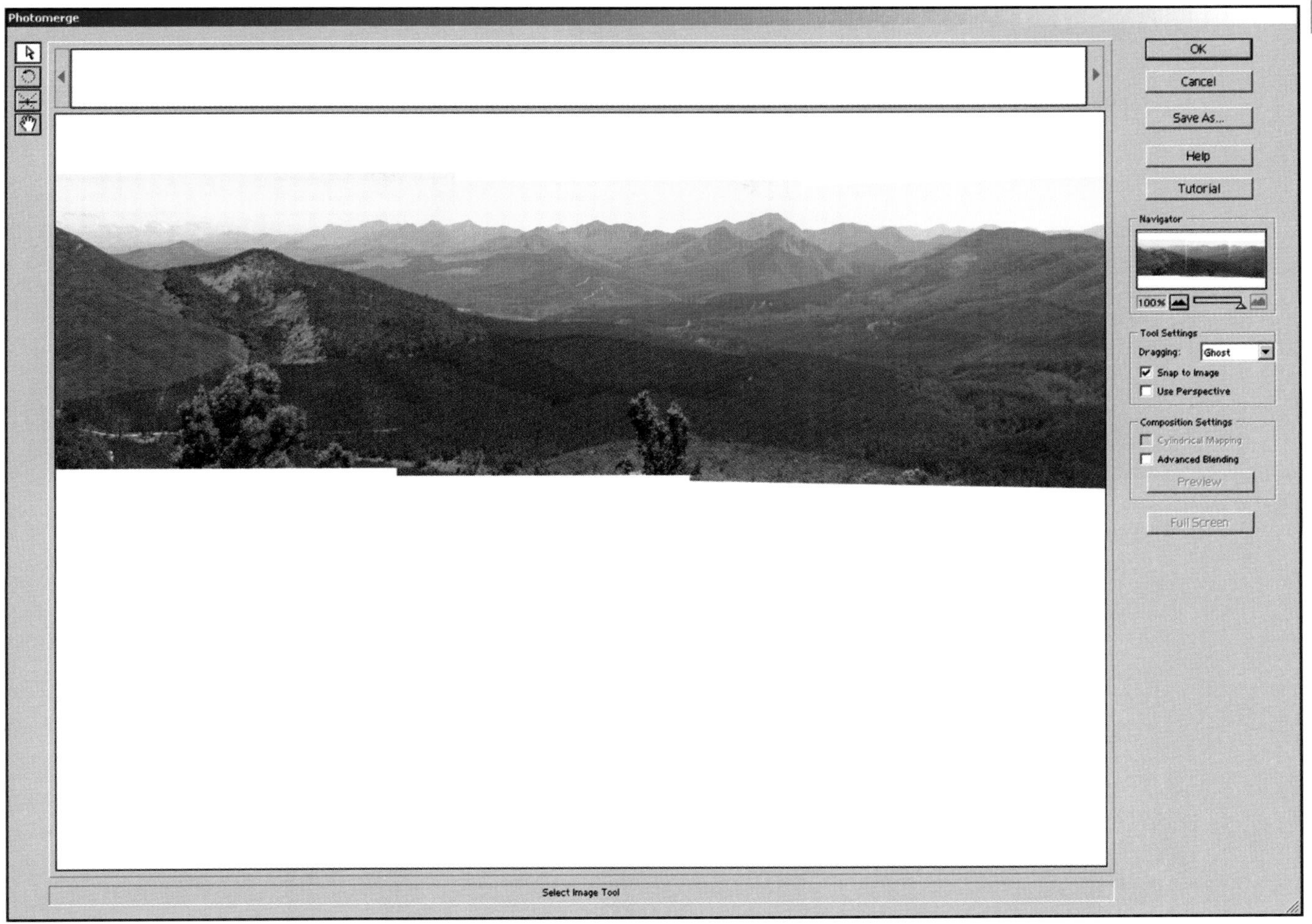

10. At this point, let's save the image – so that we can come back at a later date and rearrange the separate photos, if needs be. Once we click on OK, Photomerge will flatten all three images onto one layer. Do this now.

11. Notice that the individual photos did not all line up vertically, probably because I was a bit shaken up by the crazy drive to get to the spot, so I didn't maintain a perfect horizontal arc for each shot. No problem, all we need to do is just crop off the white bits: Using the Marquee tool, make a rectangular selection that does not include any of the white part. You will be cropping off some of your image, but this can't be helped. Using **Image > Crop**, remove this area: what we are left with is just a strip of pure image.

Well that was fairly easy. But let's expose some of the problems with Photomerge. Don't you just hate it when you try a tutorial using the pictures provided, which of course works perfectly, only to find the pictures that YOU actually took don't work even half as well? Let's use pictures that Photomerge has trouble dealing with.

1. Open up Photomerge again, and this time add the photos starting with `Knysna_sea1.jpg` through to `Knysna_sea5.jpg`. Here we see a little bit extra in the same panorama, with one important difference: I was facing into the sun for two of the shots so the lighting is drastically different.

2. Uncheck the Automatically Align box: This panorama was shot from right to left, so Photomerge will have trouble trying to align the shots. Notice now, that when Photomerge opens up, the images are at the top of the screen.

We're going to have to drag and drop the images onto the canvas ourselves. The first one to drag down is `Knysna_sea5.jpg`.

3. Position this on the left hand side of the blank canvas. Next we are going to want `Knysna_sea4.jpg`. We can immediately merge these two, by dragging the latter into the correct place. Once again, if the image jumps around, turn off Snap to Image.

4. By repeating the process, drag all the images onto the canvas in the correct order. Although we can get all the images to merge correctly, we have a problem with the brightness and contrast with the two on the left. So what do we do about this?

There are two different ways of tackling this problem:

- Option 1: we continue with the Photomerge and apply a brightness/contrast adjustment layer afterwards, masking out the left hand side.
- Option 2: we manually adjust these two images **before** adding them to Photomerge.

Option 1 is a perfectly valid way of completing this task, but the point of transition between slide 2 and 3 is very difficult to erase. Notice that the change in brightness between slide 2 and 3 is not a straight line, but a blurred diagonal area. This gradient change between dark and light will be very difficult to get rid of: We can apply an adjustment layer to the dark area (to the left) or the light area (to the right) of this zone, but what about the zone itself?

We would somehow have to apply a variable brightness adjustment to this area: ranging from dark to light. One way to do this would be to apply the adjustment layer to the entire dark area, including the gradient zone, and then use a diffuse brush to erase from the right hand side of the mask.

Doesn't this sound like an awful lot of work? It's also very difficult to get 100% right. Getting rid of that gradient zone is extremely time consuming and virtually impossible!

Let's look at Option 2, then: matching the brightness and contrast of the images **before** adding them to Photomerge. This also requires a fair amount of work, but it's much easier to get perfect results.

5. Leave Photomerge for the moment, and instead open up `Knysna_sea4.jpg` and `Knysna_sea3.jpg` in the main window.

6. Create a new image of 1024 by 768 pixels in size and drag our two jpegs into the document. Let's try to match the darker image (`Knysna_sea4.jpg`) to the lighter one.

7. The first thing we're going to do is to group a Levels adjustment layer to the darker image layer. (Refer to chapter 8 if you need to recap on levels adjustment layers in detail). So click on the darker layer to select it, then use **Layers > New Adjustment Layer > Levels**.

8. Group this layer to the darker image by clicking on the link button (second from left in the layers palette)

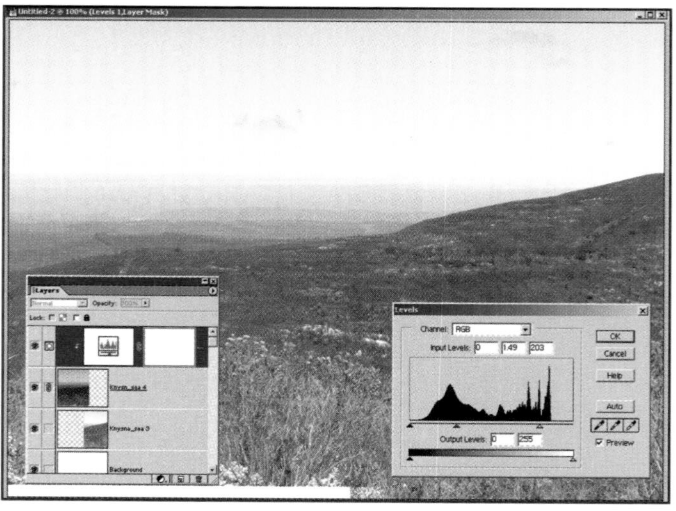

9. Playing around with the Midtones and Light tones, you'll probably find, as I did, that the **Input Levels** that work best are in the region of 0; 1.49 and 203. This is a definite improvement, but it's not looking completely perfect yet. So we're going to add a further adjustment layer: Hue/Saturation.

10. Click on **Enhance > Color > Hue/Saturation**. In the dialog box that pops up you'll notice that there are further options if you click on the **Edit** box with **Master** selected. First, let's try playing with the Master values a little. I was happy with a –16 Saturation here.

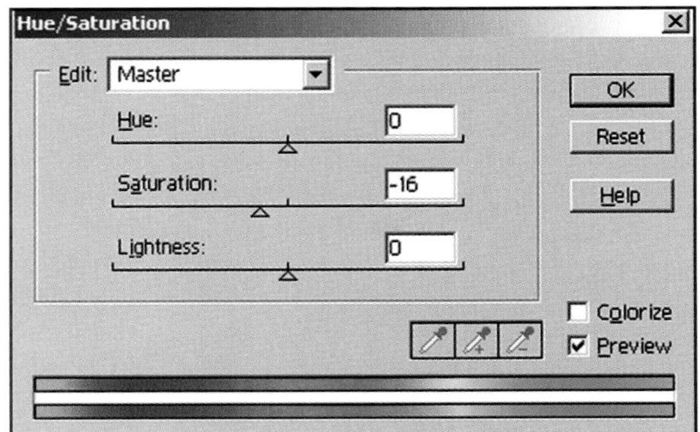

11. Now, if we're really feeling fussy (which I hope you are!), we might decide that the blue tones of the two images aren't quite matching up, especially in the sky. So in the drop down Edit menu, click on Blues. Before we mess with the greens, let's take a step back and have a critical look at the image.

12. Notice that a lot of the blues in the image are in the lighter range. So we don't just want to affect the 'Blues', we want to affect a range of color from blue to cyan. What we need to do is drag the range slider slightly to the left, in order to incorporate more cyan. The following settings work well:

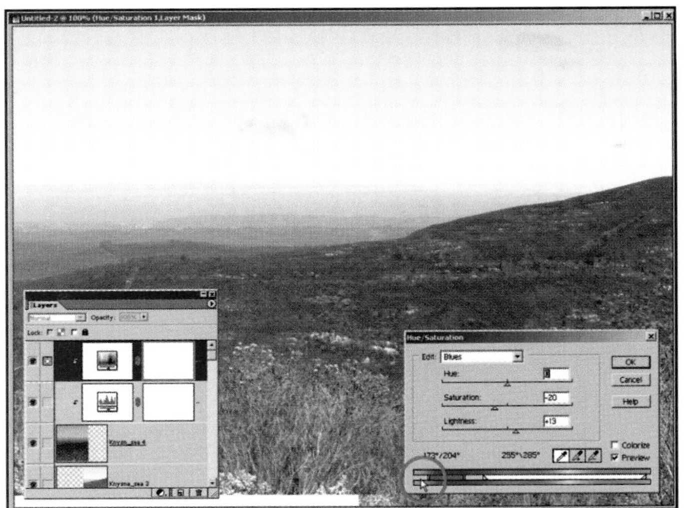

13. We've pretty much got the two images alike in color saturation and lightness. Delete the light layer (the one to which we have not applied the adjustment layers) by dragging it onto the tiny trashcan at the bottom right hand corner of the Layers palette– we no longer need it as a reference for the dark one.

14. Click on the darker layer, and, using the Move tool, drag it so that it snaps to the center of the canvas – it should be a perfect fit. We can now flatten the image (**Layers > Flatten Image**) and save our new version for use in the Photomerge.

15. Repeat this process using `Knysna_sea5.jpg` and `Knysna_sea3.jpg`. It doesn't matter that the two don't line up – just overlap them an inch or so – the same way as before. You are going to have to make the finer adjustments yourself, as in all likelihood the above settings will be slightly off when applied to a different image.

Once you have saved this image, you can now easily Photomerge them together, with a far more professional result.

The Vanishing Point tool

Our last tool to encounter in the Photomerge stable is the **Vanishing Point tool.**

1. Open up `Knysna_sea1.jpg` and `Knysna_sea2.jpg`. Don't let Photomerge automatically arrange them, but drag them and align them on the canvas yourself.

2. Once you have done this, turn **Use Perspective** on (if it isn't on already). Now using the Vanishing Point tool, click on the middle of the left hand picture, and then on the middle of the right hand one. Notice how the perspective of the two images changes depending on where you click.

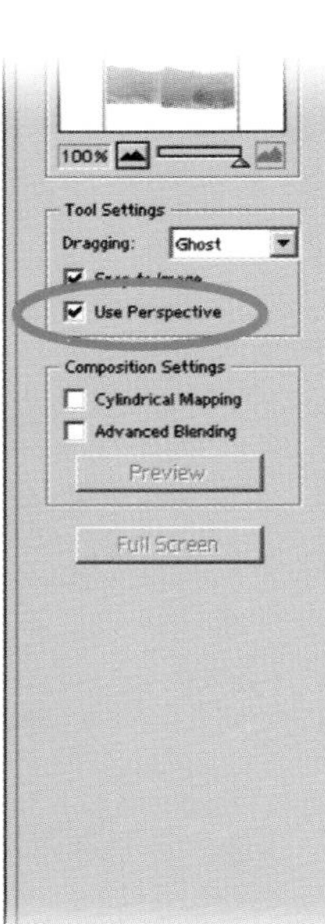

3. The Vanishing Point tool sets the point furthest from the camera, perspective-wise. This point will then appear flat, and everything else will distort around it – the further away something is from this point, the greater the change in perspective.

By combining these techniques, you can create flawless and professional panoramas without spending hour upon hour using the Clone Stamp tool.

As we have seen in this chapter, the Photomerge tool is incredibly useful for creating panoramas. An important point to watch out for though: When Photomerge completes the panorama (when you click OK) it outputs a flattened image into Photoshop Elements.

If you wish to save the panorama in an editable state, do so from within Photomerge, before you create an output. Remember, if you're not quite happy with the way Photomerge has completed the panorama, you can always do a final touchup with the **Clone Stamp** Tool. Enjoy!

11 Ageing a Photograph

In this chapter we are going to be looking at applying special effects to a modern day photograph in order to make it look like it was taken at the turn of the last century. This exercise will teach you techniques to stylize photographs, and will add to the re-touching skills, like cloning and airbrushing, that you have already learnt.

Ageing a photograph is not simply a case of putting it into black and white or sepia tone, although this is the most commonly practiced technique. In order to convincingly age a photograph we actually need to take a look at how photographs were created in the past, and the kind of effects this resulted in.

11 Old and new – photographic differences

The most noticeable difference in an old photograph, besides the absence of color, is the grain and texture. In digital times, we might call this a lack of resolution. Consequently, fine details in old images are partially lost due to slight blurring.

A brief history of photography

There are very few precisely focused old photographs, for two good reasons. Firstly, the exposure times had to be worked out manually and were very long (so if something moved, it blurred). Secondly, the lenses used were pretty rudimentary and their ability to focus was quite limited. The type of film used, and the mechanics of the camera, also mean that really old photographs often show high contrast and a fairly low range of tonality.

When photographs first started to gain popularity, the photosensitivity of the chemicals used was comparatively low. This meant that it took a much longer time to take a photograph, so subjects had to be completely stationary. Louis Daguerre (who invented the daguerreotype, one of the first photographic processes) took photographs of Paris in the 1830's and 40's, but the people in the shots moved too fast to be captured. As a result, Daguerre's photographs showed what looked like a city of the dead. Only one man, who stopped to tie his shoelace, was photographed in those shots.

With the advent of modern photography, and most recently, digital photography, these limitations have been completely overcome. Cameras and film (or digital CCDs) today are able to take photographs of objects moving at incredible speed with perfect clarity; color is taken completely for granted; microscopic and telescopic lenses give us the power to capture things our eyes cannot even see. Yet it is still astounding how good some old photographs are. Often they demonstrate really good composition and use of light, much the same way a painting would. Perhaps this was because they had to be planned very carefully as the process was so arduous and complicated.

Even at the beginning stages of photography, people were already realizing they could manipulate it. In the 1850's, a very primitive form of Photoshop was practiced. Photographers like Oscar Reilander put together complex images made from many different negatives, which they assembled before negative-positive reversal (we'll cover our own version of this in the next chapter!).

Your own time machine!

Have you ever been to the movies to watch a period piece and the actors are wearing all the costumes and moving through all the right settings, but it just doesn't look old? You also get those photographers who'll take a picture of you or your family dressed in old clothes – yet when I look at these, I can instantly tell they are not old photographs. What is it about them that gives the game away? Where does the illusion break down?

For this exercise, we're going to ask the reverse question. What is it about an old photograph that visually authenticates its age?

AUTHENTIC AGEING

As we've already mentioned, old photographs evidence high contrast, low tonality and a fair amount of grain. They also usually have some flaws in the developing – those little white or black dots you see, for example, or the occasional thin squiggly line. Furthermore, an old photograph might not have been perfectly preserved. Some scratches, stains, fading, perhaps even a slight film across the image, testify to the age of the print.

We are going to have to add these elements to our photograph for the sake of authenticity. Bear in mind also the subject matter; unless you are opting for heavy irony it's obviously no good trying to age a photograph of your brand new car, or a girl in a miniskirt! For our project, we're going to use a picture of a steam train.

1. Open up `train.jpg` from the CD.

This is a picture of the Outeniqua Choo-choo, which still operates today along the South Coast of Africa, and is only slightly less bumpy than the 4 x 4 that took me to the panoramic view in the last chapter.

2. The first task is to duplicate the background layer, as always we want to preserve our original. So do this now, either by dragging the layer down to the New Layer icon at the bottom of the Layers palette, or by right/CTRL-clicking and selecting Duplicate Layer from the drop down menu.

We are now going to add an adjustment layer above this copy of the background layer. Note that we are not going to group with a specific lower layer as we have before. We want the adjustments to apply to the entire image.

3. Create a Hue/Saturation adjustment layer by clicking on the leftmost icon at the bottom of the palette.

4. In the resulting dialogue check the Colorize box in the Hue/Saturation dialog box.

This option changes all the hues in the image on a tonal basis to reflect the chosen color, as opposed to merely tinting the colors with the chosen hue. Using the Colorize option in effect gives the impression of a duotone (a two toned image, for example, but not necessarily, black and white).

5. Next, experiment with the sliders to achieve the hue and saturation you want. We'll make the Lightness setting pretty high; we need to decrease the tonal range in order to give the effect of an over-exposed photograph. The settings I decided to use were: Hue 38; Saturation 19; and Lightness +35.

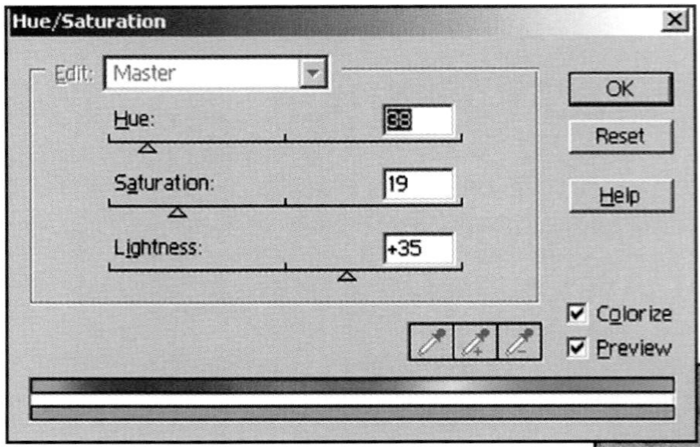

That's not a bad start – but there are still many telltale signs that this is a modern, digital photograph. Firstly, there's no grain, secondly the contrast is low (a problem we have knowingly exacerbated) and, thirdly, the image is too sharp. And that's just for a start!

Let's add the grain now. How should we do this? Well, we could use the Grain filter form the Filters menu. It seems an obvious choice doesn't it? But in fact, we'll need a bit more control than this 'quick and easy' solution.

6. Using **Filter > Noise > Add Noise**, we get the following dialog box:

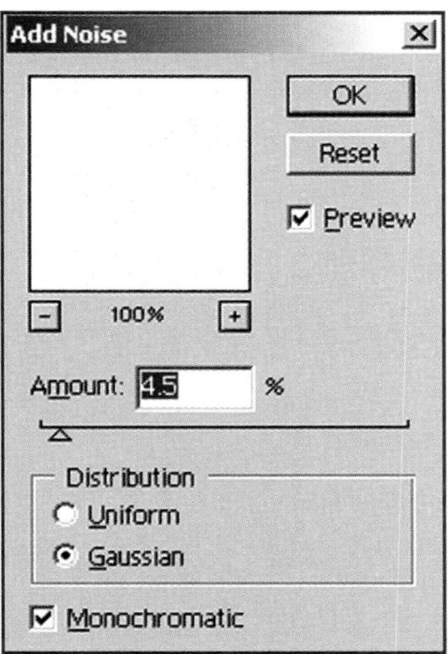

7. Check **Monochromatic** and use **Gaussian** distribution. We're going to add a subtle spread of noise, to the value of 4.5%.

8. We still need to overcome the large tonal range of our image, so let's apply a Brightness/Contrast adjustment layer, using the settings: Brightness –20; Contrast +55. Notice how this severely decreases the amount of definition in lighter areas, in particular the smoke. This is a good imitation of the effect in old photographs.

9. We've still got an image that is way too sharp to be authentic, so let's address this now. Duplicate your background copy layer (the one we're busy adjusting) and drag it so that it's the top layer in the Layers palette. The reason we're duplicating this one and not the original photograph below, is that this one has the grain we put on it.

Let's start by removing the color from this layer. We're going to work directly on it, as opposed to applying adjustment layers to it.

10. Firstly, let's adjust its Hue/Saturation, click **Enhance > Color > Hue/Saturation**, and check the Colorize box. Use roughly the following settings; Hue +30 and Saturation -25. Leave the Lightness as it is.

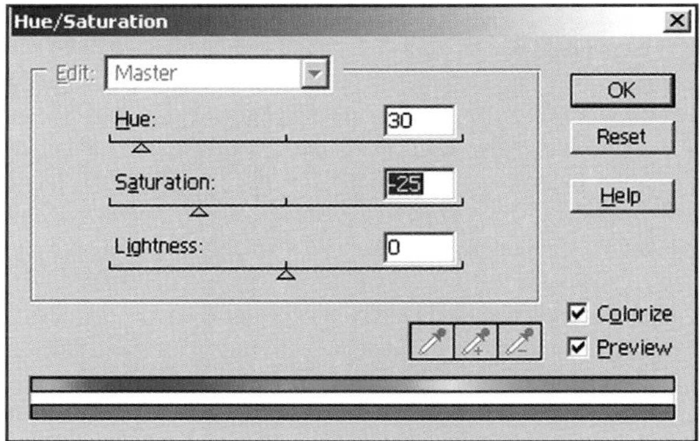

11. Now let's alter its brightness/contrast. Go to **Enhance > Brightness/Contrast > Brightness/Contrast**. Use a setting of about 50 for Contrast.

12. Finally, add a Gaussian blur to this layer too. **Filter > Blur > Gaussian Blur** using a radius of around 1.4 pixels.

13. We are now going to use this layer to affect the layers below by changing its blending mode to **Darken** and setting its opacity to around 60%.

The Darken blending mode will set any pixels that are lighter in this layer to the same darkness as those in the layers below. Pixels that are darker than in the layers below will be left alone. This will remove a lot of the lighter, more contrasted areas from our image. Notice the loss of definition in the darker areas – which is much within keeping of antique photographs.

14. We've picked up quite a bit of color along the way, which is a side effect of using brightness/contrast. Make another hue/saturation adjustment layer, and bring the saturation down to –50.

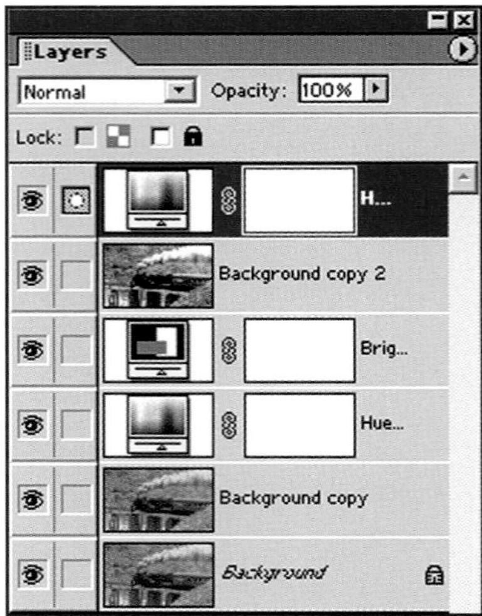

Scratching it

We've pretty much dealt with reproducing the mechanics of an old photograph. But we still need to add some real authenticity. As mentioned, many old photographs contained flaws such as scratches and fibers on the film. It would be nice to replicate these flaws, and also add some physical evidence of ageing, such as damp marks or discoloration.

In order to do this, we are going to have to create some brushes, which we can then use to stamp discoloration onto our image. What we want to do is make some really scratchy brushes and then apply them to our image.

The best brushes are often scanned-in edges of bad photocopies, textures from other photographs, pieces of faxes, etc. The effectiveness of using a brush made this way lies in the fact that you are using something real, yet not quite recognizable. Randomness, in reality, is quite different to anything you can create from scratch on a computer.

15. In the chapter folder on the CD you'll find `brush1.psd`. Open it – it's an image created in Elements using some of the filters on a few arbitrary marks made on the page.

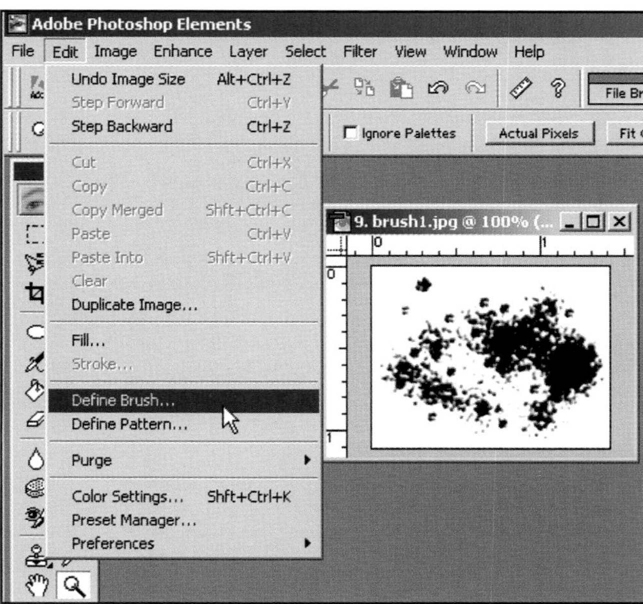

16. We're going to make a brush out of this image by going to **Edit > Define Brush**. A dialog box will pop up which allows you to give your new brush a name. Call the brush mothballs, and hit OK. Notice that when you now open up the Brushes palette, your new brush is there.

1	3	5	9	13	19
5	9	13	17	21	27
35	45	65	100	200	300
14	24	27	39	46	59
11	17	23	36	44	60
14	26	33	42	55	70
378					

We can now use our new brush to 'potato stamp' this pattern everywhere we want – creating a motley texture to things.

17. Using the new brush at about 20% opacity, with black ink, create a new layer called 'mothballs' and stamp it in a couple of places, in particular the plume of smoke above the train. In this way we've created a damp mark on our photograph.

18. Now let's add some scratches. Create a new layer called 'scratches'. Using the same technique as above, open up `brush2.psd`, and define this entire image as a brush.

Using roughly 20% opacity and white paint, let's put some scratches over the train and bridge area. This is rapidly ageing the photograph. Notice that the brush shape you use to paint with is not quite the same as the final result: Elements is basically showing you the size and shape of the brush, and not the complexity.

It's hard to believe it's the same photograph isn't it? We could have used a million different techniques to create an aged photograph. There is room for experimentation in this process, so you could try mixing and matching some of the techniques we have covered here. Some old photographs look washed out; others are beset with deep black shadows and very little halftone – basically there is no right or wrong here, so go with what you feel looks the most authentic. For instance, try turning the first brightness/contrast layer on and off:

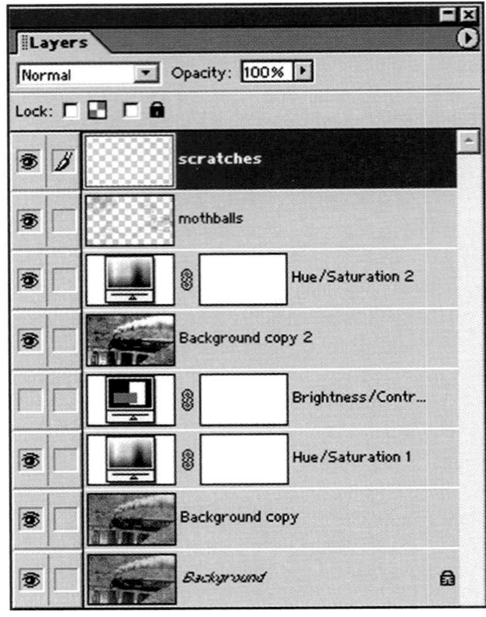

We lose a lot of the contrast for the image, and we get a very washed out look. Although this might not represent an authentic turn of the century photograph in this way, it does somehow look older to me.

Just to refresh your memory, go to the Layers palette and use the eye icons to switch the visibility off all of the other layers so you can have a look at the original.

Depending on how old you want the photograph to look, you would use different techniques. A good starting point is to do some research, and actually look at photographs from the period you're trying to imitate. Although if you do this you'll notice that sometimes antique images are in really good condition and could be mistaken for modern black and white ones. We want to exaggerate an ageing effect to bring it to the attention of the viewer.

In this chapter we have seen how hierarchies of adjustment layers create different adjustments to the image. Creating heavy stylization on an image will often require careful planning, and as we have seen involves multiple layers all acting upon one another. Experimentation is frequently the key to finding the combination that really works.

12 Creative collages

The aim of this chapter is to bring together many of the skills we have learnt over the past chapters and put them to practical use. We have seen how to improve photographs, now let's look at making our own artwork.

Design, and the use of a particular style, is a subjective thing. We are going to look at a few projects in this chapter, but it needs to be said right from the beginning: the way you choose to use your digital photographs in designs is entirely up to you. Throughout the course of this chapter, it will be valuable to constantly imagine how you would have done the tutorials differently. If you're feeling up to it, actually **do** the tutorial differently.

Recycling disappointing photos

This chapter is going to look at some of the uses for your digital photographs, and how seemingly arbitrary parts of photographs can be used to create special effects. The main emphasis on this chapter is: looking at your photographs in a different light. Yes, we've taken a picture of the windshield of a car, and a picture of an old run down shed.... But how can we use these photographs, or even parts of photographs to create something new?

While we are progressing through these tutorials, try to see the potential uses for your own photos. For example, sometimes the subject matter in a photograph isn't relevant but a light area of the photograph can be used as a layer above our main image, creating an eerie effect.

Photographs are no longer static images, no longer lifeless or isolated. They are our tools – both paint and canvas. A useful exercise, to get your mind around this concept, is to open up any two images that you've taken. Place them on the same canvas, one above the other and run through the different blending modes for the image above. Sometimes the results are fairly horrific, but other times combining images in this way gives us a really stunning collage type composite. It will also get you into the habit of seeing digital photography as a dynamic art form.

We can make so much more out of digital photography than just pressing the trigger. We can create something entirely new, like a painter, or a sculptor: photography can be both the means and the end. There is a new dimension to photography, one that involves the depth of an image, and with it the depth of an idea. This is limited only by your imagination. So for the first tutorial, let's open our minds and create something fantastical...

THRILLER BOOK COVER PROJECT

An important element in design work is to decide what the tone of the work is going to be. What kind of feelings do we want to evoke with our design? Let's consider the following scenario:

Imagine we have been asked to design the cover for a book with a creepy plot. A detective must track down a killer, with only a few sketchy clues from a traumatized witness to lead to his whereabouts. These clues lead the detective to believe that the killer is hiding out in an old shed in a forest. The book focuses on the hunt for this location – a seemingly ordinary building with an extraordinary secret, which must be discovered.

We are going to use a number of fairly different images for this project – some for subject matter and others for special effects. The most important part of creating this book cover is getting the right tone across. We would like the image we construct to reflect the essence of the book. We'll work in a slightly different way to how you would work if this were a real project: Normally we'd form a loose image in our heads of what we wanted to achieve then go take pictures to compliment this mental image. In this case, we have the images first. We are going to use the following four pictures to create something really special.

A rather strange assortment of pictures, I admit, but you'll be surprised at the results we can achieve with these. The top left picture is simply a shot of different grain papers. The top right photograph I took while on the way to work one morning. I was keen on getting a picture of the mist over the city. What I actually ended up getting was an underexposed shot of the sun rising, and drops on my windscreen. We will see later however, that even throwaway shots like this can be extremely useful – and hey, the shot cost me nothing to develop...

The third picture, in the bottom left, is a picture I took of an old watershed, and will form most of the subject matter for our project. The final picture was taken by a friend of mine as part of a study in posing, and will be used for its stark contrasts. Let's get started!

1. Create a new document **File > New**, make it 500 x 700 pixels in size, RGB mode, with a resolution of 72 dpi, and fill the canvas with black.

2. Open up `watershed.jpg`, we're going to drag this onto our project canvas. We'll need to resize it a bit, so that it's horizontal span is 500 pixels the same as our canvas, so go to **Image > Resize > Image Size**, and making sure that the **Constrain Proportions** box is checked, adjust the Width to 500 pixels.

Image Size

Pixel Dimensions: 550K (was 900K)

Width: 500 pixels

Height: 375 pixels

Document Size:

Width: 17.64 cm

Height: 13.23 cm

Resolution: 72 pixels/inch

Constrain Proportions

Resample Image: Bicubic

OK

Cancel

Help

Auto...

3. Now go to the Layers palette and literally drag and drop the watershed image into our blank canvas.

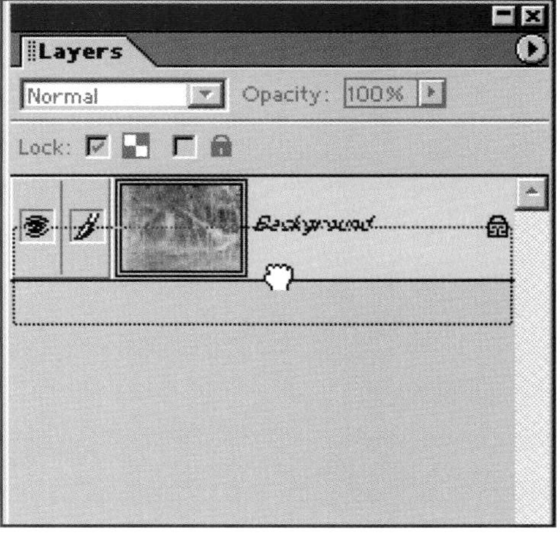

4. Call this layer 'watershed'. Use the Move tool to place it vertically in the middle of the canvas. You could use a grid to help you place the image centrally, to do this go to **View > Show Grid.** (Then select **Hide Grid** afterwards to return to normal view).

5. Let's immediately start addressing the tone of the project by making an adjustment layer, go to **Layer > New Adjustment Layer > Hue/Saturation**

We need to create a sinister atmosphere so let's colorize the image to give it a strange brown tone – almost like a memory or a dream. We're going to be looking at a memory of the watershed, through the eyes of the witness. What does she remember? It's a hazy, jumpy recollection. It was dark, and she was scared. We want to try and capture this. Use roughly the following settings for the adjustment layer:

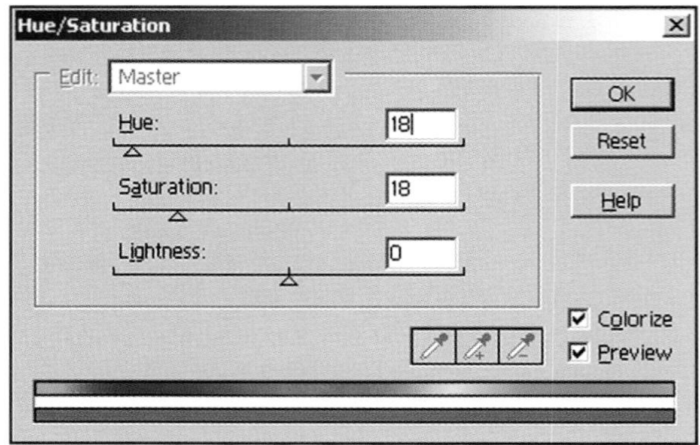

6. We've lost a bit of contrast in the image by reducing the hue range; so let's restore this by creating another adjustment layer of brightness/contrast. Use the following settings:

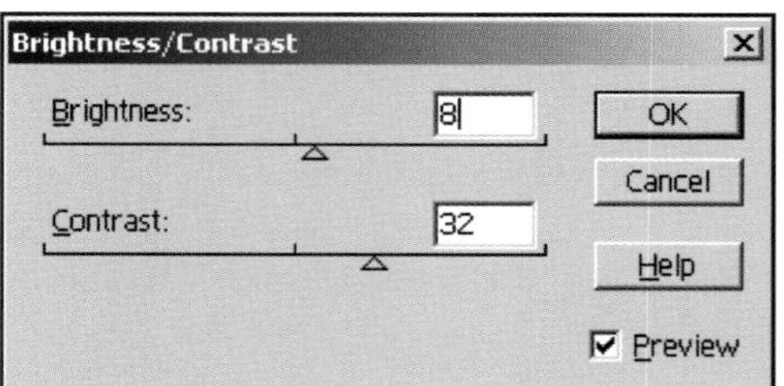

Our image should look roughly like this now:

Not a bad start. But we want the essence of our picture to be the shed. A seemingly ordinary shed, which has an extraordinary secret. We want it to stand out from the background a little bit, so we need to adjust the hue and saturation of the shed only.

7. Create another hue/saturation adjustment layer, **Layer > New Adjustment Layer > Hue/Saturation** and use the following settings:

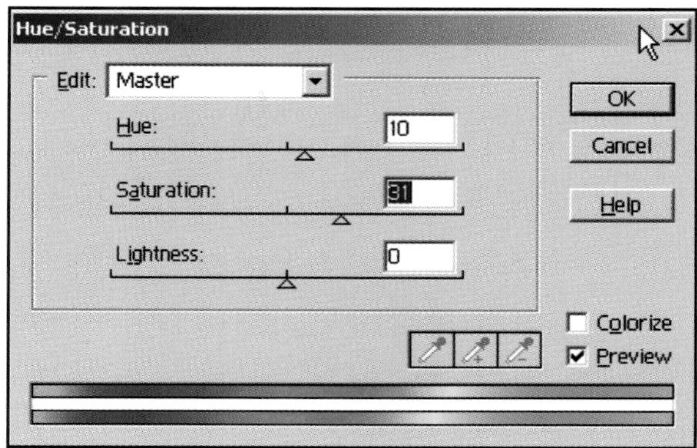

8. Fill the adjustment layer's mask with black by selecting the adjustment layer in the Layers palette and using the Paint Bucket tool. Basically this means that the mask is being applied nowhere. This may seem like a strange move, but all will become clear in the next step.

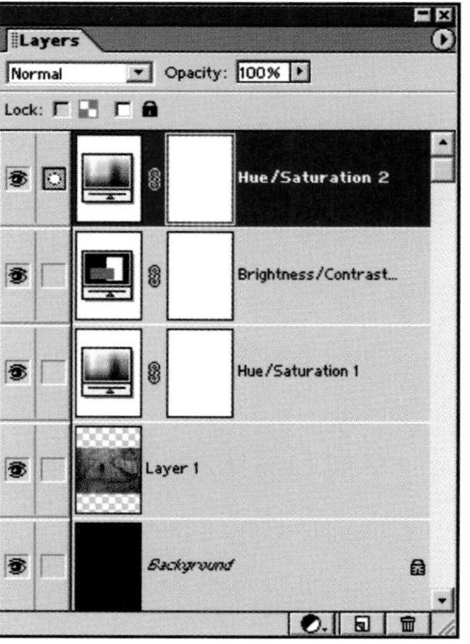

9. Making sure that you have the mask layer selected, use a white paint and a diffuse brush of size 100 with 80% opacity to paint certain areas of the shed to make it stand out. Trace over the shed, and leave the rest untouched. We now have a slightly golden hue to the shed, and everything else is in the same brown.

10. What we're going to do now is add a layer just above the black background. Open up `roughpaper.jpg`, make sure that you're on the background layer of the forest project, and drag this image to just above the background layer. If you simply drag the image onto the canvas Elements will automatically place the layer just above the previously selected layer, which in our case was the background. If you accidentally copied the rough paper image to the wrong layer then just move it in the Layers palette to the appropriate spot.

11. Let's turn off all our other layers in the meantime (by clicking on the little eye) so that we can see what we're supposed to be doing.

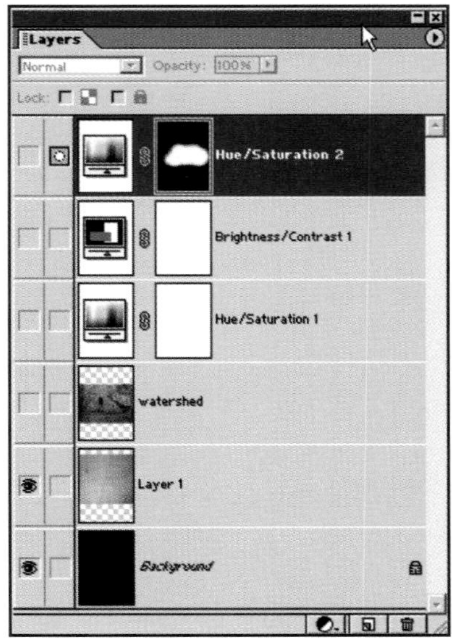

12. Duplicate this paper layer and flip this duplicate layer vertically by going to **Image > Rotate > Flip Horizontal**.

13. Now let's use the Move tool to line these two layers up so that they touch, and therefore cover the entire canvas.

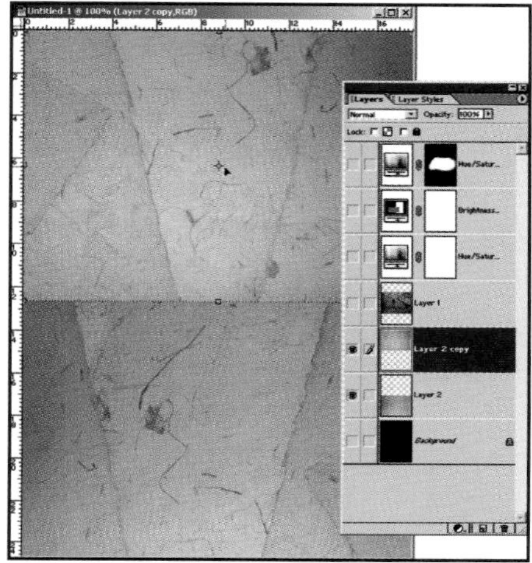

14. With this done, we will need to link them together by clicking next to the eye icon in the Layers palette, so that you see the little chain link icon appear and then merge them by going to and merge them **Layer > Merge Linked**.

15. Let's double-click on this new merged layer to rename it, in the Layer properties dialog call it 'paper'. Now set its blending mode to Hard Light. Let's turn the visibility of all our layers back on (remember you do this by clicking on the eye icon).

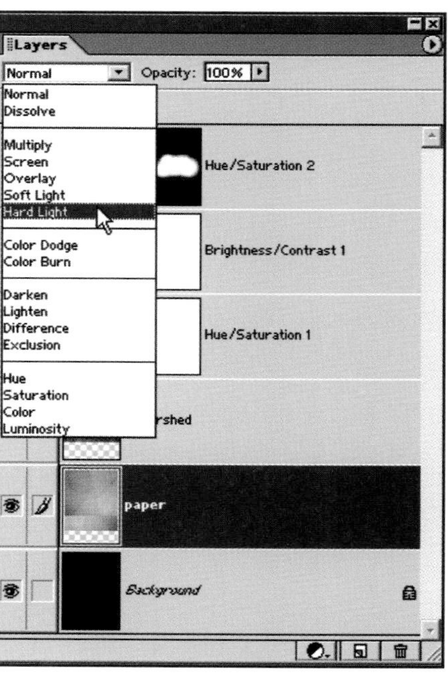

You may ask: Why not just stretch the initial paper layer so that it fits the canvas, instead of going to such lengths? If we had stretched the layer, we would have lost quite a bit of the texture and stood the chance of getting pixelation in the image. Avoid stretching images wherever possible. Even though Elements will try its best to recreate the image as a larger size, the unavoidable loss of definition is often problematic.

One more thing: We've basically created a paper layer that is the same at the top and the bottom as we have mirror imaged the layer to copy it. Because of this, the parts of the paper that are sticking out from behind the shed layer are the same at the top and the bottom.

16. To avoid this, drag the paper layer down quite a bit. The newly combined paper layer is quite a bit bigger than our canvas, and we therefore have quite a bit of room to play with.

17. Go back to the layer mask attached to our second hue/saturation adjustment layer. Select the same 100-sized white brush and paint the top and bottom parts of the mask white – the areas where the paper juts out from the watershed.

Because we are using white paint, the hue/saturation adjustment that we made to the shed itself will now be applied to the paper, giving it the same golden color. Leave about half an inch of the existing color intact on either side of the shed image. In other words, instead of painting the entire part of the mask representing the paper to white, stop about half an inch short of the shed photo, both above and below:

This allows for a better blend from the trees and leafy ground into the paper – as they are meeting with the same hues.

From a stylistic point of view, we've got to do something about the horizontal lines the watershed image makes where it meets and separates itself from the paper layer. We've partially fixed this by blending the hues together, but let's break up those stark delineating lines:

18. For the time being, turn off the watershed layer again. Create a fill layer of black just above the paper layer by going to **Layer > New Fill Layer > Solid Color**. Once again, let's fill the layer mask with black – thereby not applying the fill anywhere:

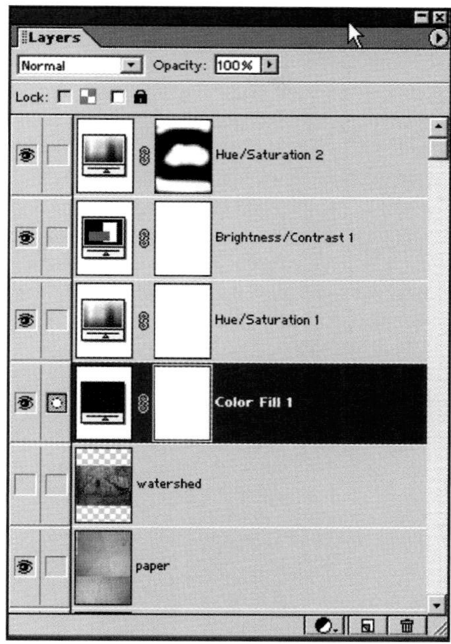

19. Let's use the brush we created for ourselves in the last chapter called 'mothballs' (the file is also in the folder for this chapter). Using white 50% opacity paint, let's stamp the middle section of the image on the mask layer, which will have the effect of making this area visible. Because our fill layer is black, this exposed paint will itself be black.

It looks like we've ripped out a piece of the paper. This is a nice visual analogy to the theme of the book: tattered clues, with the vital pieces missing.

Let's go back to working on our watershed layer. Before we do so, we'll duplicate it, as we are going to permanently alter it, so it will be good to have the original handy, in case we decide to revert back to it at a later stage.

20. Duplicate the Layer now (I'm sure you remember how to do this and don't need me to remind you!). Leave the duplicate layer just above the shed layer, and turn the visibility of the original shed layer off.

21. We are now going to work on this duplicate layer. Call this layer 'shred'. We're going to use the same brush, but this time as an eraser. Select the Eraser tool, then on the tool options bar, select Paintbrush Mode, and in the brushes palette you'll find the mothballs brush all ready to be used as an eraser.

22. Now let's stamp away pieces of it to break up those horizontal lines. Use the brush at 70% opacity. We don't want to delete much of the image, just the top and bottom edges. Notice that wherever we delete from these edges, the black area we just created shows through. So now we have a fairly good and interesting blend between the two photographs:

Now we have a fairly unusual looking building, seen as if it's in a dream. What would be nice to add is the concept of something sinister. It would be nice to show that the building itself is hiding something. That inside, it is very different from outside.

23. Let's use the 'driving to work' photo now. Open up `waytowork.jpg` and drag it onto the project just above the shred layer. Change the blending mode of the layer to Difference, and drag the layer till the highlighted area (which is the sun) is positioned over the high door in the shed. Now it looks like the shed is shining with an inner light, which is escaping into the fading twilight.

25. Once again we've got horizontal divisions where this layer ends, so use the mothballs brush again to break this up. If you want to, duplicate this layer, so that you still have a copy of the original. Call the duplicate "worked on layer: light".

We're almost there. As a matter of personal preference, I added a little bit of vertical breakup:

26. Open up `raven.jpg`. Shrink the image down to about 50% of its original size, and then drag this image onto our project, position it just above our light layer in the Layers palette.

27. Drag the layer to the top right hand corner, so that the figure is half cut off by the right hand margin of the page, and then use a Soft Light blending mode for the layer.

28. All that remains is the left hand shoulder of the model, and a black vertical strip. Call the layer 'coral'. Let's use the eraser on this layer to remove some of the 'white' area to the left of the vertical black bar, use a fairly small brush (around 35) and just dab at the area to make it darker.

We still need to add the titling to our book cover. This part of the tutorial I'm going to leave up to you. As a guideline, have a look at `book_cover.psd`. Have a look at the layer entitled 'title', and the copies thereof. This is just a starting point. Try to create your own title, keeping within the theme and style we have chosen. Don't be afraid to experiment with different fonts and sizes.

MAKING A CD COVER

For a CD cover, we want something equally eye-catching to the last tutorial, but we want to simplify the visual plane somewhat. CD covers are usually a lot smaller than book covers, so a lot of detail will be lost. We need to keep this in mind.

1. Let's go for a slightly surreal look. Open up `forest.jpg`. This is a run-of-the-mill picture of a forest path. Not for long! How about we make everything except the path, the tree and the sky, red?

2. Let's create a Hue/Saturation adjustment layer with the following settings:

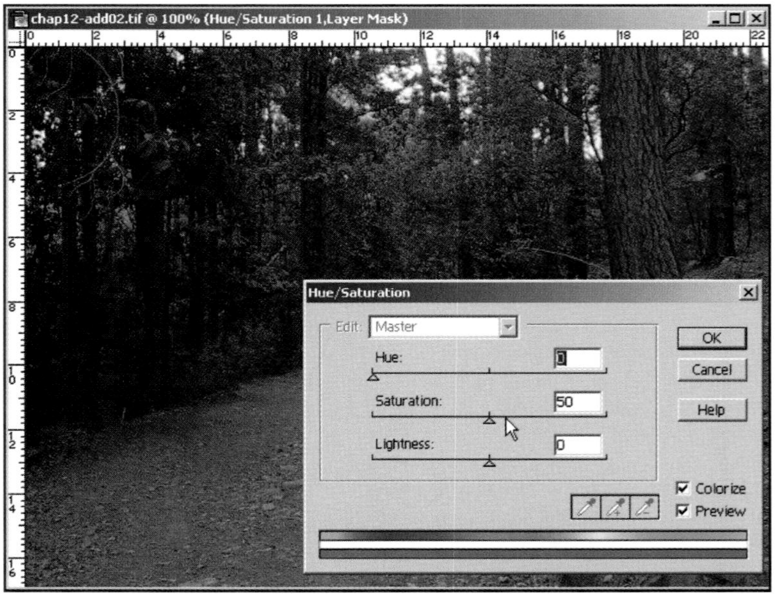

Wow. OK now everything is red.

3. Let's use a black brush of size 35 at 70% to draw on the mask where the path and tree is. Dab at the areas of the sky that you don't want to be red too – they shouldn't take on too much of the red anyhow as there wasn't much color there to begin with.

For a touch of realism (if that's possible!) leave the edges of the path with a little bit of red on them, or our path will look too cutout. This is why we're using a brush that's less than 100% opacity: if we skim over an area quickly, not all the red will be removed. Only if we concentrate on an area will all the colorization vanish.

4. The colors aren't nearly bright enough; so let's immediately apply a brightness/contrast adjustment layer:

Brightness/Contrast
Brightness: +9
Contrast: +37
OK
Reset
Help
Preview

We have a fairly strange looking scene now.

I've left a little bit of red at the top of the path – to give it a kind of eerie glow. Well seeing as how this is turning into a magical forest, let's add a magical character.

5. Open up `raven.jpg`, which we used in the last tutorial. Let's shrink this image to 50% to start with.

6. Make a rectangular marquee around the figure and drag this selection (using the move tool) to our project, placing it above everything. Let's call this layer 'Coral', after the photographer that took the pic. Shrink Coral so that she fits nicely on the path.

Now we need to get rid of that white background, what's the best way to do this? Maybe by using the Magic Wand tool and then hitting Delete? Not so fast! If you do this you'll notice that part of the face disappears as well. This happens because the face is also white, and there is no boundary between the face and the background: so Elements assumes that the white face is part and parcel with the background. Let's try a slightly different approach (if you have already deleted part of the face then use the History palette to step backwards).

7. Using the Magic Wand tool click on the background to select it, zoom in a bit and, now take the Lasso tool, hold down the ALT key to subtract from our Magic Wand selection:

8. Try deleting now, and we should leave the face intact, while the background disappears. Use the Eraser to tidy up any resilient pieces of white background that stayed behind. Notice that the figure has a faint white border. Because the figure comes from a white background, some of the blending from white to black has remained.

9. Using the Burn tool with a brush size of 13 at a 40% exposure, trace over the outline to the figure, specifically the parts that have a tinge of white to them. We just want the brush to affect the very edges, don't go too deep into the figure or we will darken parts that we don't want to affect. You might need to switch to a smaller brush size to remove this white halftone from the raven.

Hmmm. Something about the figure being there still looks a little unrealistic. We need to add a shadow. Let's duplicate the Coral layer and call this new layer 'Coral shadow'.

10. Using: **Image > Transform > Distort**, we are going to make this figure into the shape a shadow would be:

11. Lock the transparency of this layer, and then fill with black. We now have a fairly good shadow, but there are still some things we can do to improve it.

12. Firstly, drag the layer to just below the Coral layer. We now need to blur it a little bit, so unlock the transparency (if we don't we wont be able to affect anything except the interior) and use **Filter > Blur > Gaussian Blur** with a radius of about 3.5. Setting the blending mode of the layer to Soft Light will complete the process.

Now let's add some special effects. Duplicate the Coral layer, and call it 'whitecoral'. Let's lock the transparency of this layer and fill it with white. Now we're going to once again unlock the transparency of the layer and this time apply a motion blur to this layer by going to **Filter > Blur > Motion Blur**. Use the following settings:

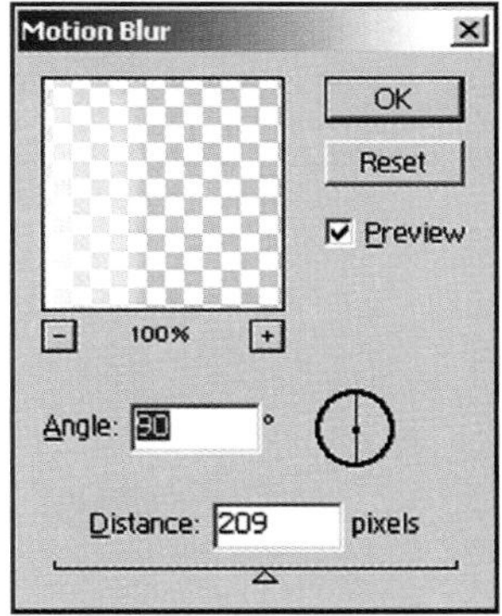

13. Use the Eraser to delete all the blurred parts of this layer that fall below the figure, so that it almost appears as if a smoke is rising up. Let's also drag this layer to just behind the Coral layer.

14. Let's draw a beam of light shining down on the figure. Create a new layer above the Coral layer and make a rectangle of white a little bit wider than the figure and starting from the bottom of her dress to the top of the screen.

15. Fill this marquee with white, and using **Image > Transform > Perspective**, narrow the top of the rectangle by pulling the top left and right toggles towards each other.

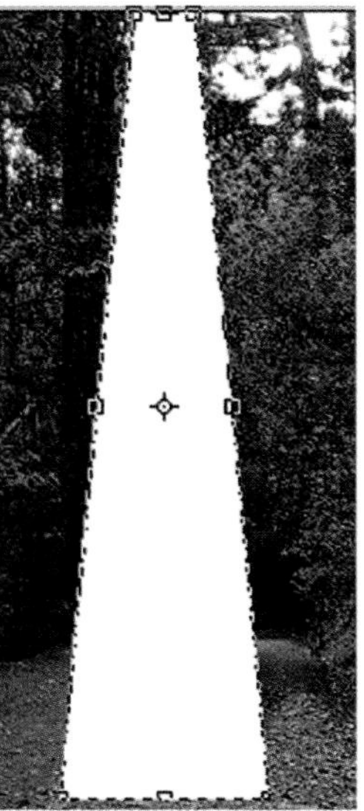

16. Now let's use a Gaussian blur of about 10 on this layer. Lock the transparency of this layer, and set the foreground color to bright orange and the background color to bright yellow. We're now going to apply a vertical color gradient using the gradient tool.

17. Select Linear Gradient from the options at the top, and then drag the gradient line from top to bottom vertically. This will fill the opaque areas (remember we locked the transparency of this layer) with a nice gradient fill.

18. Let's change the blending mode of this layer to Soft Light and set the layer opacity to 50%. Call the layer 'magic'.

How about we make the smoke a little bit curly?

19. Let's try **Filter > Distort > Zigzag**, with the following settings:

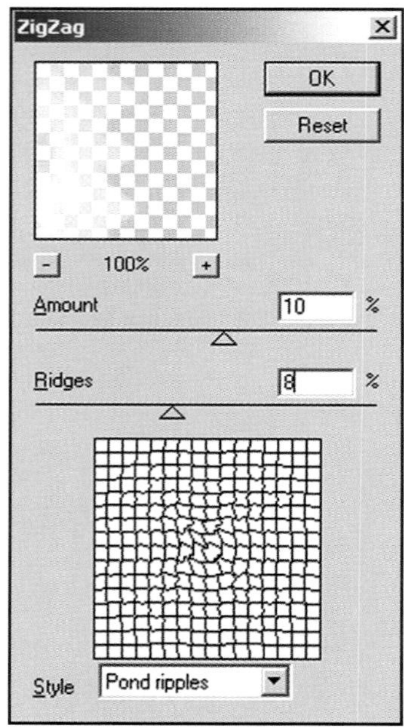

That pretty much completes our picture!

What remains to be done is to convert our picture into a CD cover. Firstly, the proportions of the image are incorrect; so we need to make it into a square.

20. Let's set the background color to Black and use **Image > Resize > Canvas Size**. All we want to change is the height, so set that to the same as the width: 640.

We now have a square canvas with a black strip at the top and bottom.

21. Create a new layer above all the others in the Layers palette, and draw two 3 pixel wide stripes in white where the image ends, and the black background begins, one at the top, the other at the bottom. These form a kind of border between the photograph and the black areas.

22. Now create a circular marquee about 145 pixels in diameter in the bottom right hand corner and delete the piece of the bottom white line that's inside this area. We're now going to stroke this area with white using a 3 pixel thickness: Go to **Edit > Stroke**

23. The bottom white line now flows into the circle. Let's fill the circle with a deep red (R=131,G=12,B=12).

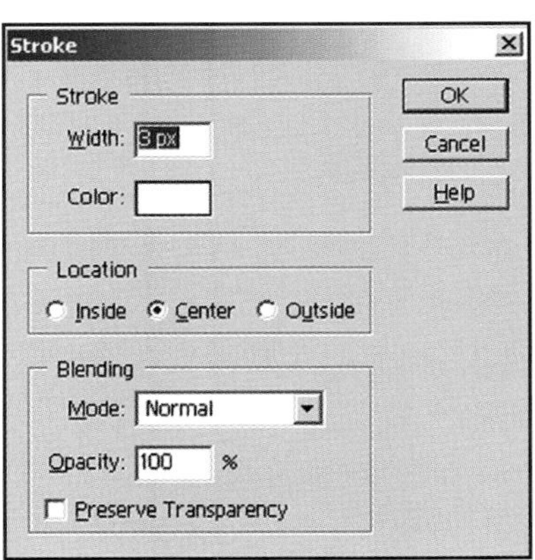

What remains to be done is insert the name of the band, the name of the album, and let's put a small yellow icon in the maroon circle. We're going to call the band 'stonefountain'.

24. Using a font size of about 48 and a nice thick white colored font, write out 'stonefountain' and position it just above the top white line, touching the left hand margin of the project.

25. Let's use the same font and change the size to around 72 points. We're going to call the album 'dimension2'. Let's write that out and position it so that it ends by touching the circle on the right. Position it just below the bottom white line.

26. I've used a very simple yellow iconographic symbol to place in the maroon circle.

27. Finally, that black background is looking a bit harsh. Let's go back to our background layer and select this black area, by using the Magic Wand.

28. Click in the top black area, while on the background layer, then hold down the Shift key and click in the bottom one. Holding down the Shift key adds to our selection.

29. We should now have both black areas selected. Let's fill this area with a nice dark maroon – even darker than the one we used for our circle. I've used R=60, G=0, B=0, but it's totally up to you.

30. Hmmm. Why didn't it work? Ah, the brightness/contrast layer just above is contrasting our nice dark maroon and making it totally black. Curses. Reselect this area, and let's make a new layer, just above the hue/saturation and brightness/contrast layers. Call it 'maroon'. Now if we fill with our chosen color, we can see it take effect.

The important thing to realize when creating your own artwork using your digital photographs is: Almost every image can be used for **something**. Even a totally blurred image can be used as a strange blending mode.

A good habit to get into is moving all your booboo pictures into their own folder. Go through them every now and again, and try and imagine what you could possibly use them for; whether it be texture, lighting or some other use. Virtually every digital photograph you take will possibly have some use in the future. For instance, in this chapter, we used the `Raven.jpg` image both for its subject matter and for its texture qualities.

I've often found that the worst pictures often end up being the most useful. Also, it's a great comeback line when someone asks you why the picture is so blurry and badly lit: "No I took this picture to use it as texture on an adjustment layer". That normally shuts them up real fast!

Another point to keep in mind is: Whenever you change the blending mode of a layer, even if you know exactly which blending mode you need, run through them all. Every now and again you'll discover a blend by mistake that will really add to your project. Experiment. Lots. While these tutorials will help you get to grips with the most useful aspects of Elements, the most powerful tutor is your curiosity.

13 Publishing your work

Once you have spent hours slaving over your work you'll want to find some way of showing others, without necessarily requiring them to use a computer and a copy of Photoshop Elements. Here we'll look at the various methods of doing just that. A few years ago a chapter like this would probably have had the mundane title of "Printing", but then a few years ago a digital camera cost thousands. These days there is not one but two principle 'publishing' routes out of Photoshop: print and the web.

Printing to paper

We'll start with the most obvious method. For all the high-tech wizardry around these days, paper is probably still the most satisfying medium. The quality of your output is dependent on your printing device, so here are some pointers to bear in mind when choosing a printer (or in assessing the potential of your printer).

Technology

Far and away the most popular and cost-effective form of printer is an **inkjet**. Canon, Epson, HP and Lexmark all produce a number of appropriate printers, though you should expect to pay more to be able to print on paper larger than standard letter/A4, or for higher quality, or speed.

Inkjet (Canon call them bubble-jet) printers work by forcing tiny bubbles of ink onto the page through a **print head**, which passes very near the surface of the paper. The ink needs replacing periodically and, as a rule of thumb, the cheaper your printer the more expensive this will be.

If cost is not an issue then **color laser** printers produce speedier, and more even results, however there is less choice in paper types. Similarly **dye-sublimination** printers produce near photographic results, but require very expensive, special paper, and only produce small prints.

Resolution

Perhaps the most significant consideration is the resolution of your printer. This is measured in dpi (dots per inch), a figure which refers to the number and size of the ink droplets that your printer uses to formulate an image. It is natural to assume that you should set your resolution in Photoshop to the same as your printer, but sadly life is a little more complex than that.

Each dot (pixel) on your monitor can represent many different colors – typically 16.8 million, though it depends on your settings. Your printer only works with four basic colors – Cyan, Magenta, Yellow and Key (Black). It mixes patterns of dots on the pages which appear to represent the colors underneath.

For this reason, there is no need to send any file to print with a resolution higher than 300dpi to, say, a supercool 2880 dpi inkjet printer. For most purposes 150dpi will be perfectly acceptable.

Working with images from digital cameras means they often have a default resolution of 72dpi (while you're working in Photoshop). Because you're working with an image that has never seen a printed page, this is effectively just a made up figure (72 is the default for monitors, and therefore web pages, which is why it often crops up).

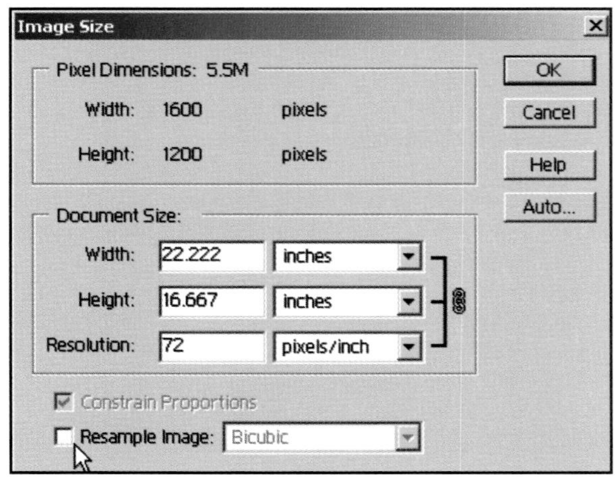

You may find it beneficial to change the resolution in Photoshop. What this does is not to change any of the pixels in the image, but tell your printer what size each pixel should be on the page. You can do this by clicking **Image > Resize > Image Size** and unchecking the **Resample Image** box. This means that you can either tell Photoshop how long you want one of the edges to be, or type in a new resolution.

It is important to remember that you're not changing the amount of detail in the image – that is determined by the number of pixels (the Width and Height at the top of this box, which become grayed out if you're not going to resample the image) but rather how large the image should be on the page. For example if we type 6 inches (the width of a traditional photo print) into the width box, the resolution figure changes to 266 pixels per inch.

If your image does not have enough pixels in the first place, you can resample the image but you'll never get any more information than when you took it. Photoshop simply has to guess as to how to fill additional pixels based on those around it, so the result will look blurred.

Paper

On a standard desktop printer the type of paper you print onto will dramatically alter your results. Standard photocopier-grade paper will never produce photo-quality results because of the texture of the paper. Photos, by their nature, have an uneven amount of ink in different areas. On low-quality paper, different quantities of ink will spread and dry differently.

On good quality photo paper, however, the results can be spectacular. Most printer manufacturers sell paper that, though expensive, is perfectly matched to your printer hardware and software settings. Your printer may well take a long time to print at its maximum resolution, but it's quicker than waiting for your photos to get back from the lab.

QUICK TASK: PRINTING A PICTURE

1. Open the image you wish to print and load your printer with the media you wish to use.
2. Click on the **Print Preview** button on the shortcuts bar.

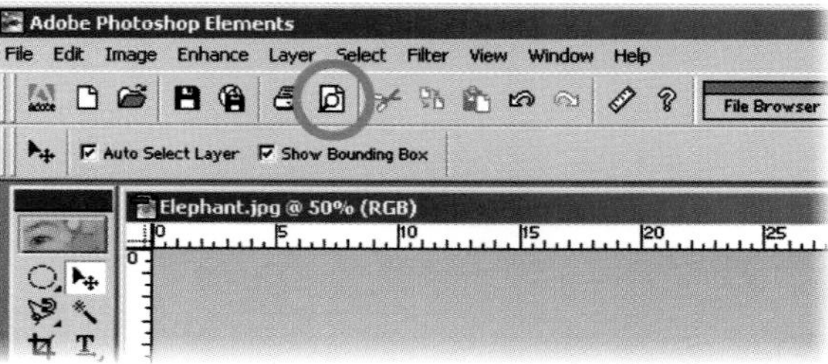

3. The preview dialog will open, showing a representation of the page as it would print, with the current settings selected. In this case the image is too large to fit on the page, but don't worry about that yet. The size is determined by the image's resolution and the number of pixels. In this case the image is 1600x1200 at 72dpi.

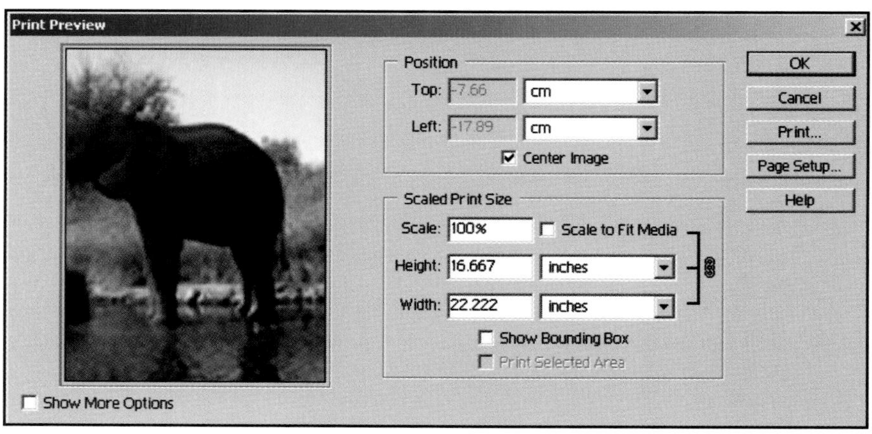

4. The first thing to worry about is ensuring we've got the correct paper size. Do this by clicking on the Page Setup button to the right of the window, which brings up a further dialog. From here select the printer you will print to (if you have more than one) and then click the Properties button.

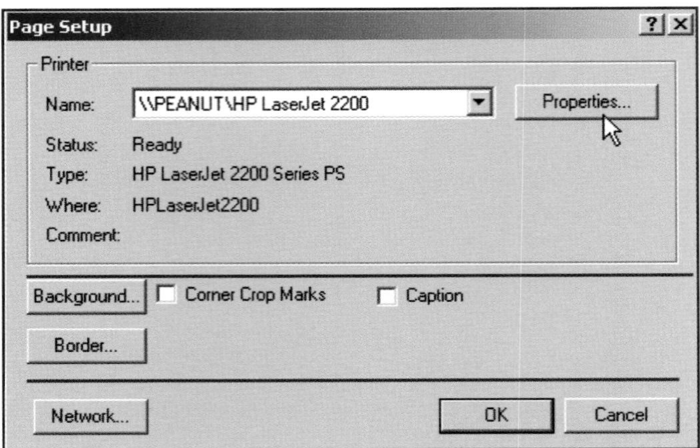

5. The options brought up by the Properties button depend on your printer, as this window is part of the software included with your printer. The options should be fairly self-explanatory, but feel free to refer to your printer documentation if you need help. You may find it useful to select landscape printing at this stage.

6. Once you have made any changes, click OK in your printer software window, and OK in the Page Setup window to return to the Print Preview window. Notice that the preview box has changed to reflect the change to landscape printing.

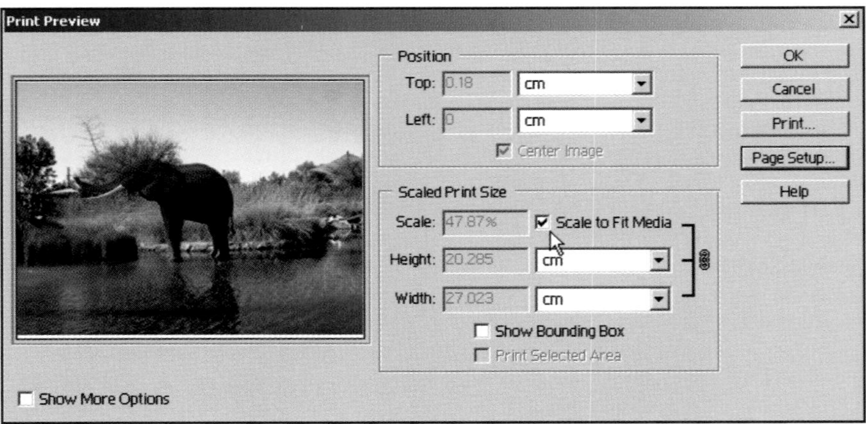

7. With you're paper size set, you are ready to scale your image to fit the page. At 100% the image will print the size you have set in Photoshop, at the same resolution as the file is set up at (you can see this by closing the preview window and clicking **Image > Resize > Image Size**). The **Scale to Fit Media** option is very handy here, as it automatically scales the image to the page size, but beware of blowing up a low-resolution image too far.

8. Once you're happy with where your image will appear on the page, click the 'Print...' button. The next dialog allows you to select a color profile (for color correction). It also offers you the choice to adjust your printer's

Setup options. Again this is specific to your printer. This time it's your last chance to tell your printer what quality settings to use and what sort of paper you have inserted.

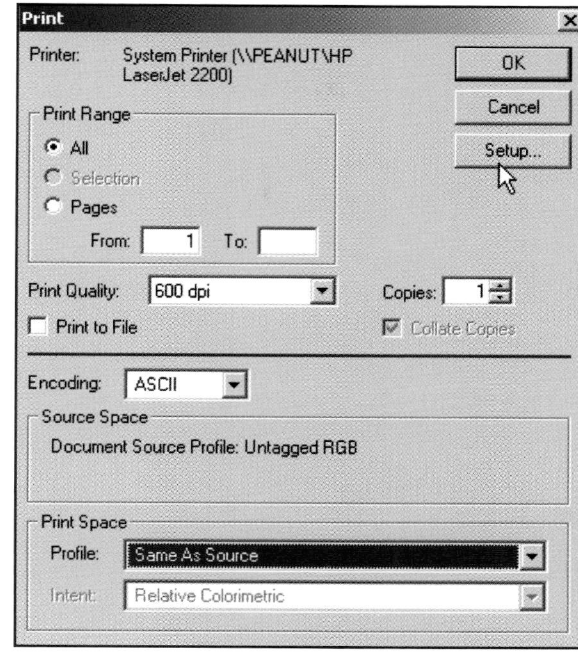

9. Click OK (from the above dialog) to finally send your document to the printer and await the results.

QUICK TASK: MULTIPLE IMAGES ON A PAGE

Sometimes you might want to put more than one copy of a picture on a page – say if you're using expensive paper and you want to cut out copies and send them to relatives. Photoshop has a built in facility to produce **Picture Packages**.

1. Open the image you wish to make a page of prints of.

2. Click **File > Automate > Picture Package**.

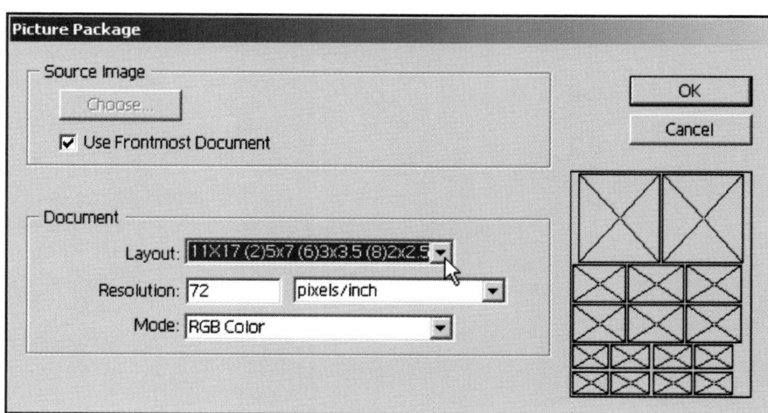

3. Check the **Use Frontmost Document** box and select a layout that suits you. The layout is the number of copies of the picture and their size that will appear on your page (and each is previewed as an 'x' in the bottom right hand corner of the window.

4. Select a suitable resolution for the new image. For maximum quality on an inkjet, 300dpi is a sensible maximum – any more is a waste, and will slow Photoshop, and your printer software, down.

5. Click OK, and Photoshop will spend a little while creating a new image with multiple copies of the old one on it. You can then print it as before.

Color Management

While we're on the subject of printing, it's worth considering the concept of **Color Management**. Color on a computer screen is made up of mixing light together, specifically blue, green, and red light. The more light you mix together, the brighter the light is going to be, and the lighter in color. Let's try to understand this visually.

1. Open up a new canvas of 200 by 200 pixels and draw a red blob in the middle of the screen. We'll use true red, which has an RGB value of R-255; G-0; and B–0. When you select the color in the Color Picker enter the exact RGB values you want in the boxes provided.

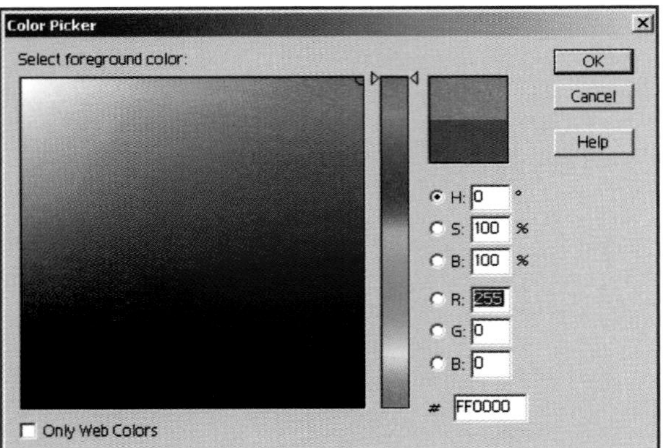

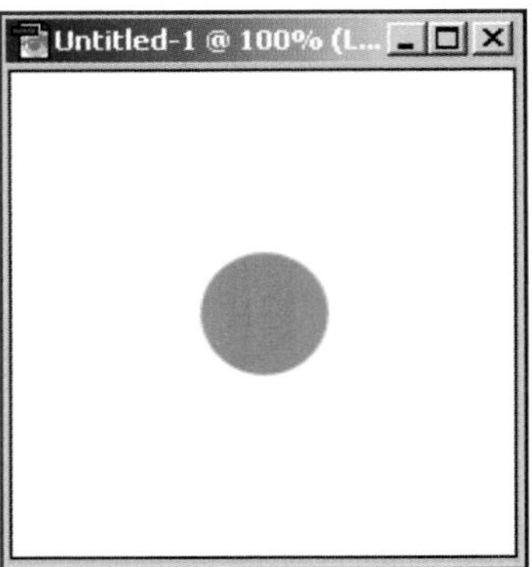

2. Make a new layer and draw a green blob over the top of it. Again we'll use true green: R-0; G-255; and B-0.

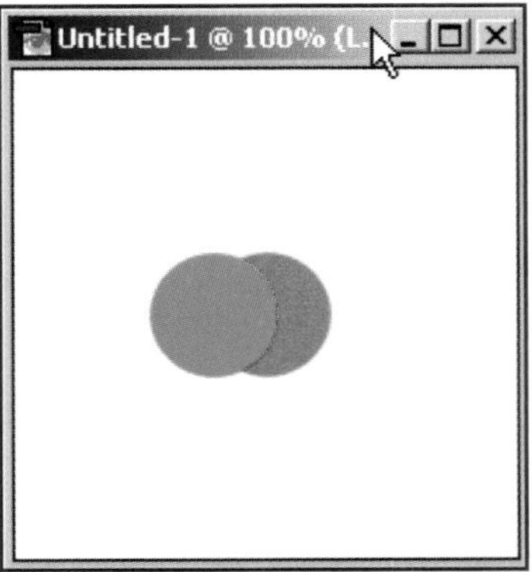

3. Now set the blending mode of the top green layer to **Screen**, you'll see that where the green overlaps with the red it appears as yellow. This is because the Screen mode is mimicking the way color works on a computer monitor, and hence adding the light together. This is called **additive color**.

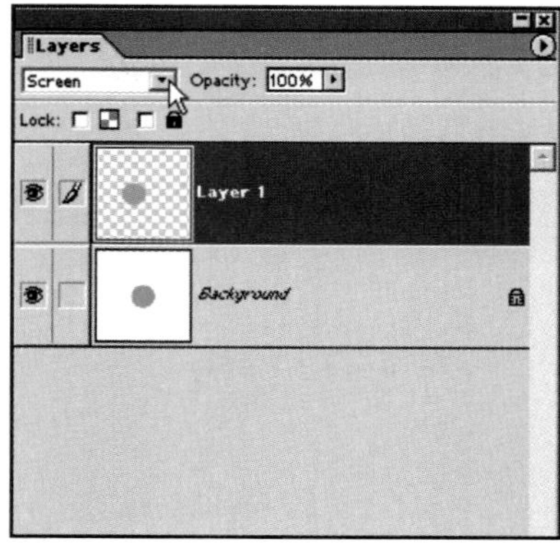

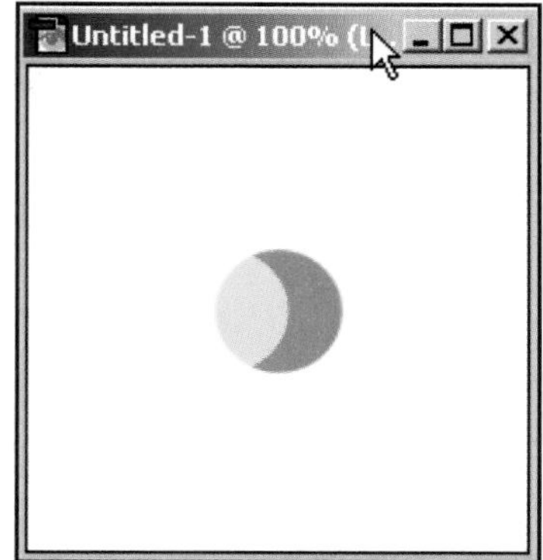

4. If we repeat the process and create a layer above both of the original layers and place a blue blob over it; when we also set its blending mode to Screen, where all three overlap the resultant color is white.

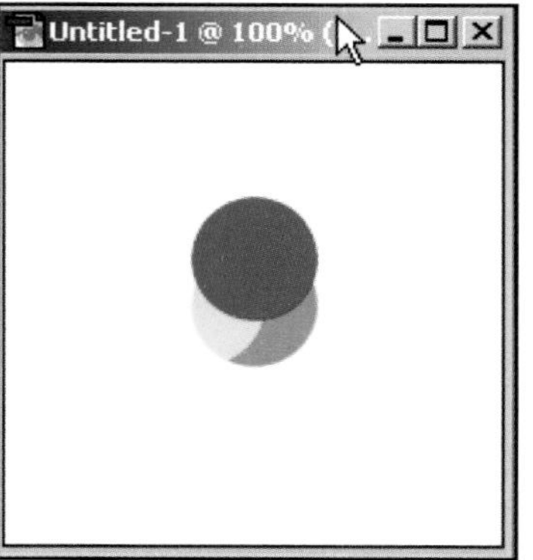

So, combining colors/light on a computer screen has the result of making things lighter. This is not so for printers. When we combine paints, the resultant is always a darker color (assuming we're not using white paint). So if we used the same three colors (red, blue and green) and mixed them together, we'd get a darker color than the one we started out with. This process is called **subtractive color**.

Now, because the way color is displayed on a monitor, and the way color is represented on a printer, are almost the exact opposite of one another, you can imagine the headache of getting what you see on the screen to print out the same way!

In order to achieve this, we use **Color Management**, which is a process that works out the correct colors for us. This process basically changes our images' colors in order to make them print more accurately on our printer. The way the colors change is dependent on the type of printer we are using.

How do you know if you need to use color management? Try printing something out, specifically with bright and dark colors, and colors that are of very similar hue, and see how the printer handles it. If you're happy with the result then look no further, go and fetch the frame...

Basically, a fair amount of the colors we see displayed on our monitor can be reproduced in print. But a "fair amount" of colors clearly does not represent all of the colors we are likely to use. A device such as a monitor or a printer can produce a certain range of colors; this range is called the gamut. Where the two ranges (the monitor and the printer) don't match up, we say we are out of gamut. It's the colors that fall out of gamut that we're worried about.

A lot of the time, however, the result can be pretty appalling. Enter stage left: Color Management. Go to **File > Print Preview**, to bring up the following dialog box, make sure that you check the **Show More Options** box**.** Select **Color Management** from the drop down list.

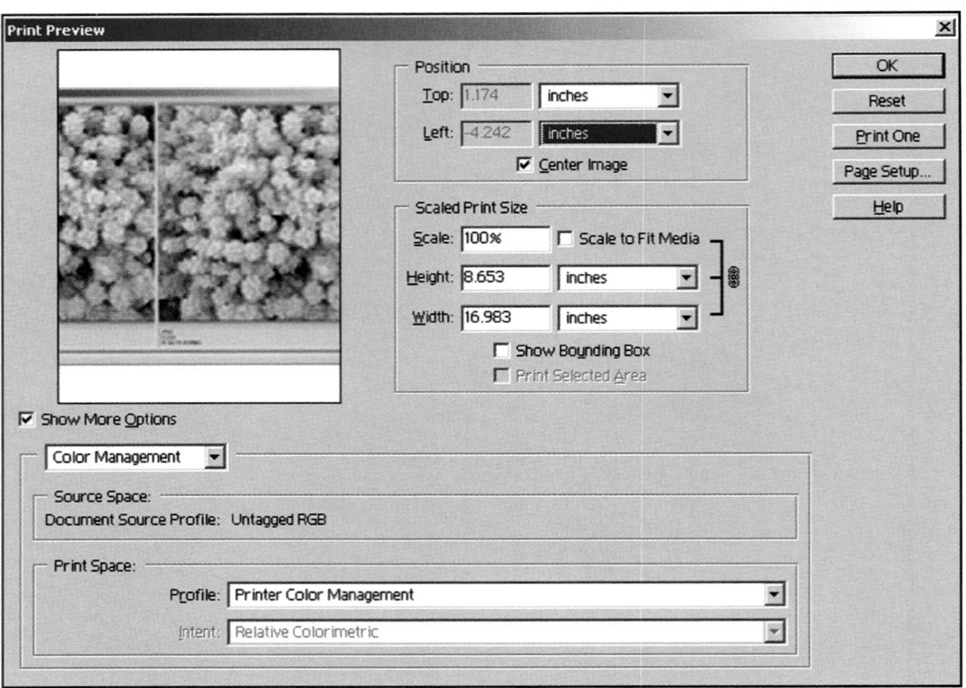

The **Print Space** area of the dialog box allows you to select a **Profile**, here we have selected **Printer Color Management**, which will use the printer driver installed with your printer to work out how the image should best combine its colors to print on your printer.

The next field allows you to choose the **Intent** of the conversion process, what does this mean? Basically, Intent will determine how the color is converted from additive to subtractive. There are three main types of intent: **Perceptual**, **Saturation** and **Colorimetric**.

- **Perceptual** intent tries to preserve colors in such a way that they are perceived as natural to us. So no matter how the colors are changed in order to print, no one is going to end up with a bright red face or green hair. (Unless that was the plan to start with). Perceptual intent will therefore try and keep color as true to nature as possible.

- With **Saturation** intent, this is not the case. If you were printing out something like glossy flashy text, you'd rather sacrifice an exact color match in favor of brightness and vibrancy of color. In this case, natural color is replaced with unrealistic but brighter colors.

- **Colorimetric** intent focuses on preserving the colors that are within both gamuts (the monitor and the printer) as much as possible, even at the expense of the relationship between colors, so colors that are close together tonally might end up much further apart or be composited into the same color.

These are fairly technical considerations, but worth keeping in mind should you ever need to reproduce your images in print accurately. To be honest many people find color management an extremely complicated process, and will generally end up manually adjusting the brightness and contrast of the image till it prints the way they want. This can also be due to having a poor quality printer, and a good deal of color management depends on having a really effective printer driver. If yours is not great then you may need to resign yourself to making manual brightness and contrast adjustments to get the best out of your printed images.

Even though its tempting to try to print an image in the highest possible resolution that the printer can handle, consider the fact that it's going to probably take ages if the file size is huge. Also, there is a structural limitation imposed by Elements of a maximum of 2 GB in size or 30,000 pixels squared, per image.

Of course if you're trying to print something this size off your home computer, you're going to be making a few cups of coffee before your printer finally manages to print anything! However, if your printer only supports 300 dpi, printing something at 600 dpi will not improve the quality of the final print in any way, all it will do is increase your file size.

The Internet

These days, of course, paper isn't the only way we can get images to others people. As a visual medium the web naturally lends itself to displaying photographs, we've spent the last few chapters weaving our photographs into artwork, well, why not showcase this artwork on the web? Or perhaps you've got a business, or an event that you'd like to publicize with your photos. This book is not the place for a full-scale discussion about designing your own website, but we will cover the important points to consider when preparing your digital photographs for the Web.

If you find the idea of publishing to the Web a little daunting then you're in luck, Photoshop Elements can help us to create our own, online photo album. By using the Web Gallery feature we can automatically create a simple web site, containing a home page, thumbnails of our images, the full size pictures, and simple navigational links. If you are familiar with HTML, then you can customize this site to suit your own needs.

QUICK TASK: WEB GALLERY

The **Web Gallery** function is designed to work on a folder of images, so before starting you need to save all the pictures that you want to put into your Web gallery in one folder on your computer somewhere. Save any changes you have made in Photoshop.

1. Click **File** > **Automate** > **Web Photo Gallery**.
2. Select the style that you want for your web pages. There are 4 options: **Horizontal Frame**; **Simple**; **Table**; and **Vertical Frame**.

You can see a thumbnail of each style, to the right hand side of the dialog box.

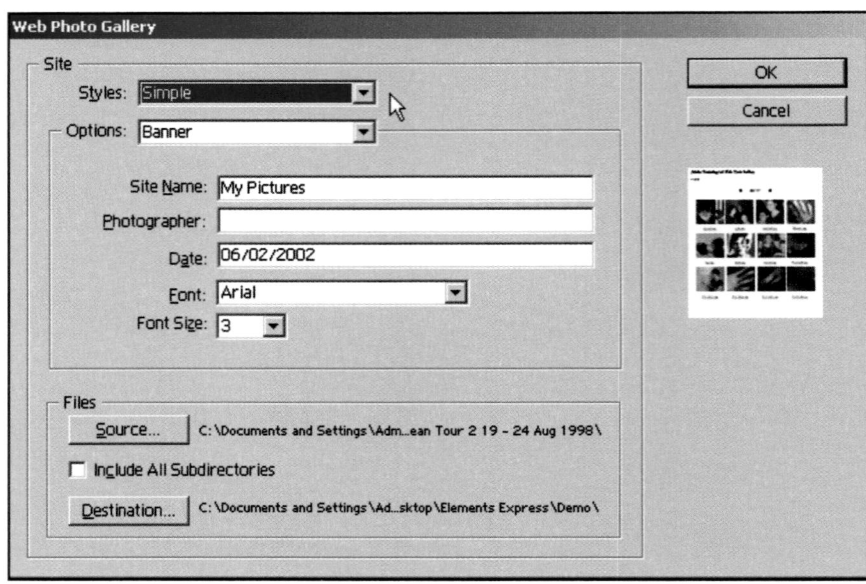

The **Options** pull-down menu has four separate headings, allowing you to define several different elements of your Web gallery. We'll look at all four of these option sets.

- Using the **Banner** option set, add a personal caption to the web pages we're creating in the top three boxes, and select the font and size in the bottom two. Bear in mind that you can't rely on another user having the font you choose unless you stick to the defaults.

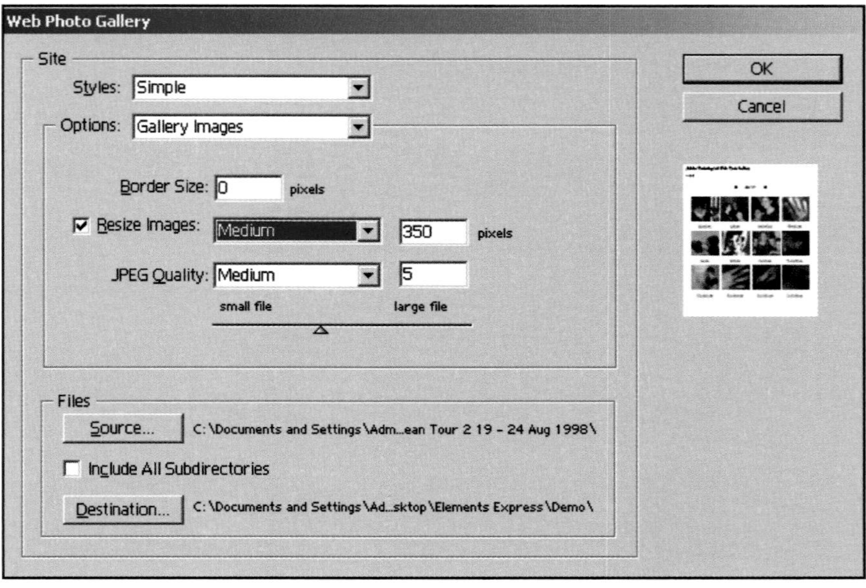

- Now select the **Gallery Images** option. Here we can choose the size and quality of the main images, set here at a width of 350 pixels. It's a good idea not to make it too much bigger because of the file size, but if you know all the viewers have high-speed access, then you can set the size, and even the quality, a little higher.

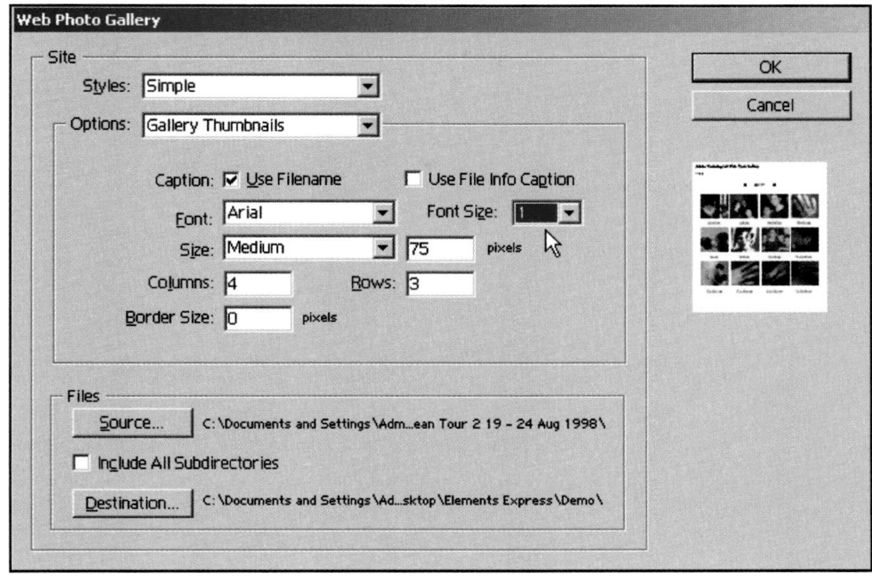

- The **Gallery Thumbnails** option allows you to set the size of thumbnails. It's a good idea to set the font size quite small, in order to get as much of the name on screen as possible. The Columns and Rows options have no effect on the Horizontal and Vertical frame styles.

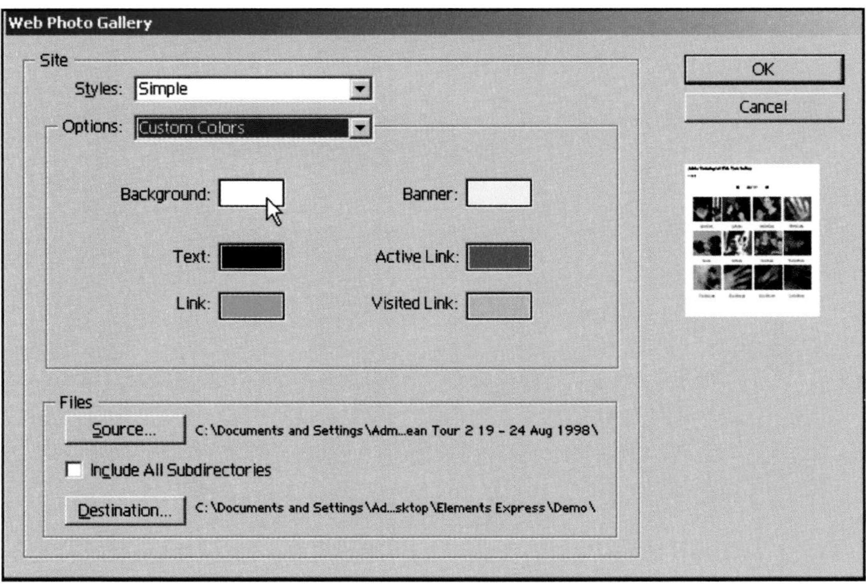

- The **Custom Colors** option allows you to define a different appearance for your pages. Clicking on a color brings up the color picker, from which we can select a color. It's a good idea to check the Web Safe Colors in the bottom left corner, as this will ensure we select a color that can be reliably reproduced on other computers.

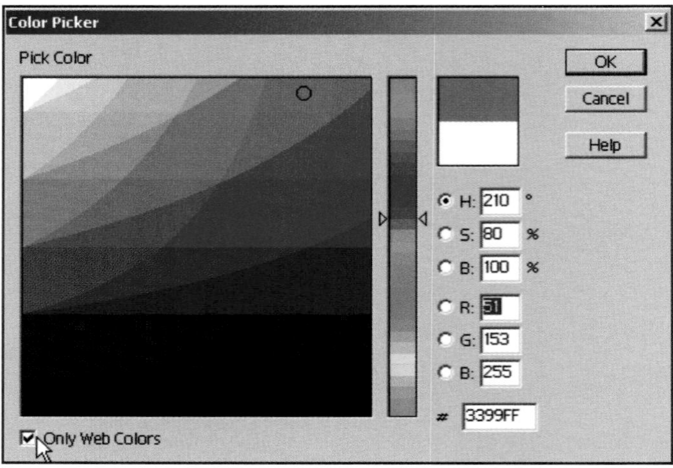

8. Once you're happy with the colors, all that remains is to select the folder that you want to create the web page from (the one with all the images in) and the output folder. Click on the Source button (near the bottom left) and use the pop-up window to select the folder where you keep your images. The computer will use these but leave them untouched.

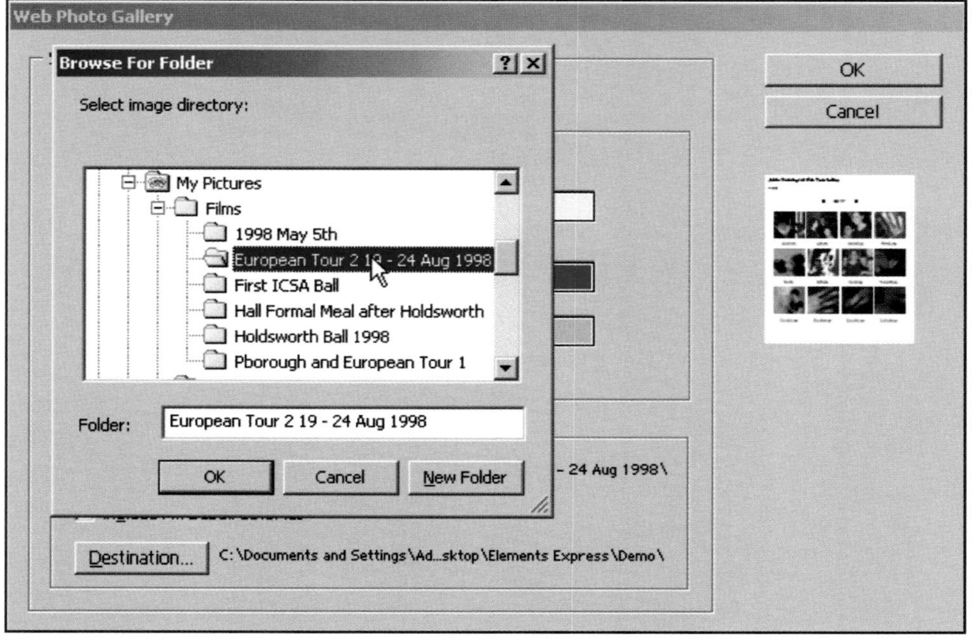

9. Repeat this process with an output folder (it's best to save this in a new empty folder somewhere on your computer before uploading files to the internet). This is where all the new files that form the web pages will be placed. Now click Finish.

Your own web site

The Web Gallery function is clearly very useful, but it is somewhat restrictive, and you probably are ready now to flex some serious creative muscle. So, you have an idea for a great web site, and you have all your all new digitally re-mastered photographs, but before jumping in there, here are some important points to consider when preparing your images for the web.

- First up is the file size question; Photographic images make for notoriously bulky files. No one likes waiting ages for a web site to download, the larger the file size, the longer it will take. File size is dependent on physical size, file type and resolution; we'll look at ways of compressing files in a few moments.

- Secondly, if your web site is one that is chiefly concerned with information, an overpowering use of graphics can both confuse and irritate the viewer. So do consider what you are trying to achieve with your pictures and designs.

- Thirdly, remember that a visitor to your web site may not have the same sized browser window or screen resolution, so your images may be viewed at a different size to the one you originally intended. As a general rule, you should design for the current standard monitor size, which is 800 x 600 pixels, so our images should not exceed 750 x 500 pixels.

Optimizing your images

As mentioned above, file size is possibly the most important factor when preparing images for the Web. Graphics files are always hefty; they contain all that pesky information about color and shade, so how do we overcome this weight issue? Well, we compress the files, and in doing so we have to strike a fine balance between picture quality and file size frugality.

The first step in compressing your files for the web is to change the resolution to 72 dpi, which is standard screen resolution size. This ensures a lower file size, but no loss of quality. Even if you did save your files at a higher resolution this would not be shown on most monitors. If however you want visitors to your site to be able to print your images out, then you may wish to revert to a higher resolution.

The next question is to choose an appropriate file format. There are three main file types used on the Web. These are **JPEG** (Joint Photographic Experts Group), **GIF** (Graphics Interchange Format), and **PNG-8** or **PNG-24** (Portable Network Graphics with 8-bit or 24-bit color). Each of these formats uses compression techniques to reduce file size, and therefore download time for your images. But how do you know which one is the appropriate one to choose? Let's look at each of the file types in detail.

JPEG

JPEG is the best format for saving photographs, and any naturalistic images with continuous color variations as it supports full color (24-bit/millions of color). It reduces the file size by discarding any "unnecessary" color information in order to compress it.

In theory the information that is lost is not really discernable to the human eye, but in practice this depends on the level of compression that you use: JPEGs very often lack sharpness, and we can sometimes lose detail if we greatly reduce the file size. Because this compression technique involves the loss of information the JPEG is known as a **lossy** format. It is always a good idea to have the original image saved elsewhere before saving to a JPEG as once the information has been discarded it cannot be recovered.

Photoshop Elements will let you decide the level of compression, and therefore the amount of information that will be lost; we will cover that process shortly. One major drawback with the JPEG format is that it cannot support **transparency**. You can overcome this problem if you know the background color of the web site for which it's destined, as you can replace the transparent areas with this color.

GIF

GIF files use a different method of compression that works best on large areas of pixels that are all exactly the same. This makes it the ideal file format for images that have a lot of flat, solid color; like line drawings or logos, but it is not so well suited to photographs or naturalistic drawings because of their sensitive gradations of color. The color range of a GIF is also restricted to 8-bits/256 or less, so clearly this is an unsuitable format for images that contain a lot of color variation.

GIFs do support transparency in images, and they also can be used to create animations, which can add character to your web site, they also are the natural format for displaying images with very sharp edges.

PNG

A new file type entering the web arena is the Portable Network Graphic, or PNG. This format has the best of both worlds, being good at displaying full color images and also able to show transparency. PNGs can also handle varying levels of transparency, unlike the GIF, which allows for only 100% transparency or none at all. In some situations, however, a PNG is slightly larger in file size than the JPEG or GIF so it is still not widely accepted as a web standard, even though most modern browsers support it.

Let's just summarize the distinguishing features of these three file types now:

	JPEG	GIF	PNG
Color Support	Full-color, 24-bits/ millions of colors	8-bits/256 colors or less. Use Web safe colors when preparing images for the web	PNG-8 supports 8 bits/ PNG-24 supports 24-bits.
Compression	Lossy; some color information is lost during the compression process	Lossless: no data is lost	Lossless
Supports transparency?	No	Yes	Yes
Drawbacks?	Lossy compression can lead to blocky images, or lack of sharpness	Limited color palette.	Not supported by all web browsers.
When to use	Photographs or any full color image with continuous variation in color.	Use for images with flat solid color; line drawings, text images, or logos.	In the future PNG is likely to replace GIF for flat color images.

Save For Web

Now we've had a look at some of the important distinctions between file formats, let's have a look at what happens when it comes to crunch time in Photoshop Elements. There is a very useful feature for this particulartask: the **Save for Web** option.

Using this option brings up the following dialog box:

The Save for Web dialog allows you to actually see how your image will be affected according to which file type you use. The image on the right is the optimized one, which you can compare with the original on the left. Notice that the bottom of the JPEG Options pop-up dialog box tells you the size of the file and also roughly how long it will take to download on a modem.

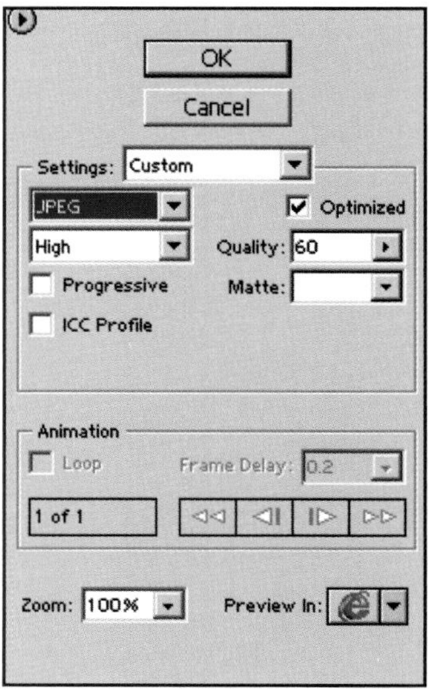

If you look at the drop down boxes on the right, you can select what type of file you'd like to save the image as: GIF, JPEG or PNG. Also, you can decide what quality you'd like the image saved at. For JPEGs, this is a simple slider, from high to low quality, with the option of using a **Progressive JPEG**. This is a JPEG that first displays a really low-resolution copy of the image, before it draws the higher resolution image.

This at least allows the viewers to see *something* while the image downloads. The low-resolution copy appears in progressive bands as the image downloads. Without this, viewers would simply be staring at a blank space. The **Progressive JPEG** effectively saves as two copies – one with a very low resolution, and very fast download time, and another with a custom resolution. Because of this, the file size of the images increases slightly.

If your original image contains an area you wish to be transparent, you can set this using the **Matte** drop down box and picking the color you wish to be transparent. If you are saving a file that is already on a transparent background, Elements will automatically complete this operation for you.

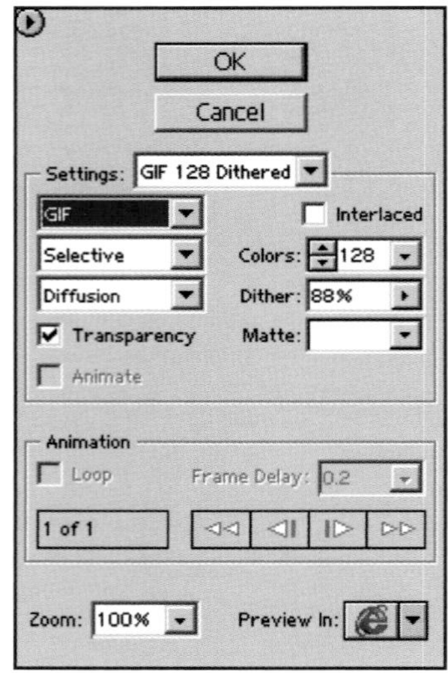

If you choose to save your file as a GIF, you'll see that there is an additional check box allowing you to opt for an **Interlaced GIF**, this performs the equivalent function of a Progressive JPEG. Another choice available under the GIF file format is the **Dither** option. What does this refer to? Well, a GIF only uses 256 colors or less, and so very little room is available to render gradients and other fine color changes. If we try to save an image with gradients (such as a sunset) using the GIF option, what we get is large bands of flat color instead of the gradient. One way around this is to dither the image. What this means is that colors that are not available in the GIF palette of 256 are simulated by using a checker board of two different colors that, when viewed from a distance, merge to look like the required color.

As you know, if you look at a black and white checkered pattern from a distance, it will appear to be gray, just as a red and yellow one will appear orange. Using dithering in this way, we can, to some extent, overcome a GIF's limited range of colors and prevent banding from occurring.

One more thing to note about the GIF format is that we can reduce the file size reducing the number of colors that the GIF uses. This is often not at the expense of resolution, (although depending on the nature of the image, it may affect the perception of image quality). For example, if the image only contains four colors, we can set the GIF to save only four colors and cut out unnecessary color information which increases the size of the file.

PNG options – there are two available. PNG-8 is fairly similar to a GIF, with limited palette, while PNG-24 is more similar to a JPEG. Some web browsers still do not support PNG, so it is not recommended that you save your images as PNGs, although in the future this is likely to change.

One final point to bear in mind is that you should save all of your original artwork as a PSD, and not JPEGs. Not only is the PSD format the only one to support layers, but also each time you save a JPEG, even at maximum quality, the image algorithm the JPEG uses to compress the file will reduce the file size and image quality slightly.

Conclusion

We've seen how Photoshop Elements can help you refine your digital photographs, through color correction, removal of unwanted features, and even the addition of attractive features. Remember that Photoshop Elements is also a powerful creative tool: it allows us to age photographs convincingly; to create digital panoramas, even design CD covers. Hopefully, you're already proud of the work that you've designed over the course of these chapters; well this is just the beginning. Armed with a digital camera, and Photoshop Elements you can enjoy a level of creative freedom which was once only accessible to professional photographers.

Now you know how to go about preparing your images to the Web, and you're a dab hand at printing them out, you must be keen to put the book down and start distributing your art to the world at large. We're always keen to hear from our readers, and if this book has inspires you to create something really special, then you can share it with us at our gallery at www.friendsofed.com/photoshop. We look forward to being impressed!

Index

The index is arranged hierarchically, in alphabetical order, with symbols preceding the letter A. Many second-level entries also occur as first-level entries. This is to ensure that users will find the information they require however they choose to search for it.

J

L

M

N

U

V

W

Z

Registration Code: 08029F2V0U1T0WT01

friends of ED writes books for you. Any suggestions, or ideas about how you want information given in your ideal book will be studied by our team. Your comments are always valued at friends of ED.

For technical support please contact support@friendsofed.com.

Free phone in USA: 800.873.9769
Fax: 312.893.8001

UK Telephone: 0121.258.8858
Fax: 0121.258.8868

Digital Photography with Photoshop Elements – Registration Card

Name ....
Address ....
City ....State/Region ....
Country ....Postcode/Zip ....
E-mail ....
Profession: design student ☐ designer ☐
photographer ☐ other ☐
other (please specify) ....
Age: Under 20 ☐ 20-25 ☐ 25-30 ☐ 30-40 ☐ over 40 ☐
Do you use: mac ☐ pc ☐ both ☐
How did you hear about this book?..........
Book review (name)..........
Advertisement (name) ....
Recommendation ....
Catalog ....
Other ....
Where did you buy this book? ....
Bookstore (name) ....City..........
Computer Store (name)..........
Mail Order..........
Other..........

How did you rate the overall content of this book?
Excellent ☐ Good ☐
Average ☐ Poor ☐
What applications/technologies do you intend to learn in the near future?..........
....
What did you find most useful about this book? ....
....
What did you find the least useful about this book? ....
....
Please include any additional comments..........
....
What other subjects will you buy a design book on soon?
....
....
What is the best design book you have used this year?
....
....
Note: This information will only be used to keep you updated about new friends of ED titles and will not be used for any other purpose or passed to any other third party.

D E S I G N E R T O D E S I G N E R™

N.B. If you post the bounce back card below in the UK, please send it to:

friends of ED Ltd.,
30 Lincoln Road, Olton,
Birmingham, B27 6PA. UK.

NO POSTAGE
NECESSARY
IF MAILED
IN THE
UNITED STATES

BUSINESS REPLY MAIL

*FIRST CLASS MAIL PERMIT*64 CHICAGO,IL*

POSTAGE WIIL BE PAID BY ADDRESSEE

friends of ED.
29 S. LA SALLE ST.
SUITE 520
CHICAGO IL 60603-USA